Dan Sickles

1890 McCulloch

LHC, AZ 86403

SERIOUS MONEY

The Art of Marketing Mutual Funds

SERIOUS MONEY

The Art of Marketing Mutual Funds

BY
NICK MURRAY

Editor
Robert A. Stanger

Publisher
Robert A. Stanger & Co.
Shrewsbury, New Jersey

Other Publications From Robert A. Stanger & Co.

Periodicals:

STANGER'S INVESTMENT ADVISOR
SELLING MUTUAL FUNDS
THE STANGER REPORT: A GUIDE TO PARTNERSHIP INVESTING
STANGER'S PARTNERSHIP WATCH
THE STANGER REVIEW: PARTNERSHIP SALES

Books:

SHARED PERCEPTIONS: THE ART OF MARKETING REAL ESTATE PARTNERSHIPS
HOW TO EVALUATE REAL ESTATE PARTNERSHIPS

Published by Robert A. Stanger & Co.
1129 Broad St., Shrewsbury, New Jersey 07702

Printed in the United States of America.

Library of Congress Catalog Card Number: 91-65977

ISBN 0-943570-11-5

**This book is for
JOAN,
who always believed**

Contents

Acknowledgments

People who write books seem always to thank their families, more or less ritually, at the end of the acknowledgments. I'd like to reverse the process. I tried, in a very small way, to acknowledge my wife Joan's contribution to this book — and to my life — in the dedication. But my daughters Karen and Joan, no mean writers themselves, have also been wonderfully encouraging. And, whenever I was sitting there staring at a blank sheet of paper, my son Mark instinctively showed up and took me out for a game of racquetball.

At Bear Stearns, Jonathan Barnett was typically kind and supportive of my nights-and-weekends efforts to produce this book. I literally could not have completed the task without Andrea Ricigliano. And Hoda Zahid instantly tracked down all manner of arcane statistical information, always making it look easy.

Bob Stanger gave me the idea for the book; his and Keith Allaire's fine editorial hands add much value to a manuscript that clearly showed the enthusiastic haste with which it was written.

I became familiar with the work of Aaron Hemsley Ph.D. in 1983 when I took his "Psychology of Maximum Sales Production" course. Aaron's work is specifically for financial planners and investment salespeople, and I believe it is critical to your success in the 1990s.

Marvin Brown taught me to sell mutual funds twenty years ago. More than that, he showed me that there was such a thing as "the sales process." This book is a continuing exploration of that process, so it owes much to Marvin.

In the acknowledgments for my previous book, *Shared Perceptions,* I thanked my friend Gordon Joblon for his critical intervention in my career. His response was the last letter I had from him before he died. I miss him and am just glad I got to say "thank you" in time.

If thinking about writing a second book were the same as writing a second book, this book would have been done two years ago. I'm grateful to Kenneth Schwartz M.D. for helping me get on with it.

Finally, I think I'm a better businessman and a better investor (and even, perhaps, a little better person) because of the opportunity to work for Alan C. Greenberg at Bear Stearns for the last six years. **But, of course, the beliefs, opinions and mistakes in this book are mine alone. They certainly do not necessarily reflect the opinions or business practices of Bear Stearns, which is not responsible for the content of this book in any way.**

— N.M.

"Ironically I believe Clive <u>was</u> sorry … He believed that facts were the only kind of information and he despised whoever was not ruled by them.

Whereas Ned was all the other way, and more at risk on account of it. He was by temperament and training an agent runner and captain of men … In that sense he was the determined primitive, as people who deal in human nature have to be …"

John LeCarré
The Russia House

FOREWORD

The Death Of
Do-It-Yourself Investing

On October 19, 1987 the Dow Jones Industrial Average fell 23% on New York Stock Exchange volume of six hundred million shares.

* * *

In mid-May 1989, Eastern Europe's most honored living playwright, Vaclav Havel, was a political prisoner in a Prague jail cell. On December 29 of the same year, he was elected President of Czechoslovakia, becoming his country's first non-Communist leader in nearly half a century. During just a few months, from the Atlantic to the Brandenburg gate, and on to Moscow itself, Communism had virtually collapsed.

* * *

In September 1989, after nearly a decade of unprecedented corporate takeover mania, the stock of UAL Corporation, parent of United Airlines, was trading at $300 per share. The company's unions were negotiating to acquire the airline, but Wall Street was speculating that even more aggressive bidders would soon appear. No one knew it at the time, but UAL was about to become, in relation to the 1980's leveraged buyout craze, what Pickett's charge was to the Confederacy: the high water mark.

On the afternoon of Friday, October 13, 1989, bankers advised the unions that the acquisition of UAL at $300 per share was not financeable. Period. When the story hit the news tape, the Dow Jones Industrial Average went down 7% in two hours on huge volume. Takeover stocks — real or imagined — lost twenty and thirty percent in value. Toward the end of the day, the market in many junk bonds —

issued to finance the wave of highly leveraged takeovers — simply ceased to exist.

One year later, loans for hostile takeovers were unavailable on any terms from any traditional lender. The brokerage firm which virtually created the concept of junk debt vanished into Chapter 11. And UAL stock touched a low of $84-1/4, down 70% in thirteen months, as doubts arose that any takeover was possible at any price.

* * *

In mid-July 1990, the price of oil was under $17 per barrel and falling freely. After almost four years of weak oil prices, public opinion had written OPEC off. It was seen as a cartel that had failed under the weight of oversupply.

Few people realized that four years earlier, when oil traded briefly below $10, at least a dozen of the 16 members of OPEC produced over quotas. But in 1990, only two were cheating. And one, Kuwait, began to realize neighboring Iraq was moving troops toward its border.

Within thirty days, the price of oil was near $40.

* * *

All of these events, and many more, tend to drive home the lesson that the world has become too complex, and events are unfolding too suddenly, for the individual investor to function comfortably. The volatility with which markets respond to change, and the advent of phenomena like "program trading," create an investment climate which the investor hates and fears.

The individual investor has ceased to believe he can manage his own investments. Instead, he has turned to "managed money" — investments where the individual turns his money over to someone else to manage. While mutual funds are the most common example of "managed money," the concept embraces a broad universe of investments including variable annuities and "investment" life insurance, real estate investment trusts (REITs), closed-end funds, "wrap" accounts, and even unit investment trusts. The investor will not be back to picking individual investments anytime soon. And, he is almost certainly correct.

But will the individual investor handle his investments in managed money accounts any better than he ran his own portfolio? Will he be able to sort out the bewildering, and proliferating, variety of managed money vehicles? Not a chance. **Without an adequately compensated advisor to help with selection and discipline, the individual investor will simply make all the classic, horrendous mistakes he made in his own portfolio** ... he'll just do it one step removed.

The unguided investor will still throw every dime he has into an aggressive growth stock fund in the summer of 1987. Then, when stock prices crash, he'll liquidate in a panic ... forcing his portfolio manager to sell even more stock at even more depressed prices. With interest rates already down, he'll hide out in a bond fund for a year or so until the stock market is up 40% from its lows. Then, he'll read about this nifty little equity fund written up in *Money* magazine ... and away we go. Again.

This is where you come in. The investor needs a confident, seasoned professional like you, keeping him on the right track ... making sure he stays diversified and insulated from his own tendencies toward greed and fear.

In that sense, the trend toward managed money is perhaps the most positive development of recent times for securities salespeople and financial planners. You can do what you're best at and what you're really paid for: gathering and allocating assets. And, you're freed from having to do what most of us aren't particularly good at and aren't paid for either: managing money.

FILL THE SKILL GAP

Yes, the investor needs you now more than ever, and for all the right reasons. The trouble is, he doesn't necessarily realize you're the solution. And a lot of you are finding you don't know how to convince him. Your uncertainty is the reason for this book.

In general, the financial services industry has always been much better at communicating product knowledge than in training salespeople and planners in the psychology and practice of selling. Even the sales process itself is in disrepute among many in the financial planning community.

But, as I travel around the country talking to planners as often as salespeople, I keep hearing the same complaints — that marketing and sales skills training just hasn't kept pace with the development of new investment instruments and strategies. What difference does it make to your income if you're an expert on international bond funds but are so paralyzed by rejection you've stopped picking up the phone? What good is it if you know great asset allocation techniques but can't get people to trust you? What value do you provide if you've identified the best growth stock fund of the 1990s, but you can't get people to make a decision?

In the end, our profession rewards us not for what we know, but for what we do, and for what we are able to convince other people to do ... a very different set of skills.

The help you're probably getting from money management firms isn't likely to be the right kind. A bright young wholesaler shows up at your office sales meeting, eager to prove conclusively (with the help of a couple of dozen well-chosen charts and graphs) why his particular energy stock fund is better than all others. Only you realize the issue of *which* energy fund to recommend to your clients is about 50th on the list of 50 client questions/objections. You need answers for the other 49 which are far more important:

(1) Why energy?
(2) What if oil goes back to $10?
(3) What percentage of my assets should be in energy?
(4) Why do I have to do anything now?
(5) This fund owns Texaco, and I bought Texaco once and lost money.
(6) Shouldn't I buy a no-load fund?
(7) Who are you, and where did you get my name?
(8) I only buy bonds ... CDs ... real estate ... wine futures ... Confederate autographs ...
(9) I don't need this; I'm buying Exxon stock.
(10) My accountant says I shouldn't buy any mutual fund.
(11) What's the minimum I can buy?
(12) Why is the commission so high?
(13) I can do better on my own.
(14) What if the net asset value goes down?
(15) The current yield is only 2.5%. I need income.
(16) I lost money in an oil income limited partnership once.
(17) What if Iraq invades Israel? ... Russia invades Saudi Arabia? ... Venezuela invades Argentina? ... Texas invades Oklahoma?
(18) The oil price is manipulated ... oil is too geopolitical ... oil

companies rape the environment.
(19) My brother-in-law sells mutual funds.
(20) I just want to watch it for a while.
(21)(22)(23)(24) ... etc.

I think you see my point. Most mutual fund wholesalers are trained to help you sell *their* mutual fund. They unconsciously assume that you already know all about selling mutual funds in general — not always a valid assumption.

Product wholesalers are nice people but aren't necessarily trained — nor do they necessarily have a lot of direct experience — in helping you address the basic issues:

- making a real prospecting plan and sticking to it;
- handling rejection;
- telling a real objection from a stall;
- what "essentials" to know versus what's "nice" to know;
- making an emotional connection with your prospect; and
- getting people to trust you.

This book will teach you how to tackle these basic issues.

PUT TO REST THE MOTIVATION QUESTION

You've probably invested in this volume with your own money (in this day of radical cost-cutting, few firms would buy you this book) because you're not satisfied. Imperially slim people don't buy diet books; perfectly successful salespeople don't usually buy how-to-sell books. Dissatisfaction arises from realizing there's a gap between what you have accomplished and what you would like to accomplish. And that's very healthy.

But don't worry about whether or not you are sufficiently "motivated." You have more than enough motivation to last three lifetimes. The proof? In your career choice, you've voluntarily signed up for "The Great Trade-Off." You get all the benefits of living entirely by your own wits and by your own energy (side A of The Great Trade-off) at just one price — nobody ever has to pay you anything (the flip side).

The benefits are what first attracted us to our profession — what we love about it:

- **No income limit** — An astounding attribute, but true. The only limit on your potential income in this business is the limit which you set, consciously or unconsciously, for yourself.

- **You are your own boss** — None of us has a real "boss." Nobody can tell you how much money you can make or what to do. You make your own hours, set your own work pace, decide what kinds of investments you want to work on and what kinds of clients you want to work with. You decide how much sales assistance you want, and what you want to pay for it.

And if you find yourself, one fine day, completely confused by the markets, and you have no investment strategy at all, you can just park everybody in a money market fund and go fishing for a month until your head clears or the market makes up its mind. Who's to stop you?

- **Never unemployed, always in demand** — A good planner/salesperson can never be unemployed. Indeed, all through the retrenchment of the last few years, when the financial services industry eliminated tens of thousands of jobs, the competition to hire good salespeople reached a fever pitch.

Demand for good salespeople will always be there. The cost structure of the financial services business is becoming a harder and harder nut to crack, so everyone will always be eager to obtain (and retain) an established professional with a good, clean, growing business, as opposed to incurring the awful expense of training new people.

- **Opportunity for self-expression** — Outside of the arts, and possibly trial law, I know of no profession beside ours that offers as much capacity for self-expression. Nor does the job entail a long, arduous apprenticeship before you have access to that benefit. From the very first day you're licensed, you can define how people see and hear your own potentially unique way of communicating good investments. And you can go on developing, expanding and refining your mode of self-expression long after most people's careers have topped out . . . even after many people have retired.

But to get the benefits of The Great Trade-off, you have to go up on the high wire all alone, and practice your own special artistry in your own totally unique way, before thousands of upturned eyes — with no safety net. You've chosen to look The Great Trade-Off right in the eye and say, not just "This is what I *want* to do" but, "This is what I *need* to do." That puts you way up in the 99th percentile of human motivation.

Remember: Our business offers genuinely limitless rewards to people who have curiosity, realism, flexibility, love, a high tolerance for ambiguity and a relentless drive for self-examination and self-correction. But, like life itself, a career in our business is terribly unforgiving of self-delusion, of the comfortable excuse, of going through the motions.

> *"Only where love and need are one,*
> *And the work is play for mortal stakes*
> *Is the deed ever really done*
> *For Heaven and the future's sakes."*

— Robert Frost

And, as for the challenges of this rapidly changing investment landscape, in the end what counts isn't what changes — technology, institutions, governments, markets, investment products, the facts. What counts is what doesn't change — people, their hopes for the future, quality, integrity, judgment, discipline, a long-term perspective, diversification, asset allocation — and the terrific power you have to enhance the financial well-being of the people who rely on you.

I hope this book serves your best interests ... and theirs.

1

Why Managed Money?

In 1980, U.S. gross national product was $2.7 trillion. The Dow Jones Industrial Average closed at about 950, and the daily volume on the New York Stock Exchange averaged 45 million shares.

Imagine going to a meeting at the end of 1980, and the speaker tells you, as a matter of absolute fact, that in 1990:

(1) GNP will be $5.5 trillion, up 104%;
(2) the Dow Jones Industrial Average will reach 3000;
(3) the average NYSE volume will be 157 million shares; and
(4) most securities salespeople and financial planners will have a difficult time earning a superior income.

Chances are you'd have laughed out loud, and so would everybody else in the audience. In fact, a lot of people would have said, "Give me the Dow at 3000 and you can keep the other two. If stocks are going up so much, that's all I need to know." Others may have said, "Give me volume three times today's, and I don't care where the Dow is; there'll be more than enough business to go around, and I'll get my share."

During the 1980s, economic growth, the accretion of household wealth, stock prices and volume have all exceeded everyone's wildest dreams. Then why are your client base, assets under control and income all far below the level you feel you deserve, as well as far below the level you'd expect after a decade of such prosperity?

Lots of reasons. One has to do with your own psychology, and thus your expectations, work habits and reactions. (We'll explore this issue later.) Another reason comes under the heading, "Be careful what you wish for; you may get it." (Remember the short story we all read in high school called "The Monkey's Paw"?) You wished — if you even dared to imagine such things — for the Dow to reach 3000. And you got it . . . accompanied by unimaginably horrifying volatility.

Then there's another reason, and it is the motivation for this book. During the 1980s:

THE WHOLE WORLD WENT TO MANAGED MONEY. IT WILL NOT BE BACK TO STOCK PICKING ANYTIME SOON. AND THE WORLD IS ALMOST CERTAINLY RIGHT.

The growth of mutual funds may be the most unequivocal and dramatic illustration of this phenomenon. (See Table 1-1.)

Table 1-1 GROWTH OF MUTUAL FUND INVESTMENT		
Year	Number of Mutual Funds	Fund Assets
		($ in billions)
1980	564	134.8
1990	3,108	1,069.1
Source: Investment Company Institute. Data includes equity, fixed-income and money market funds.		

The growth went on all through the 1980s, and that's important. Because you could easily say, "Sure, the individual investor gave up after the '87 crash, and went to money management in a panic. But, he'll be back when things settle down again and a new bull market starts."

First of all, you will grow old, gray and destitute waiting for things to "settle down again." Second, that's not even the point! **The individual investor has been steadily turning over increasing amounts of money to professional managers for a good ten years now.** (The percentage of household financial assets held in mutual funds has quadrupled since 1980!) And this trend is *not* based on the direction of securities markets.

Nor is the trend a broad, subtle, institutional change in the behavior of large pension funds, something that has nothing to do with the individual securities salesperson or planner. The trend is Reality with a capital "R."

The great American individual investor you're looking at here is voting with his feet ... and with his IRA, his Keogh, and his 401(k), too.

He feels there is a better use of his time. He's saying, "No matter how much time I spend, I can't figure out what the Japanese stock market, the price of gold, and the Fed funds rate are doing to my $75,000 of ten-year Treasuries and my 300 shares of IBM. I could be spending an extra two hours a week in the office, or teaching my grandson to fish, or reading a book, or watching the sunset, if I didn't have to pay attention to this stuff. Bag this; I'm out of here."

And, whether we like it or not, he's right. So, we'd better take a lesson from the general who asked which way his troops had gone, so he could go out and lead them. Managed money is where your clients have gone. But make no mistake about it, they still need your leadership. The threshold decision to go to managed money avails your client very little if he makes the same dreary litany of mistakes that characterized the way he ran his own account.

Properly counseled, the investor will find very important benefits to managed money. And the benefits help you, as well, in your struggle to keep the investor on the right course, save him from his own excesses of greed and fear, and create a superior income stream for yourself in the process.

MAKE ASSET ALLOCATORS OUT OF TREND FOLLOWERS

By offering managed money, you inevitably focus investors on asset allocation — one of the surest ways to keep the investor from spending his whole life chasing the current trend over a cliff. People always put all their "new money" into whatever is "working," while assiduously selling out of — and then avoiding like the plague — what's "not working." That's because the individual investor is The Great Extrapolator. As an avid reader of the financial press and magazines (those great expositors of everything that happened yesterday), the investor is always up too close. He extrapolates from his most recent experience to his expectation of tomorrow. In the process, he loses long-term perspective.

For instance, in 1980, after a few years of high inflation and high interest rates, investors were loaded with oil and gas programs and real estate tax shelters, whose fundamentals were "working." Equity mutual funds experienced net liquidation in 56 of the 60 months from 1975 through 1979 ("not working"). And bonds? Everybody knew, net of inflation and taxes, bonds were the only financial instrument ever invented which could, if held long enough, totally extinguish your purchasing power (*really* "not working"). So what happened? Of course: inflation and interest rates cratered, oil and real estate wiped everybody out, and stocks and bonds soared. So much for the wonderfulness of extrapolation.

On the other hand, by the summer of 1987, the stock market had gone straight up for five years. People were now extrapolating that trend indefinitely into the future. All the "new money" was chasing the next hot takeover stock. Was the Dow Jones Industrial Average already at 20 times earnings? No problem: the Japanese Nikkei Index was selling at 40 times earnings. Don't worry; be happy.

As you'll remember, Halloween came a couple of weeks early in 1987 .. and it was a trick, not a treat. The 1987 Crash, more than any single event, finished off the individual investor thinking he could be his own portfolio manager.

Using managed money to implement asset allocation helps you control the investor's tendency toward extrapolation, as well as his capacity for knee-jerk over-reaction to startling events. And it lets you create and maintain a disciplined program of adding to positions in out-of-favor asset classes during periods of deep undervaluation.

For instance, the same investors who took second mortgages to buy oil in 1980 at $38 per barrel were convinced in 1986, when the price cracked $10 on the downside, that oil was a carcinogen. So, sure enough, it was $38 again — if only momentarily — by 1990.

Had you followed a strategy of allocating, say, 5% of your portfolio to energy all along, you did superbly well in an asset class that killed almost everybody who touched it. (And then, in a manner of speaking, killed everybody who missed touching it.)

Now, I admit it's tough to have discipline, and tougher to convince the investor to follow the discipline. But you might have convinced him to invest programmatically in an energy mutual fund. And if you had, that client would today be one of the great referral sources of your career, when he wasn't naming grandchildren after you.

(What you'd have been doing, of course, is "dollar-cost-averaging," which is a virtually flawless way of making long-term investments in cyclical asset classes. And since all asset classes are cyclical, you're right to conclude dollar-cost-averaging is an extremely smart way to invest.)

Tell your client again and again ...

DOLLAR COST AVERAGE
THROUGH INVESTMENT CYCLES,
AND, LONG-TERM, YOU'RE ALWAYS RIGHT.

Look at the Bailard, Biehl & Kaiser diversified portfolio of U.S. stocks, bonds, cash equivalents, real estate, and foreign stocks. By following an asset allocation discipline (keeping 20% in each asset class regardless of the prevailing investment wind — the BB&K Index in the table below), the portfolio produced virtually the same return as stocks alone, but with a great deal less volatility.

THE BENEFITS OF AN ASSET ALLOCATION DISCIPLINE

Stock market and bond market returns compared with returns for three diversified portfolios maintaining a strict asset allocation discipline and held from 1971-1990.

Year	Stocks[1]	Bonds[2]	60% Stocks 40% Bonds	Stocks, Bonds, Cash (1/3 each)	BB&K Index[3]
1971	14.31%	13.23%	14.14%	10.83%	13.7%
1972	18.98%	5.68%	13.54%	9.38%	15.1%
1973	-14.66%	- 1.11%	- 9.11%	- 3.03%	- 2.2%
1974	-26.47%	4.35%	-14.88%	- 5.44%	- 6.6%
1975	37.20%	9.19%	25.65%	17.04%	19.6%
1976	23.84%	16.75%	21.18%	15.19%	11.5%
1977	- 7.18%	- 0.67%	- 4.57%	- 0.94%	6.1%
1978	6.56%	- 1.16%	3.65%	4.40%	13.0%
1979	18.44%	- 1.22%	10.28%	9.14%	11.5%
1980	32.42%	- 3.95%	17.45%	13.17%	17.9%
1981	- 4.91%	1.85%	- 1.99%	4.06%	6.4%
1982	21.41%	40.35%	28.98%	23.97%	14.4%
1983	22.51%	0.68%	13.43%	10.52%	15.5%
1984	6.27%	15.43%	10.11%	10.75%	10.4%
1985	32.16%	30.97%	31.85%	23.38%	25.4%
1986	18.47%	24.44%	21.11%	16.61%	23.4%
1987	5.23%	- 2.69%	3.59%	3.92%	8.7%
1988	16.81%	9.67%	13.97%	11.01%	13.2%
1989	31.49%	18.11%	26.24%	19.22%	14.1%
1990	- 3.17%	6.18%	0.57%	3.61%	- 1.4%
Compound annual return	11.15%	8.71%	10.52%	9.55%	11.20%
Number of Years With Positive Return	15	14	16	17	17

[1]Standard & Poor's 500 index
[2]Long-Term Treasury Bonds
[3]20% U.S. stocks, 20% bonds, 20% cash, 20% real estate, 20% foreign stocks
Note: Results assume portfolio allocations are re-balanced annually.
Sources: Bailard, Biehl & Kaiser; Ibbotson Associates Inc.

FOCUS ON BASIC TRUTHS

Will all your clients maintain the asset allocation discipline? Probably not — unless you tell clients some "basic truths," make them believe you, and keep them acting on those truths. Inject managed money into the relationship like truth serum, and your clients' attention will focus on the basics:

- **Stocks, bonds, real estate, and international equities are among the core holdings of all successful portfolios.** You may want to give them different weightings at different stages of your life. But these core holdings are like milk — you never outgrow your need for them.

- **Cyclical change never stops.** At any given time, some core holdings will be working better than others. Then, cyclically, the star performers will lie down and bleed while the laggards jump up and start shooting the lights out. And almost every time this happens, it will surprise you. That's why you don't want to manage your own money.

- **You can hire great people to run each of your core holdings.** The professionals will almost always do better than you would — usually a whole lot better. So hire the pro's. And then don't second guess them.

- **Maintain reasonably consistent asset allocations by investing regularly.** You will always be buying fewer of the assets that are very expensive and more of the assets that are very cheap. In other words, dollar-cost-averaging tricks you into being relatively aggressive near market bottoms and relatively cautious near market tops.

- **What else is there?**

The answer is, of course, "There isn't anything else. Everything else is commentary." But, without your active, constant guidance and reinforcement, this approach simply won't happen.

One of the enduring myths of our business is that the salesperson or planner becomes *less* important to the client if "all he's doing" is channeling money to other managers. In fact, as I hope you're beginning to see, **your involvement is even more critical when you adopt the strategy of handling clients with the concept of managed money.**

GET PARALYZED INVESTORS MOVING

As in football and war, "nothing" is almost always the wrong thing to do in investing. Act or you will be acted upon, usually in ways you won't like.

Paralysis is the ultimate form of panic. You might say a guy running up the aisle of a crowded theater screaming "Fire!" is panicking. But his impulse to get out and warn others isn't wrong. Yet the guy in the front row next to the screamer *who is still sitting there,* staring into the middle distance with unblinking eyes as the smoke starts curling up around his ears … he's in the grip of the ultimate panic. He's panicked so bad he has no chance.

How often have you heard an investor say: "This stock market is a disaster; it's going much lower; interest rates are going higher; the economy is in for a big recession; everything is going to hell in a handbasket … so I'm not buying or selling anything. I'm just standing pat."

Although this guy's mouth is moving, it is clearly not connected to his brain in any useful way. He's like the guy sitting in the burning theater, about to become toast. The more horrifyingly volatile the markets are, the more of these soon-to-be crispy critters you're going to run into.

Offering managed money is the most reliable way to get these people ambulatory again. You can say to the client, "You don't have to suffer in silence, nor bear this burden alone. There are very smart people around, with records of doing relatively well even in times like these. And you can hire some of them, right now, to be opportunistic and to hunt up some of the really undervalued assets and businesses that are only available in times like these."

Notice how much more elegant, encouraging and non-judgmental this approach is than saying, "Dude, you're a zombie. You better get to a financial psychiatrist quick, or they're gonna mail what's left of you home to your loved ones in a Glad sandwich bag." And let me say here, for the first of many times in this book, that in selling managed money, the *feelings* you communicate are to the *facts* you communicate as nineteen is to one.

THE WAY YOU SAY WHAT YOU SAY
IS INFINITELY MORE IMPORTANT
THAN WHAT YOU SAY.

But I digress. I'm simply trying to drive home the point that people are apt to have extreme emotional reactions to today's jagged markets — reactions which are made even worse by the perpetual doom-saying of the media. But **you can snap the investor out of it by interposing a money manager between him and the fire.** Remember, however, like the problem it solves, this appeal is to the investor's emotions, not to his intellect.

RESTORE A LONG-TERM STRATEGIC PERSPECTIVE

By offering managed money, you can help end the neurotic and futile quest for "tops" and "bottoms."

When the books are closed on professional investing in the second half of the twentieth century, the greatest investor of the period may well turn out to be Sir John Templeton. Templeton is often asked, "When is the right time to buy stocks?" And he always says exactly the same thing: "When others are urgently and anxiously selling." In other words, great value in stocks (or in any asset class) exists only when the great plurality of market participants fears and loathes them, and will sell regardless of price.

Well, if that's good enough for Sir John, it ought to be plenty good enough for your average individual investor, right? Wrong. Because, again, the individual investor's perception of the cycle — of the inexorable ebb and flow of values in all cyclical markets — isn't very clear. Instead, he's an extrapolator. If stocks (or bonds, or whatever) are going up, they'll keep going up. "You're not at the top yet." Are they going down? Then it's the end of the world. "It's over. No bottom is in sight."

The stock of AMR Corp., the parent of American Airlines, was $107 a share in September 1989. Gee, that seemed a little pricey, didn't it? — a highly recession-sensitive company, after eight years of economic expansion, selling at over twenty times earnings, in a purely commodity-driven business where a small increase in fuel prices costs millions in lost earnings?

"Nonsense," scoffed the individual investor. "Don't you know anything? United Airlines is being taken over. And my brother-in-law's broker hears that Donald Trump (yes, Donald Trump!) is about to bid $120 for AMR. Hang on, we're not at the top yet."

Alas, The Donald must have had other things on his mind, because he never made that takeover bid. And, as we now know, he couldn't have financed one anyway.

Never mind that. Look at the fundamental lunacy here. AMR is 107; the theoretical risk, therefore, is $107 per share. But the investor is holding the stock, betting it will go up another 13 points to the rumored takeover price of 120. In other words, the potential reward, if everything goes right, is about 11%. So the investor is risking 107 points to make 13, just so he can't be criticized for "missing the top."

Just one year later, in September 1990, we have war, chaos in the oil market, a very palpable business contraction ... and AMR at $40 a share. Joe Topchaser is buried, having lost upwards of $67 in his attempt to make $13.

But look at the company in September 1990. American is, at that point, the largest privately owned airline in the world, second only in size to Russia's state-owned Aeroflot. Debt is only about 40% of capitalization — good financial shape. The stock sells at around 30% below book value — and book value, in American's case, may be meaningfully understated. The company's single largest asset, the state-of-the-art SABRE reservations system, is worth well north of $1.5 billion, but is carried on the books at zero.

Sure, American's earnings have disappeared for a while because of the spectacular run-up in fuel prices. But look at what's happening to American's marginally financed competitors. Midway, desperate for cash, has sold American some landing slots at New York's La Guardia and Washington's National, where landing slots are like crown jewels. Eastern is already in Chapter 11. Pan Am and Continental are making noises that sound a lot like death rattles.

So, all in all, you look at AMR and you say, "Gee, this is a great company in a business that's growing very rapidly around the globe, and AMR will pick up their share of the marbles if some weaker players are shaken out. Sounds like something I might want to start pecking away at, right?"

Of course not. Because now Joe Bottomfisher is saying, "Forget it. Book value, schnook value; this market's going lower. The company's losing money. We're not at the bottom yet." And he'll keep saying that, right up to — and then beyond — the bottom. Then, after it's clear that a new uptrend has begun, he'll say, "Too late. We missed it." — just before the stock doubles.

(If this sounds like 20-20 hindsight, go back and read the papers from September 1990. This stuff was all front page news. And sure enough, within six months, Eastern was gone. Midway, Pan Am and Continental had all declared bankruptcy. And AMR stock was $60 — up twice as much as the overall market.)

Oscar Wilde defined a "cynic" as someone who knows the price of everything and the value of nothing. Oddly enough, the individual investor is Wilde's cynic. Most investors isolate on the price of the stock and always lose. They should isolate on the value of the company. But they don't know how.

That's why most investors need a money manager who knows how to assess the values of companies. Give the manager the money — he'll know what to do.

I'm just using stocks as an example of the neurotic quest for tops and bottoms, but you know that all asset classes work the same way. Take bonds, for example. When interest rates go up, bond prices go down. By committing more money in such a down debt market, the investor can buy higher current yields, as well as appreciation on the bonds when interest rates cycle down again. But will he do it?

Of course not. "I'll wait . . . rates are going higher." When rates are 8.5%, he's waiting for 9%. At 9%, he thinks 9.5% is a shoo-in. And, as sure as you're sitting there, at 9.5%, this market sage will confidently assure you they're going to 10%.

Whereupon rates go back down to 9%. And the guy says, "Never mind, it's too late now. I'll just put my money in a money market fund until rates go up again." Which you know is a sure sign they're going straight to 7%, without leaving a skid mark.

Contrast the market timer with an investor who knows he should always have about 30% of his capital in bonds. With your help, he's chosen a high quality bond fund. And, with a little gentle prodding from you, he tops it off every so often, whenever the amount allocated to bonds drops more than a couple of percentage points under 30%. Here again, without the investor really sweating over the decision, he's acquiring more shares when interest rates are high and the price of shares in his bond fund is low . . . unless he starts reading the headlines and watching FNN. Whereupon even the most resolute investor can start unconsciously blurring the managed money decision into a surrogate market timing attempt.

Whenever the investor is anxious to put more money with a manager because the market is so great, or reluctant to put any more money in because the market is so bad, you know he's once again trying to bastardize a money management/asset allocation strategy into market timing ... and hoping you won't notice.

Here, again, is where you come in, reminding the investor that ...

**✳ IT'S NEVER THE WRONG TIME
TO PUT SOME MORE MONEY
WITH THE RIGHT MONEY MANAGER. ✳**

SUMMARY

- The individual investor has given up. He knows he needs managed money. But, left to his own devices, he'll try to out-think his own managers. That's where you come in.

- Money management products help make asset allocators out of trend followers. Investing only in "what's working" means you're always climbing aboard the investment vogue du jour just before it crashes. Asset allocation with money management products saves the investor from himself . . . but only with your constant guidance.

- Money management products help the investor get moving when he's paralyzed. Terrifying volatility and negative media increasingly immobilize the investor. A consistent strategy of putting new money with great managers keeps the investor moving and dollar cost averaging.

- Smart people are always capable of doing dumb things. The investor's intellect is not the problem; it's his emotions. You are the bridge. The feelings you communicate are to the facts you communicate as nineteen is to one. And the *way* you say what you say is infinitely more important than *what* you say.

- Money management products help restore a long-term perspective, instead of a neurotic and futile search for "tops" and "bottoms." All you ever need to do is buy more when most folks are selling, and vice versa. Asset allocation with money management products tricks the investor into doing the right thing, through the medium of dollar-cost-averaging.

- It's never the wrong time to put some more money with the right money manager.

2

What Managed Money Can Do For You

Keeping your own interests in proper balance with your client's is an important theme. On one side, if you put your interests ahead of the client's, you are buying a one-way ticket out of the business, if only on the installment plan. Less obvious, but equally true, you damage yourself by excessively subordinating your interests to those of your clients.

So, in the interests of a balance-of-benefits approach to the business, let's look at what managed money can do for you.

"PURIFY" YOUR WORK

Most of us are good at gathering and allocating assets and are less good — maybe a lot less good — at managing portfolios of specific securities. And, as you successfully build a client base, you must spend more time managing assets.

The commissioned stockbroker is probably the most painful example of this dilemma. He wants to be selling as much of the time as he can, but he has to spend effort keeping up with the market, reading research, staying on top of the news on companies whose stocks he owns, and reacting to unforeseen events. Ironically, the more he builds his business, the more insistent and important these demands become. And the larger the client base, the greater the need for services of various kinds (dividends, taxes, portfolio evaluations, etc.).

Offering managed money lets you concentrate on your strength and on the activity most financially rewarding — not the one you don't feel particularly good at. When you explain that to people, you sound very professional:

> "Mr. Prospect, I feel I have certain strengths to offer investors. I'm good at helping people define goals. I can create rational investment strategies to attain those goals. I think I excel at selecting superb money managers to handle each segment of my clients' portfolios in a successful way. Last, and most important, I've learned to help my clients stay the course and not get blown this way and that by the investment fads — and fears — of the moment.
>
> That's a lifetime's work. And inevitably, I haven't had time to develop some other skills. I could never figure out the short-term swings in the stock market, or what interest rates will do in the next six months, or whether to buy Apple or IBM. I never thought trying to outguess the market mattered much anyway, compared to a long-term, patient strategy of hiring great money managers and letting them do their job. Does that sound like a reasonable approach to you?"

You can say all that in a minute and fifteen seconds. Or you can say:

> "I can pick stocks better than your other broker can. I have a better idea what the markets are going to do. You should invest with me because I'm going to be more right."

Sounds pretty awful when you put it that way, doesn't it? Yet, that's what most securities salespeople feel they have to say when they're running the money themselves.

Pitting your investment selections against the pro's . . . is that how you want to position yourself for the next ten years?

TALK TO LONG-TERM SERIOUS MONEY

The managed money approach automatically de-selects the crazies (well, most crazies) and forces you to talk to "serious money." Take another read through the presentation above. Can you see yourself saying this soliloquy to someone who wants to beat the options market? Chances are, such an investor will be gone long before you finish. He'll be off talking to some other salesperson who will have a couple of good months while the guy trades himself into oblivion. In the next scene, the other salesperson is taking part in meaningful discussions with the compliance department about overtrading the fish's account. Only then will this salesperson notice he hasn't opened another account in two months.

Meanwhile, you'll keep forging ahead, putting under management serious money from real people.

TAKE AN ASSET-BASED APPROACH

In the long run, gathering assets is all that counts. People who succeed in our business have a large amount of assets under control and don't try to turn it over very much. And, people who fail have a small amount of money under control and try to turn it over a lot.

The managed money approach keeps you out there gathering assets versus managing portfolios — the thing you are paid to do. And the more time you spend gathering assets, the more opportunities you will have to do business over the years — in good markets and bad — as people's needs change. Even when another salesperson prospects your clients, they'll come to you to see what you think. Because **he who controls the assets ultimately controls the account.**

The more assets you control, the less potential for conflict of interest in your relationships with clients — because the more money you control, the more sensible opportunities you can find to put it to work in a way that benefits everyone.

CREATE INSTANT CREDIBILITY

For younger salespeople/planners, or anyone who's been in the business for a relatively short while, offering managed money provides instant credibility. Instead of having to feign expertise you haven't got — and not fooling anybody in the process — you're selling experienced, well-known management. **If the person who's going to run the money has twenty-five years experience, the fact that you only have twenty-five months doesn't matter.**

Properly conditioned, a client will always see you in the light of your recommendations. The quality and seriousness of the investments you choose for people form their view of you.

But, be sure you're channeling that potential credibility in a way the investor can really feel. Your own confidence is the emotional bridge that connects the investor and the money manager you are selling. Most people will not invest their confidence one step removed. And don't ask the investor to invest his confidence in spite of you; he won't do it.

To buy an international bond fund from you, the investor doesn't need to feel you know all about international bond markets. (In fact, you'll have assured him you don't.) But unless he gets a very strong sense of *informed belief* that you and your firm have chosen this particular fund wisely, he probably won't play. You're asking him to make an act of faith, for which the ultimate support has to be you. Prospectuses, "mountain charts," glossy brochures and other pieces of printed matter don't do it for people — people do it for people.

Realize that the "instant credibility" managed money offers you is purchased at a price — you must stand up confidently for the manager you're representing. You may be daunted by the amount of "product knowledge" you don't yet have. That's understandable, and, in a way, laudable, because it means you want to learn more so you can serve investors better.

Product knowledge will surely come in time, as you continue to grow and experience this phenomenally instructive business. Meanwhile, take comfort from the fact that product knowledge can never be the ultimate answer, because …

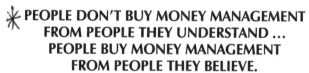

PEOPLE DON'T BUY MONEY MANAGEMENT FROM PEOPLE THEY UNDERSTAND … PEOPLE BUY MONEY MANAGEMENT FROM PEOPLE THEY BELIEVE.

LEVERAGE YOUR FIELDS OF EXPERTISE

The stock market is a lifetime's study, and even then you never master it. You just learn to make your peace with the market as best you can. But once you learn to sell a great long-term growth stock fund (or a great money manager), you can move on, because that's all you'll ever need to know about the market.

The same is true of sectors. You could spend an awfully long time trying to understand health care technology. And given the speed of technological change, you might never understand it. But find one superbly managed health care mutual fund, and you've instantly mastered what you really need to know.

Health care, the environment, media and communications, and energy are all sectors you may think belong in a well-diversified equity portfolio. But you'll probably never master any one, much less all, of these vital businesses. And why should you? If you know who the consistent, high-quality managers in these sectors are, you've learned all you *and your clients* need to know. And you can go on and learn something else.

ELIMINATE THE BURDEN OF "KNOWING"

As I said earlier, our business rewards us not for what we know, but for what we do. And offering managed money liberates you to do what is essential for your success — prospecting, selling, counseling — without the burden of "knowing."

Both securities sales and financial planning put a tremendous premium on your willingness and ability to get yourself in front of the prospect and talk to him about his hopes, dreams, fears, investment experiences … how he reacts to you, tries to avoid making decisions, fears making a mistake … and a hundred similar concerns.

What does any of that have to do with what you know, or don't know? Nothing. The fact is that product knowledge never made anybody a good salesman of anything. Besides, the individual investor doesn't invest with his head. He invests with his heart, and then justifies what he's done (or hasn't done) with his head.

You can't learn anything about the sales process from a prospectus, book, or a tape. You learn to ski by skiing; you can only learn how to sell (or counsel clients effectively) by getting out there and listening to the prospects. In time, you'll infer what product knowledge you need from the questions people ask you. Just remember:

SYSTEMATIC SELLING EFFORTS
ALWAYS LEAD TO BETTER PRODUCT KNOWLEDGE …
IT NEVER WORKS
THE OTHER WAY AROUND.

SELL EXPOSURE INSTEAD OF PROOF

By offering managed money, you avoid one of the most insidious obstacles to the development of client relationships — the "burden of proof" syndrome.

Listen to what a transaction-oriented salesperson sounds like:

"My firm is very positive on the stock market. We believe that natural gas stocks will outperform the market over the next twelve months. Our favorite natural gas stock — the one we think will perform best — is Unocal. It's got the largest concentration of U.S. natural gas reserves, and great management, too. I think you should buy 1,000 shares."

Now, this presentation is not hard-sell or hyperbolic. The assertions about Unocal are quite true. But look at all the things you predict are going to happen: (a) the stock market will go up; (b) natural gas stocks will go up more than other stocks; (c) Unocal will go up more than other gas stocks. Well, maybe that's going to happen; maybe it's not. At the very least, this salesperson has a terrible burden to carry. All the client has to say is anything that sounds like "Prove it," and you've had it. Because you've let yourself be cast in the ultimate false position: *trying to prove what's going to happen in the future.*

Subliminally, this false position is very bad for your relationship with the client — because you've pressed the button that says, "I don't know if I can trust this person." The client isn't thinking about your firm, or your research department, or Unocal. You're the bridge; he's thinking about you.

Incidentally, even if you can overcome the client's fears and get the order, you are by no means out of the woods. If Unocal doesn't go up now, you're a bum. You gave the client the right to judge your professionalism and commitment based on the movement of one particular stock over the next few months. Dumb.

Now, listen to the managed money approach:

"Mr. Client, I'm afraid energy is going to be one of the megatrends of the '90s. The world underinvested in energy in the 1950s and '60s, because oil was so plentiful and cheap. We paid a terrible price for that in the '70s, when prices rose 1000% in just a half-dozen years because the world was undersupplied.

The cycle turned, as it always does. In the '80s, we had huge oversupply, because high prices led to over-investment. Prices crashed, and exploration stopped.

Energy demand will experience enormous growth in the '90s, as the world economy goes global and the third world industrializes. The supply is there, but the production capacity isn't. So, cyclically, the '90s will be a period of increased investment and an upward bias in energy prices.

No portfolio will be properly balanced without some meaningful exposure to energy. In all but the most extreme circumstances, a 5% to 7% portfolio weighting should be enough.

The hard part is not letting ourselves get too bullish when spot oil prices shoot up, nor too bearish when oil prices crater. That's where a consistent 5% to 7% weighting comes in. We'll keep focused on a long-term strategy and prevent getting stampeded by the headlines.

We could try to pick one or two energy stocks, I suppose, but that doesn't seem to me to be the really smart way. Instead, I'm putting about 5% of my clients' portfolios in the Gronsky Energy Fund. Over the last ten years, the management team of the fund — who spend all their time studying the world energy situation — have really performed brilliantly. (Example: Gronsky Energy Fund performance vs. unweighted oil stock index.)

Am I right that 5% of your portfolio would be about $ _____? Then I'd like you to buy $ _____ in Gronsky Energy Fund shares this morning."

The presentation takes two minutes and fifteen seconds. But, look at all it encompasses:

(1) why energy now;
(2) a cyclical appreciation of energy prices;
(3) suggested portfolio weighting;
(4) the need to stay the course;
(5) full-time management versus us picking stocks;
(6) the manager I've chosen, and why; and
(7) request for a specific order, or "trial close."

The presentation is perhaps most notable for what it *doesn't* contain:

(1) any suggestion of where oil or natural gas prices are going to be one, three, five, or ten years from now;

(2) any suggestion of where stock prices, much less oil stock prices, are going;

(3) any suggestion that Gronsky Energy Fund is the "best" energy fund; and

(4) anything at all that smacks of "proof."

Does this presentation try to answer all the client's questions and objections in advance? No, of course not. You don't know what questions or objections you'll face, and you can't find out until you shut up and listen. (Most people outside the sales profession — and a few sad souls inside — think the great salesperson is a great talker. Nonsense. The great salesperson is a great listener.)

No, the message of this presentation is: Cyclically, energy is about to hurt you, unless you participate; you participate by creating and maintaining a certain portfolio weighting, not by zigging and zagging with the price of crude; I know a superb manager who does nothing but energy; he's going to do better than we are, so let's stop knocking ourselves out and give him the money.

Offering managed money lets you sell exposure, not proof. The client feels better, and you'll live longer.

PUT UP THE "FIREWALL"

Even good money managers, under pressure to perform, sometimes bet the ranch on a bad poker hand. When poor performance happens in a managed money context, though, you and the client are on one side and the manager is on the other — that's the *firewall effect.* "He let *us* down," has to be your attitude. "If *we* think this through clearly, and regroup *together, we'll* come out OK."

You don't want to end up like the Lone Ranger, the time he and Tonto were set upon by a war party of Sioux. They galloped away into a little-known canyon, only to find it occupied by hostile Comanches. Dashing out again, they ran right into a band of screaming Apaches. "Looks like we're in real trouble this time, Tonto," the masked man said. To which Tonto replied, "What you mean *we*, white man?"

SUMMARY

- A healthy balancing of both your clients' interests and your own is vital to a successful client relationship.

- Managed money purifies the nature of your work by placing a premium on what you're good at and what you are paid for: gathering and allocating assets.

- Managed money forces you to be talking to long-term, serious money, and to the owners thereof. Such an emphasis tends automatically to de-select crazies from your book-building program.

- Managed money gives you an asset-based approach to the business, and in the long run, assets are all that count. Successful practitioners of our business have a lot of assets under control, so they don't have to turn the assets over very much. Losers have few assets under control and try to make them work too hard.

- Managed money creates instant credibility. But you have to earn your credibility. You must beam a strong sense of informed belief at the client, which is not a function of what you know, but of how you feel and how you make the client feel.

- People don't buy managed money from people they understand. People buy managed money from people they believe.

- Managed money leverages your expertise. Learn where a sector belongs in an overall portfolio. Learn who are the consistently credible managers in that sector. Give them the money. And then go learn something else.

- Managed money frees you to do the only things which make you successful — prospecting and selling. Systematic selling efforts will always lead to better product knowledge, but no amount of product knowledge will get you up and out the door.

SUMMARY *(continued)*

- Managed money lets you sell exposure, not proof. The "burden of proof" syndrome is toxic and will poison any incipient client relationship at the roots.

- If worst comes to worst, managed money creates an emotional firewall, with you and the client on one side and the manager on the other. "What you mean *we*, white man?"

3

The Six Absolutely Critical
Things You Need To Know

If you are preparing to make a major push into selling managed money, you may be worried about all the things you don't know yet. Funds or "wrap" accounts? Asset allocation or market timing? Foreign stock or bond funds? What countries, when, and why? What's standard deviation? Is risk-adjusted return important? Where are the snows of yesteryear?

The answers to these and hundreds of similar questions are the same:

(1) I don't know.
(2) It depends.
(3) You'll find out as you go along, or you'll find out you don't need to know.
(4) Those aren't the threshold issues.

You absolutely have to know only six things to begin the quest for success in selling managed money. Here they are:

1. FIRST AND FOREMOST, YOU ARE SELLING YOURSELF.

Mario Gabelli, Dr. Martin Zweig, Sir John Templeton, and the next dozen great money managers you can think of, all have one thing in common: Not one will ever sit at your client's dining room table or in his office at the back of his shop. None of them will draw your client out so he'll tell you what a terrific artist his daughter is turning into, and how he'd love to accumulate the money to have her study art in Florence. Or how the client's father worked until the day he died, and how the client wants to make sure he and his wife will have long years of comfortable retirement. Or how he'd like to arrange that his married son won't have to worry about his children's education, the way the client did.

No, great money managers can't do that. But you can, and you must. Because **people buy managed investments with their serious money for the attainment of their most serious goals.** And when life's goals are the issues at stake, people invest with somebody who shows he understands their goals, who cares deeply about helping them achieve those goals, and who will be there in good times and bad to help them stay the course.

Will you please tell me what any of that has to do with what you *know*? I'm convinced it has entirely to do with *who you are*, and how you make the client feel.

If you can demonstrate empirically (with charts, graphs and a computer print-out) that dollar cost averaging into a high-beta aggressive growth stock fund will produce such a low average cost that, in nine of the last ten five-year periods, the track record of the fund clearly indicates the client will be able to keep his daughter in pasta and paint brushes for three years in Florence … well, my hat's off to you. I wish you luck. But I think the client is an even-money bet to go catatonic on you … and his wife is likely to run screaming from the room.

I'd prefer to say something like this:

"I see what you're trying to accomplish. More than that, I sense how deeply important it is to you. Achieving the goal you've set for yourself isn't going to be easy. But I'll commit myself to helping you, if you'll allow me.

First, you're going to need to invest in high-quality common stocks, because that's about the only way to accomplish real growth of your capital. Next, you will want to hire the finest, most reliable money managers you can find to manage your stock portfolio.

*Then, we're going to need the discipline to keep adding systematically to your account, month in and month out, even when prices are falling and the headlines are scary … which at times they will be. The most important thing to remember is that the prices of great common stocks often **go** down … but they never **stay** down. And the same monthly (or quarterly) dollar investment buys more shares when prices are low.*

I suggest that the most sensible vehicle for your goal is the Gronsky Quality Growth Fund. I've come to rely on the Gronsky Group extensively over the years, to the point where I try (note: say only if true) to get back to visit them in Boston a couple of times a year (or, to host a dinner for my clients with one of their senior people a couple of times a year).

In fact, my wife and I are investing in Gronsky Quality Growth shares for our own children's education. (Again: say only if true.)

I'm not suggesting that Gronsky Quality Growth will be the number-one, best-performing stock fund of all time. Frankly, I have no idea which fund will be the top performer. And, when the figures come out every 90 days, it's always somebody new who shot the lights out. Often they fade away.

I'm not interested in that. The Gronsky Group follows a long-term, consistent strategy that stresses avoiding the big mistake. Stellar short-term performance doesn't matter much if you turn around the next year and give it all back. My attitude is: I don't have to do the "best," as long as I do very well over the long term … and avoid the big mistake. Don't you agree?

Gronsky Quality Growth tries to buy shares in great companies when they're undervalued, and hold them through major upward cycles. In other words, just what you and I would do if we had the time, the knowledge, the patience and the discipline.

But the fact is we don't have all those qualities … at least not all the time. That's why, when it comes to goals as serious as yours, I don't feel I can afford not to hire the Gronsky Group.

Does an initial investment of $10,000 and $2,500 a quarter feel comfortable to you? Or, after the initial investment, is $1,000 a month easier for you?"

That whole presentation takes two and a half minutes. Sorry, but because I was trying to bring it home efficiently, I had to leave out a lot of stuff like: track record (the dreaded "mountain chart"); beta; stocks the fund owns; the sales charge; how Gronsky Quality Growth compares to the Lipper 109 Big-Cap Growth Funds over the last 1, 3, 5, 7, 10 and 17-1/2 years; what they did in the fourth quarter of 1987; and where the portfolio manager got his MBA. Et cetera, et cetera.

You see, in two and a half minutes, all you've got time to cover is everything the folks really care about. Does the prospect want to know about any of the stuff I left out? Fine. He'll surely ask, and I'll be happy to answer. But, I try not to answer questions nobody asks me. And my first premise is:

PROSPECTS DON'T CARE WHAT YOU KNOW UNTIL THEY KNOW THAT YOU CARE.

So, I elected to use my 150 seconds to tell the prospect:

- I understand you.
- I feel what you're feeling.
- It's not going to be easy.
- I'll help you, if you'll let me.
- Only good stocks will get you there, managed by a first-class manager.
- We're going to have to be disciplined.
- I know some great people, and I do mean *I know them personally.*
- I invest with them myself (if true).
- Keep "performance" in perspective. You don't need to shoot the lights out, but you do need to avoid shooting yourself in the foot.
- Whatever it costs, you can't afford *not* to do it.
- Do it!

Managed money is about the deepest needs of people. People have to invest their confidence in another person before they'll invest serious money in anything. You are the bridge. First and foremost, you are selling who you are . . . not what you know.

2. YOU MUST SET THE AGENDA.

In today's tremendous universe of money management products, you can't be all things to all people. Nor should you even try. You have to have a consistent, strongly held notion of what people can reasonably ask you to do.

Chuck Yeager was the pre-eminent test pilot of the era which took us from propeller flight to a manned landing on the moon. And yet, throughout his long and supremely distinguished career . . .

NOBODY EVER ASKED CHUCK YEAGER TO BUILD AN AIRPLANE.

Yeager did what he did better than any man alive. So, no one would have dreamed of asking him to do something else. Everybody was happy to have him do what he was great at. And that must be your attitude in setting your own professional agenda for selling managed money.

For instance, you may know that foreign stocks were one of the best-performing *financial* asset classes during the last ten years (we're not counting Van Goghs or Etruscan coins, here). With all trade barriers falling in Western Europe in 1992 and with the freeing of the East European economies, you may feel the trend will continue apace. So, with your firm's help, you've picked out a global stock fund with high-calibre management and a superior record. And you're trying to sell clients a 10% portfolio weighting in that fund.

Suddenly, a client starts asking you if the track record wasn't built primarily in West German stocks, or what if the new unified German currency falls against the yen, or what percentage of the portfolio will be in British stocks, or what if the Russians make the ruble convertible, and things like that.

A tremendous natural defensiveness and frustration breaks out in all of us when this happens. We're torn between self-recrimination that we didn't study these issues more fully, and resentment that the client is cross-examining us about issues that probably ought to be left up to the fund manager. We start beaming a lot of confused, negative vibes at the client. The interview ends in very palpable discomfort and no sale. That experience can end your global stock fund effort. Because if this one guy asked all that stuff you didn't know, heaven knows what the next client might ask, and the next ...

Stop. Wake up. You're having a nightmare. In it, you're the only fielder in a baseball game where there are nine batters on the other team ... and no foul lines. Any ball that drops anywhere in the park will be a hit ... unless you catch it. But you can't possibly reach them all!

Wake up. There *are* foul lines, but you have to set them. And you can have plenty of veteran professionals on your team, ready to play their positions and back you up so you can continue to the close rather than retreat from the scene. (You'll see how in the chapters on Q&A.)

You're a salesperson/planner, not a professor of international economics or the European editor of the *New York Times*. You're not the portfolio manager, or the chief economist of the money management company. Let clients know ...

✳ YOU FLY 'EM, YOU DON'T BUILD 'EM.

You have to set your own agenda and not let clients and prospects set the agenda for you. You cannot be the technical expert on the myriad of economic, market and tax questions that inhabit the universe of managed money. That's why you've drafted a money management company on your team — so the money manager can master the "micro" issues.

3. PRODUCT KNOWLEDGE IS VIETNAM.

It's absolutely fatal to think of product knowledge as a precondition of a successful sales effort. **What's most important is what you do, not what you know.**

Product knowledge is the tar baby — a quagmire with a capital "Q." You never arrive on a firm footing, and you can never turn around and walk back out. You just keep slogging in deeper and deeper until the primeval ooze closes over your head, and you disappear forever. Which is a real shame, because product knowledge is the wrong war to begin with.

Most salespeople and planners try to use product knowledge the wrong way: as a defense against the terrifying prospect of looking foolish when asked a question they can't answer. We say, "Well, my relationship with people is based on their confidence that I know my stuff. I can't go out shooting from the hip. I'll look terribly foolish if they start asking me a lot of questions I can't answer. So I've got to do a great deal more homework before undertaking such an effort."

Vietnam. First of all, you never get "enough" product knowledge this way. You can never know what "enough" is until you talk to a lot of prospects and find out what they need to know and what they really don't care about. So, in searching for "enough" knowledge, you're waist-deep in the Big Muddy, and the big fool (yourself, in this case) says to push on. It's just a very elaborate way of avoiding the real work of going up the learning curve interview by interview.

The movie *National Lampoon's Animal House* takes place at the mythical Faber College. In the first scene, the camera pans past the statue of Mr. Faber, the college's founder. A quote from him is inscribed on the pedestal. Do you remember what it says? — *"Knowledge is good."*

I kind of agree with that. Knowledge is, well, *good* — not great, not bad, not all that really matters, but… *good*. Only don't make knowledge an end in itself. And don't think that real knowledge comes any other way but through talking to lots of real prospects and clients. We all worry, at the start of a new product program, that we don't have the power to bring it off. But, we find that Emerson was right: "Do the thing, and you'll have the power."

I promise you that later in this book I'll offer you a 100% effective way to turn a question you can't answer into closing the sale. So stop worrying about it.

**A QUESTION YOU CAN'T ANSWER
CAN'T HURT YOU …
THE ONLY THING THAT CAN HURT YOU IS
NOT MAKING THE PRESENTATION
BECAUSE YOU'RE AFRAID OF THE QUESTION
YOU CAN'T ANSWER.**

4. THE CONCEPT IS THE MAGNET.

You have to know, and be able to state clearly, THE CONCEPT, because it's the magnet which draws people toward you. Let's go back to the presentation of the Gronsky Quality Growth Fund to the client who needed growth of capital. After you made the all-important statement of empathy and commitment, you said:

> *"First of all, you're going to need to be investing in high-quality common stocks, because that's about the only way to accomplish real growth of your capital. Next, you will want to hire the finest, most reliable money managers you can find to manage your stock portfolio."*

Observe what you *did not say:*

> *"You need a high quality common stock mutual fund."*

This is the beginning of appreciating the difference between selling an investment — no matter how well-chosen, correct and perfectly suitable that investment is — and selling THE CONCEPT.

**THE CONCEPT IS
THE SOLUTION TO THE CLIENT'S PROBLEM;
THE PRODUCT IS
THE BOX THE SOLUTION COMES IN.**

Apprehend the difference and incorporate THE CONCEPT into your conversations with clients, and you will immediately see a radical change in the way people relate to you. If the difference still seems arbitrary or even semantic to you, just put this whole notion on hold until the next big birthday party you go to, or until next Father's Day, Mother's Day, or Christmas. Then just sit in a corner, and watch the presents being opened, and observe that the presents generate much more attention and excitement than the boxes and bows.

You see my point. People relate to the notion that you understand and know how to solve their financial problems. Next to that, the *form* of the solution holds relatively little significance. The form may, in fact, be a complete abstraction to your prospects. That's why the Universal Five-Point Managed Money Presentation we will build later flows out of THE CONCEPT.

Concentrate on THE CONCEPT and you forge a great link in the chain of understanding and trust that completes a relationship. Concentrate on the product and you remind people of everything they don't know — and every bad thing they ever heard — about the product. You throw people back onto their preconceptions, which is the last place in the world you want them.

5. WHEN YOU BELIEVE, YOU'LL BE BELIEVED.

I've been in the securities business for a bit more than half my life, and "when you believe, you'll be believed" is absolutely the single most important thing I've ever learned. It's also a big part of the reason I trash product knowledge so mercilessly. People never seem to want to buy investments I *understand;* people want to buy investments I *believe in.* (They most particularly want to buy investments I *love.*)

You probably experience this phenomenon without necessarily recognizing it. Haven't you noticed, when you're presenting something to your best clients, they say things like: "Do you really like it? Do you really think this is good for me?"

What's going on here? Clearly, some sort of bond of trust has already been established. And the bond sounds pretty powerful to me. I don't hear the client asking you what depreciation schedule the company's Canadian widget division uses, or asking to read the bond indenture, the prospectus, or the research report. I don't hear him asking about the

Lipper rating, the Morningstar rating, or the Motion Picture Association of America rating. Most pointedly, I don't hear him asking what the load is. Finally, I don't hear him asking if you *understand* the investment.

Nope. I just hear the client asking the only two things he ever really cares about, *once he trusts you*: "Do you really like it? Do you really think this is good for me?"

But here you are, wanting to get started on a major expansion of your money management business. You decide to begin with a great long-term growth common stock fund, because you know that even folks who *think* they want safety and income really need the safety from inflation that only growth provides.

So you pick up your firm's list of growth mutual funds ... and all the energy and enthusiasm run right out of you — there are *twenty* of 'em! And, as hard as you stare at all the statistics, you can't tell one from the other, much less figure out which one is the "best."

So you start talking to the wholesalers. The guy from the Monticello Fund says their track record beats the Hermitage Fund, the Mount Vernon Fund and the Sagamore Hill Fund. Sounds simple enough, and you're really getting stoked.

Until five minutes later, when the Hermitage Fund guy drops by. You thank him politely, but inform him you're leaving on a great crusade to bring the Monticello Fund to the masses. "Not so fast," he says. "You didn't fall for the 'best track record over the last 10 years' jive, did you?"

Well, you have to admit you did. "Look closer," says the Hermitage Fund guy. "We were 64 basis points behind Monticello Fund, I'll grant you. But we held an average of 30% in cash over the ten years. So our *risk-adjusted* return is astronomically higher, don't you see?"

Yes, you do. And so you experience a second-stage-rocket type of religious conversion. The burnt-out shell of Monticello Fund falls away, as you prepare to go into the stratosphere with Hermitage Fund.

Then you remember you had a lunch date next Tuesday with the Mount Vernon Fund wholesaler, so you call to cancel, and politely explain why.

"Mirrors and blue smoke," says he, pityingly. "They're hypnotizing you with the cash position to keep your eye off the performance in '87 and '90, when they were down 10% and 14%, respectively. Our worst year was -2%. So, although our total return is a few basis points lower, we did it with a lot less *volatility.* And volatility, my lad, is what your clients hate the worst."

At this point, you make the only logical business decision possible, which is to go across the street and have a stiff drink. But as you approach the door, you find it's blocked by someone coming out. Oh no, don't let it be . . .

But it is . . . the Sagamore Hill Fund wholesaler. And he's coming straight toward you . . .

In this process, you're acquiring a bushel and a peck of product knowledge, aren't you? Why, just look at all you're learning about the ins and outs and sophisticated nuances in evaluating mutual funds. So how come you don't feel so good?

Well, I'll tell you. And when I've finished telling you, I'm afraid you'll conclude, as I have, that it's your fault.

See, you went (albeit unconsciously) on a quest for the "best" growth fund. Your unconscious reasoned (if you can call it reasoning) as follows: "I'll pick out the best one; no one will ever be able to compete with me because I'm selling the best one. Therefore, I will make all the sales, have a 100% closing ratio, and be rich and famous and live forever." Or something along those lines.

Won't work. You see, "best," like beauty, is very much in the eye of the beholder. Besides, you weren't really looking for something to sell. *You were looking for something to hide behind.* You wanted the statistics to sell for you, so you wouldn't have to stand up and ask your prospects and clients to trust you. *I hate that.* So, it gives me great pleasure to tell you **the search for proof is a dead end street.**

Try something different. Pick six likely candidates from among the firm's "top 20" growth funds. Call each of the six wholesalers and schedule an interview to ask who the people are, what the philosophy is, why the wholesaler likes his company, what kind of client the fund appeals to, how the wholesaler presents it, what the common objections are, and what support the wholesaler is prepared to give you. Oh, yes, and what the track record is.

Set the agenda, and give the agenda to the candidates. Then turn your mind off — listen to what they say and how they say it. Then, see which presentation strikes you as being the best *for you.*

That's the one. It may take you a long time to figure out why. Indeed, you may never figure out why. But, as the Carly Simon song says, "Turn down the noise in your mind," and you'll find the "right fund."

✳THE FUND THAT INSTINCTIVELY SUITS YOU IS THE FUND PEOPLE WILL LOVE TO BUY THROUGH YOU.

Why? Because you believe in it. And, when people feel your belief, they believe, as well.

Fall in love. Tell a love story. You can't be "wrong" (provided the proper due diligence was done upstream from you, and provided you don't underdiversify by putting too much of your clients' assets in one fund). And, as your depth of conviction leads to greater and greater success, (a) you'll learn more (isn't that what you always wanted?), and (b) you'll acquire the drive to talk to more and more people — which is something no amount of product knowledge can ever do for you.

When you're out there, talking about an investment you love, only two outcomes are possible. One is that people respond warmly to your depth of conviction and invest in the fund. The other is that people feel your conviction, respect you for it, but don't feel this fund is right for them, and tell you why. Which leads me to the sixth and last of the absolutely critical things you have to know.

6. WHEN A PROSPECT TELLS YOU WHY HE WON'T BUY YOUR IDEA, HE'S TOLD YOU WHAT IDEA HE WILL BUY.

In our profession, there is absolutely no such thing as "no sale." Isn't that astounding? The greatest salesperson working for IBM is going to walk out empty-handed if, upon mature reflection, his prospect simply has no proximate need for more computing capability. If all your brushes are in great shape, the Fuller Brush Man is only going to get a cup of coffee out of his sales interview with you. Ditto the Avon Lady, if your collection of scents and cosmetics is quite complete, thanks.

And even if the product is desperately needed, all those salespeople will strike out if the prospect doesn't have — and can't borrow — the money.

We, on the other hand, are always dealing with people who have more money than they plan to spend. The issue is never that these delightful folks don't have money, it's that they're not sure how to deploy money optimally.

More to the point, whenever our clients tell us why they prefer not to invest in what we're recommending, they're invariably telling us:

(1) they don't understand yet why our recommendation is exactly what they need; and/or

(2) what they *will* invest in.

Let's put alternative #1 aside for the moment. (We'll handle that one in our discussion on Q&A.) For now, just focus on alternative #2.

When you are in front of a prospective client, you sound him out about his most fundamental financial needs, and you come back with a clear, crisp, deeply felt, and enthusiastic recommendation. Suppose the prospect can show you that the recommendation doesn't fit.

What a great moment! Who knows why it happens? Maybe he just didn't put all his financial cards on the table from the get-go. But suddenly, you both can clearly see that the recommendation you first made is genuinely inconsistent with what the prospect really needs. Spectacular! Why? Because ...

WHEN A PROSPECT TELLS YOU
HIS REAL NEEDS ...
HE'S TOLD YOU WHAT HE'LL BUY.

You simply have to acknowledge that the new information changes your view of things, and then start again from THE CONCEPT. Get the prospect's assent that your new version of THE CONCEPT is the correct one. Then, roll right into the managed money product that *is* the ideal one, as you can both now plainly see.

How did this happen? Easy. You went out, saw the prospect, and, with the best heart in the world, showed him the wrong product. He told you so, and showed you why ... and, in the process, the prospect clearly asked for another solution which you had close at hand.

This process has nothing at all to do with what you know. **The critical event is to get in front of the prospect and show yourself to be the concerned and dedicated professional you are.** That's what the client sees. He doesn't blame you when you initially present the wrong solution. He focuses, instead, on all your best qualities ... and tells you what he really needs.

* * *

So, in light of all you've read, shouldn't this chapter be titled "What

You *Don't* Need To Know To Be Successful Selling Managed Money?" I guess so. But, I was afraid you'd conclude this book was going to be hard-sell, or lacking in intellectual rigor, or something awful like that.

I can tell you this chapter is absolutely vital to an appreciation of the rest of the book. And if I were you, I'd stop here, go back, and read this chapter again.

SUMMARY

- First and foremost, you're selling yourself. People invest their serious money for the attainment of their most serious goals. So they invest with a professional who empathizes, shows he cares, and commits himself to helping them. None of the above has much to do with what you know — it has to do with who you are.

- People don't care what you know until they know that you care. Reach your prospects emotionally first. Then you can educate them.

- You have to have a consistent, strongly held notion of what people can reasonably ask you to do. Nobody ever asked Chuck Yeager to build an airplane. Set your own agenda. Concentrate on what you're good at.

- Product knowledge is Vietnam, if it's your precondition for a marketing effort or your defense against a morbid fear of being asked a question you can't answer. Knowledge is good, but it's the means, not the end.

- You're always going to be asked questions you can't answer. That can't hurt you. The only thing that can hurt you is not going out and seeing people.

- You have to know and be able to state clearly THE CONCEPT. THE CONCEPT is the solution to the client's problem. The product is the box the solution comes in. THE CONCEPT draws people toward you; without the conditioning of THE CONCEPT, the product turns them away.

SUMMARY *(continued)*

- When you believe, you'll be believed. Forget about the "best." Find a good fund that feels right to you, and you'll quickly find it also feels right to the people who rely on you.

- When people tell you why your money management idea doesn't fit, they've told you which one does. There's no such thing as no sale. See the people. Let them see what an honest, talented professional you are. They'll like you, even if they don't like your initial idea. They'll tell you (if not in so many words) what they want. And then they'll buy it from you.

4

Pre-Prospecting:
Attitude Conditioning

You may have purchased this book because you are dissatisfied ... because you see a gap between what you've accomplished in this business and what you want to accomplish. We've already established that, as an enlistee in The Great Trade-off, you are *highly* motivated. So, what's the problem? Just this:

YOU THINK YOU'RE IN THIS BUSINESS
FOR FINANCIAL REWARD ...
BUT YOU'RE REALLY IN IT FOR APPROVAL.

People who choose our profession tend to share a very powerful need for approval. When clients accept our financial plan or buy the investment we're selling, we get a rush of approval ... next to which the financial reward tends to pale.

But there's a fatal flaw in any psychology in which you allow people's apparent approval of you to be a critical source of your sense of self-worth. Why? Because you are also giving them the power to reject you.

And that is the central psychological problem of our profession. If you're keeping score, albeit unconsciously, by whether people accept you or reject you, I guarantee you'll end up a paralyzed failure sooner or later. Because, whether you are prospecting in order to build, re-build, or expand your business, **you are bound to be rejected most of the time**.

Don't worry — I'm not about to re-hash the vapid, futile advice of sales trainers and managers who always counsel us not to take rejection personally. "The prospect is rejecting your idea, he's not rejecting you," they cry, as generation after generation of potentially fine professionals wash out of the business. Given our emotional make-up, this advice can simply never be accurate or meaningful.

You can't get a big rush of warmth and satisfaction when the prospect says "Yes," without being exposed to a personal sense of loss and pain when he says "No." They are two sides of the same emotional coin. And since prospects say "No" a large preponderance of the time, you may readily conclude that this process is a real bad way of getting your self-esteem topped off.

So, if you've not yet been sufficiently successful at financial planning — or at selling stocks, bonds, or even mutual funds — realize that the forces retarding your success come from the way your psychology influences your behavior. No amount of product knowledge, sales techniques, "motivational" programs or anything external can change you in a meaningful way.

ALL CHRONIC PRODUCTION PROBLEMS ARE BEHAVIORAL PROBLEMS. THEREFORE, THEY MAY ONLY BE CURED BY ALTERING BEHAVIOR.

THE GREAT RULE

Your success will ultimately be measured not in who you call, or what you say, or what investments you pick, or what the "market" does, but solely on *how many prospective investors you speak to*. So, the behavioral goal is simply to talk to enough prospective investors, and you'll have no lasting problems in this profession.

The converse is also true: If you don't talk to enough people, no matter what you know or what else you do, you're not going to make it.

Reluctance to make calls can come from many different psychological sources. But, for purposes of this discussion, hypersensitivity to rejection is the umbrella covering all of our most troubling behavior problems. Think about two critical facts:

(1) **Given our emotional make-up, a heightened sensitivity to rejection is natural and unavoidable.** But, you can find constructive ways to deal with rejection.

(2) Since prospecting is the purest imaginable numbers game, **the more you are rejected, the more prospects and clients you'll have.**

Therefore:

✳ REJECTION IS AN ESSENTIAL MEANS TO SUCCESS.

If, for instance, I'll convert one well-qualified client out of every fifteen prospecting calls I make, then to succeed I must be rejected as often as possible every day. If I'm rejected 14 times, I'll have one client.

Your attitude just has to be: "I don't know or care why people reject me. And, as I grow and learn this endlessly fascinating business, I become steadily more convinced that people who reject me are making a terrible mistake. But I can't worry about it. I have to let them disqualify themselves, if that's what they're bound and determined to do."

Not long ago, I talked with an experienced securities salesman who had an exceptionally thorough knowledge of the relationship between the American dollar and the Japanese yen. He had a very clearly thought out notion of what the two currencies were going to do in relation to each other over the next several months. And he'd picked out a particularly smart way to play the move: a currency exchange warrant trading on the American Stock Exchange.

I let his monologue go on for a while, and then, when this chap paused for breath, I asked him just one question. How many clients and prospects had he told this story to in the past week? After a long silence, he answered, "One." See what I mean?

A great deal of the time and energy spent by experienced professionals on reading research, charting, programming and re-programming your PC, and similar pursuits are really an elaborate avoidance of the real work of prospecting and selling ... and the sting of rejection.

WHAT DISTINGUISHES WINNERS

What is the one critical element that differentiates the people who achieve great success in planning and investment sales from everybody else? Let's answer by process of elimination.

Clearly, intelligence isn't the critical variable. The general level of intelligence in the financial business is very high. But, brains and the bottom line do not necessarily correlate. Throughout your career, you'll see extremely bright, well-educated people consistently outproduced by plodders. (Hint: The plodder is somehow always on the phone.)

Nor is the critical element being "right about the market," whatever that means. In fact, many accomplished producers trace the beginning of real success to the point they gave up altogether on the idea of "beating" the market . . . or thinking that beating the market was their job.

Geography, social and family background, "connections" and all the other easy guesses don't stand up to scrutiny, either. Nor do abstractions like "desire," "will power" or "competitiveness." The answer is much more subtle and much more important.

Above all, **real winners seem to have a relentless willingness to take full responsibility for what happens to them.**

Winners suffer the same hurtful, frustrating, daunting experiences that befall everyone else. In fact, because they're talking to far more people every day than mediocre planners and salespeople, they are rejected far more often. And when a favorite mutual funds goes south, the financial damage has to be greater. That's simply because winners are dealing with more accounts with larger sums invested.

The difference is fundamentally one of personal responsibility. The salesperson with sixty accounts holding four hundred thousand fund shares built the position by calling large numbers of people and putting himself on the line by personally recommending the investment. (He did not, among other things, mail out 300 copies of the prospectus, tell himself he was selling, and wait for people to call in with orders.)

Watch what the winner does in adversity. If a position goes sour, the winner won't just sit there staring at the Quotron, afraid to call his clients. Instead, after consulting his sources and getting the best reading he can, he'll be back on the phone.

Perhaps he'll encourage clients to add to positions at today's lower prices. Or maybe he says he now believes he was wrong, and reminds clients that when you're wrong you should cut losses quickly and get to the sidelines. And, sure enough, he'll soon be a production leader again *because he accepted responsibility* and presented the clients with his best judgment on what to do.

Will he lose a few accounts? Maybe. If so, the winner tends to be philosophical, feeling that sooner or later he'd have lost them anyway. (Whenever a client signals that you're only as good as your last recommendation, the account is already gone; the only issue is when.) But you can bet the ranch that the amateur who folds up emotionally and doesn't call his clients when a big position heads south will lose far more ... and he can afford to lose far less.

Taking, rather then evading, responsibility isn't something winners do out of an artificial concept of nobility. Instead, winners instinctively realize that ...

WHEN YOU ACT IRRESPONSIBLY
BY AVOIDING REALITIES,
YOUR ANXIETY LEVEL GOES UP FAR MORE
THAN IF YOU JUST BITE THE BULLET.

The winner knows that success is, first and foremost, a battle against his own anxiety. The course of action producing less anxiety invariably involves attacking the problem rather than evading it. Not making the call is ultimately more painful than making it. The code of taking personal responsibility is not the easy route — far from it. But, the alternative is a form of slow but certain death.

By taking personal responsibility, the winner closes himself off to the effects of external circumstance. He doesn't like rejection one bit more than the rookie who dials the phone a few times, hears himself analogized to everything from a Fuller Brush Man to Blackbeard, and then goes for a two-hour lunch.

The winner's reaction to rejection is what makes the difference. Rejection itself can never be the issue. When the winner runs into a streak of ten straight harsh dust-offs while prospecting, he shakes his head, laughs ruefully, and thinks, "Well, if I can just get four more people to abuse me quickly, I'll be statistically eligible for the one good prospect I always find out of every fifteen calls."

Cultivate these two traits distinguishing the winner:

(1) Acknowledge rejection as the distasteful but inevitable means to a statistically certain favorable outcome. In other words, prospecting is a numbers game and the numbers always work.

(2) Manifest a steadfast unwillingness to internalize the rejection.

The amount of rejection you will face is limitless. In fact, the more prospecting and the tougher the markets, the more you'll be hammered. But the winner distinguishes carefully between people's unthinking reactions and his own vision of himself. The winner knows, above all:

(1) you can experience an infinite number of failures, but

(2) you can never *be* a failure, unless

(3) you stop prospecting and selling, which will only happen if

(4) you *voluntarily* elect to allow the failures to hurt you rather than teach you.

The key point: **The winner becomes impervious to rejection over time. He wasn't born that way; none of us is.**

TAKE A LESSON FROM SANDY KOUFAX

One of the most dominant pitchers of all time, Sandy Koufax, walked off the mound and out of baseball at the end of 1966. He won 27 games in the regular season, with an earned-run average of 1.73. Koufax was baseball's Player of the Year his last season ... just as he had been in each of the three previous years. "He was not at the top of his game," said the sportswriter Thomas Boswell, "he was somewhere above it."

Yet I've met, over the years, more than one guy who played high school ball against Sandy in Brooklyn. And with only slight exaggeration they say they hit him pretty hard, on those relatively rare occasions when Sandy got the ball over the plate.

Koufax simply became steadily better — studying and systematically eliminating each of his countless faults one by one — over the next ten years. There was no dramatic breakthrough, no magic formula, no quick fix. Every loss, every wild pitch, every home run Koufax gave up taught him something *because he let them.* He didn't seem to pay much attention to the boos, the derision, the pitying looks from teammates. He didn't have the energy for it — he was too busy getting progressively better by learning from each failure.

Sandy Koufax couldn't stop kids from booing and laughing, any more than you can stop fourteen out of fifteen people you prospect from expressing the devout hope that you'll go and jump in a lake. But today Koufax is immortal, while some guy who hit four for four against him in sophomore year just retired from the Malverne (Long Island) Sanitation Department.

Becoming a winner is a process. It doesn't come in cans, like the spinach that instantly makes Popeye invincible. The investment business is phenomenally instructive, because markets (which ultimately reflect the economy) keep repeating the same cycle. Your knowledge of markets, of investor psychology and of yourself increases substantially each time. Hang in there and the result is inevitable: **You will become successful** — as, indeed, anyone who signs up for the Great Trade-Off deserves to be.

ANOTHER LESSON FROM A BASEBALL GREAT

During his final year as manager of the Mets, New York City threw a gigantic party for Casey Stengel. At City Hall ceremonies, the "Old Perfessor" opined how nice we were to honor him while he was still active and alert. Because, he said, "You gotta remember that a lot of guys my age are presently dead."

Well, to paraphrase Casey, a lot of guys who've been in the business as long as I have aren't in the business anymore. During my early years in production, which were dominated by the bear markets of 1969-70 and 1973-74, I constantly inherited accounts from people who left the business. In fact, many were among the highest quality accounts I ever had. And I always wondered: What could those brokers have been thinking of? What awful, self-inflicted sadness kept them from realizing that, if they kept opening accounts like these, no matter how slowly, they'd someday be at the top of their profession?

Give it time. Believe in the process. Believe in yourself. Knowledge is cumulative, but so is *character*. And character begins and ends with your commitment to accepting responsibility for what happens to you. Emerson said, "Life consists of what a man is thinking of all day." I believe our professional life consists of what we're *doing* all day.

Every time a prospect brushes you aside and you hang up the phone, you have complete control over how you're going to react to the "failure." The wrong reaction is to say, "I should have had a pertinent, convincing answer to the patently obvious dodge I was given. But I didn't, and it's *my fault*. People always say that to me, and I'm always stumped. Frustrating and humiliating. I bang my head against the wall all day long. Damn, I'll *never* get the hang of this business." The cumulative effect will have you working in a bank a year from now.

The alternative is to hang up the phone and say, "That's interesting: I've heard the same objection six times in the last week. I should have a pertinent, convincing answer to this patently obvious dodge, *and next time I will*. I'm going to see my sales manager right now, or talk to the biggest producer in the office. Or, I'll call a couple of people I went through training with to see what they're saying, or bring it up at next Monday's sales meeting, or all of the above. But, by next week at this time, no one will ever turn me aside with that silly (or even serious) objection for the next twenty-five years. Now, bring on another objection!" Then you'll jump on the phone again, because only on the phone will you hear something else from which you can learn. The cumulative effect of staying on the phone is inevitably strength, knowledge and success.

You have no control at any time over what the prospect says. At all times, you have control over how you react and what you do next. *You are responsible*. You can't change how often you'll be rejected. But you can completely change the effect of rejection, by changing the way you keep score.

SUMMARY

- All chronic production problems are behavior problems. Therefore, the only cure is altering your behavior.

- You think you're in the business for financial gain, but in a deeper sense approval is more important. Therefore, rejection is the central psychological problem of the profession.

- To succeed, all that matters is how many prospective investors you talk to, and the process entails a lot of rejection.

- The critical issue is accepting responsibility for your own future. You can experience many failures, but you can never be a failure, unless you stop prospecting, counseling and selling. You must let failure teach you, not hurt you.

- Success is a process; it doesn't come in cans. Give the process time. Believe in yourself. Knowledge is cumulative; so is character.

- You can't change how often you are rejected. But you can change the effect rejection has on you by changing the way you keep score.

5

Prospecting 1:
Changing The Way You Keep Score

How many times in your career have you started a new prospecting program, begun a major new product effort, or just tried to move your business to an entirely new level? What was the first thing you did? Of course: You sat down and drew up a long-term goal.

Didn't work, did it? Ever wonder why? Well, the work of a whole new generation of behavioral psychologists is discovering why. (One of these pioneers, Aaron Hemsley, Ph.D. of Santa Ana, California, has refined this research specifically for financial salespeople and planners. In nearly a quarter of a century in securities sales, I've found Hemsley's programs more valuable than all the other sales training I've experienced, put together.)

In all the literature of sales advice, no concept gets more lip service than goal-setting. "You have to have goals," they tell you. "If you don't know where you're going, you'll never figure out how to get there" — as if the mere existence of a goal will, in and of itself, make you behave any differently than you do now.

If this were just the normal run of vacuous non-guidance we're all used to, maybe it wouldn't be so bad. But, the fact is the conventional notion of goal-setting is a pernicious fraud that does incalculable damage. And no one who encourages conventional goal setting has any idea of how our salesman/planner psyches really work.

First of all, we tend to set goals in a very dreamy, idealistic place in our minds. We see ourselves being the way we'd like to be if we weren't the way we are. We focus on where we "wannabe," but don't examine what we'll have to do every day (which we're obviously not doing now) to get there.

Far from helping us re-define reality in a positive way, conventional goal-setting is nothing but an escape from reality. **Goal-setting is to the planner/salesperson what New Year's Resolutions are to the rest of the population** — a highly predictable bad joke.

And that's the *good* news. The bad news is that the conventional mode of goal-setting, focusing on a relatively remote payoff (e.g. doubling your production next year), ignores the immediate effect of increased rejection. So if anything in the last chapter is psychologically accurate, goal setting is just the worst combination you could ask for: very deferred gratification and immediate, painful rejection. Yippee. What fun.

A month into this program, you can virtually be assured the goal will already be out of reach. And the crestfallen salesperson/planner will be in a black depression, replete with angry, confused self-recrimination.

What went wrong here? Only everything that *can* go wrong, that's all. See if this analogy works for you:

A guy weighs 165 pounds on his 30th birthday. Then, slowly, without doing very much wrong, he gains three pounds the next year. And the next, and the next … comes his 40th birthday, and the guy steps on the scale. He's 195.

Boy, is he mad. Damn, how could he have let this happen to him? 195?! That tears it. Hey, it's Labor Day and this is *war*: 165 by New Year's Eve!

Think he'll make it? No, neither do I, for three important reasons:

1. **He doesn't know how he got there, so why would he think he knows how to get back?** He hasn't analyzed the very gradual but very effective chain of long-term behavior changes that put the 30 extra pounds on. But you have to figure a very powerful, deeply engraved habit is at work here. How can he expect to turn it around on a dime?

2. **He's focused entirely on the goal, with no idea what behavior he needs to reach the goal.** The goal is an escape mechanism with no psychological reality at all, because the goal is not accompanied by a specific, practical plan. By the Monday morning after Thanksgiving, when this guy is still tipping the scale at 195, he's not going to be much fun to be around.

3. **He's trying to effect too much change too fast.** Because the system of behavior that led to the weight gain is deeply set in the guy's unconscious, only a gradual process will work the system loose. Lasting change can only be effected slowly. Fast cures just won't "take."

TRAIN WITHOUT PAIN

You're in danger, at some point, of clapping this book shut, jumping up and saying, "Got it! From now on, I'm going to make ten mutual fund presentations a day. So if I close just one out of five and average $5,000 a ticket, I'll be doing $200,000 a month!" This affirmation is from someone who may now be making four or five presentations *a month*.

Completely doomed. You're trying to effect too much change too quickly. You're exposing yourself to the pain that comes with a huge blast of rejection you're not used to, and an onslaught of questions you can't answer.

It's exactly like jumping up off the couch after ten sedentary years and saying you're going out and run five miles. You just can't — haven't got the wind, haven't got the legs, haven't got the stamina.

Instead, you need to go out every morning and *train*. Start with an open mind and find out what you can do without killing yourself every day. Soon, you'll feel a little stronger, run a little longer. A couple of weeks more, and you'll find your endurance is better.

What makes this process successful? Break it down into component parts:

(1) You tested your endurance, didn't try to be a hero and stayed within your comfort level.

(2) The next day, you did the same thing. No more, but no less either. Then you repeated the process the next day, and the next.

(3) Then, slowly, your endurance started to increase — what training is all about. When you felt you were sustainably at a higher level, you set a new daily standard.

Keep on this path and one day you'll be way beyond any goal your self-recriminating couch potato mind could ever have hallucinated initially.

That's what a truly successful, sustained, long-term change in your prospecting looks like, as well. And don't tell me the analogy is no good "because in running you're competing against yourself, whereas in prospecting you are exposed to the vagaries of other people." Wrong. There's no difference at all — **the battle to control your prospecting behavior is purely a battle with your own anxiety.**

What we're really doing here is completely *changing the way you keep score.* You see, all we over-achievers who voluntarily sign up for The Great Trade-Off are awfully tough on ourselves. We've been acculturated to regard a call that results in an order as successful — and a call that doesn't as a failure. Since the majority of prospecting calls will not result in new accounts or orders, you're bound to get down on yourself and look for ways to avoid going on. (Operational problems and paperwork have an uncanny way of cropping up precisely at times like this.)

What's really at work here? It's the malignant effect of the fatally flawed way we keep score. Sandy Koufax didn't say, "I'm only going to pitch in games I know I'll win." He said, in effect, "I'm going to pitch every chance I get. Each time, win or lose, I'll learn something and get better."

So must you. And here, for the rest of your career, is the new way of keeping score:

**A PROSPECTING CALL'S OUTCOME
IS COMPLETELY IMMATERIAL.
EVERY CALL YOU MAKE IS A GREAT SUCCESS,
BECAUSE YOU MADE IT!
THE ONLY FAILURE IS THE PROSPECTING CALL
YOU DO NOT MAKE.**

From now on, you will **reward the behavior that leads to change**, because rewarding behavior gives you the ability to really change behavior.

You'll get a kick out of every contact with a prospect because your new reward system scores every such call a success. You are going to feel, sound and even look different. Your anxiety — born of fear of rejection and "failure" — is gone, and that makes an enormous difference in the quality of energy you give off.

Your objective, therefore, should just be to create a prospecting program you can comfortably follow without disrupting the conduct of your present business. And the reward you look for should simply be the act of completing your prospecting program.

Forget about your closing ratio for a while. Try to see the point of any prospecting program:

**CONSISTENTLY MAKE THE SAME NUMBER
OF PRESENTATIONS EVERY DAY ...
EVEN IF, AT THE OUTSET,
THE NUMBER IS ONLY ONE.**

You're in training. So, you need to create a system that makes you train every day. Here it is — the five Rs system, which helps you:

- **regulate** your activity;
- **record** the activity;
- **repeat** the activity;
- **reward** the activity as an end in itself; and
- **raise** the activity a notch ... each time you're ready.

Let's discuss each component of the system.

REGULATING YOUR ACTIVITY

Just like the first morning of a running program, you have to find the base level at which you can comfortably function every day. So, for the first week of your managed money program, just make a presentation whenever you feel like it — no pressure, no pipe-dream goals, no fancy plan.

Whenever the spirit moves you, say to somebody — a client, prospect, the dry cleaner who does your suits, the guy next to you on an airplane — "Do you have three minutes to hear about a terrific way to save enough for your kid's college education?" Or, "I know a great way to make sure you have a carefree retirement. Got three minutes to hear about it?"

Then, roll right through a shortened version of your basic presentation (which we'll build in later chapters). Finish up with, "I'd love to give you a little brochure that explains how the program works, and then let's sit down and see if it really fits you. Sound OK?" Light, bright, breezy, confident, upbeat, non-threatening. And why not? See, **you only make an approach and a presentation if you feel like it**. If you don't feel like it ... don't do it! Wait until the next time you're ready, because then you'll have fun, and you'll sound correspondingly good. (This business was supposed to make you feel good, remember?)

RECORDING YOUR ACTIVITY

During this first week, make a note of each time you approach somebody — even if the person wouldn't let you make the presentation. Remember, **the only possible failed approach in this new scorekeeping system is the approach you don't make.**

The approach counts even if the dry cleaner says, "Sorry, Jack, I don't mind dry-cleaning your fading double-knit leisure suits, but I prefer to have my investments handled by a native of *this* planet." Write it down in your notebook. You scored. You felt like making a presentation, and you asked someone's permission to do so.

Don't add any commentary ("I shoulda said …") to your notes, because in your current mindset that would be too depressing. Did you *feel* like approaching somebody on managed money, and *did* you approach him? Bingo. You're on the scoreboard.

At the end of the week, look at the record. Maybe you did two on Monday, four on Tuesday, three on Wednesday, six on Thursday, and none on Friday. You made fifteen approaches in a week. Not enough, you say? I've got news for you: By definition, if fifteen was all you could comfortably do, for now, that's enough. What's more, I'll bet a dollar to a doughnut that fifteen is more approaches on managed money than you made all last month.

Look what you found out. For one week, at least, you were able to make fifteen approaches comfortably, with no anxiety build-up, no tension, no rejection shock — in fact, with no undesirable side effects at all. "Ah," as the bumbling Inspector Clouseau always said when presented with some entirely meaningless non-clue, "Now we are getting somewhere."

REFINING YOUR ACTIVITY

Now let's see how to smooth out the peaks and valleys, and arrive at a level number of anxiety-free approaches you can make every day. The simplest way is to take the total number of approaches you made in your "let's-just-try-it-on-and-see-how-it-feels" week, and average them over a five-day work week. So your fifteen calls that week (peak: 6;

valley: 0) become three a day in the next week.

You have to talk to three people a day about managed money. It doesn't matter what they say — doesn't even matter what *you* say. If it's 3:00 p.m. on Friday, and you've only made two approaches, Hemsley suggests you call somebody up and say, "Hey, you don't want to buy a mutual fund today, do ya?" The guy will say no, and you can go home. (If you can't have a little fun with your own foibles, you're hopeless. Lighten up, for crying out loud!)

But you *must* talk to three people a day — not three on Monday, one on Tuesday, and five on Wednesday to catch up. This system won't work that way. We're creating a low-level, day-in-and-day-out, lifetime chain of an anxiety-free habit here. Just don't fool around with it.

REPEATING YOUR ACTIVITY

Let's say you make three approaches a day for a week. OK, now do the same the second week. Then again for a third, and a fourth. That's it — sixty managed money approaches in just four weeks. Consistent, relaxed, comfortable, spontaneous, smiling and worry-free. Sixty beautiful checkmarks. Aren't you proud?

What's that? Let me understand the question you just formed in your mind, if not actually on your lips. *"What will my closing ratio be?"* How the hell do I know? And, more importantly, what's that got to do with anything? Maybe you closed six. Maybe you closed none. Maybe I'll get elected Pope. Who knows? *Who cares?* Get with the program; once and for all, **change the way you keep score.**

You may not have made sixty approaches on managed money (or anything else) evenly over twenty working days in years, if ever. But now you're cooking. You're starting to feel on top. And you're *learning.* Twenty-two of the sixty people gave you some version of the "stocks are too risky" objection to equity mutual funds. Thirty-four were really shifty about the load. **Now you're starting to know what's really on people's minds.** (And when I get through training you in Q&A/objection handling, you're going to powder those objections. I mean, you're going to be like the Terminator: *Nothing can kill you. Ever.*)

OK, now what happens if you can't make three approaches a day every day for four weeks? Well, then we can conclude you pushed too hard in your "let's-try-it-on" week. Something about the nervousness of a new program or the white, empty spaces in your little scorekeeping notebook made you press. Your over-achieving unconscious got ashamed and made you "paint the tape" with a lot of extra calls that you probably knew weren't sustainable. And you were right. So now what are you going to do?

Well, there's always suicide, or going back to trading the Kodak August 45's. (But I repeat myself.) I've got one other idea: Drop back to two a day.

Let up on yourself. So you couldn't do three a day for a whole month — your spouse is not going to leave you, at least not on this issue. You're not going to be fired or creamed by a cross-town bus being driven by a vengeful God. You're just like Edison, after his first ten thousand failed attempts to produce an incandescent light bulb: *Now you know what won't work.*

Great. Drop back to two a day. See if you can sustain that level for four weeks. (Go ahead, I dare you: Ask me what that will do to your closing ratio, and I'll break your face.)

Can't do two? That's OK, too.

MAKE JUST ONE MANAGED MONEY APPROACH A DAY ... BUT DO IT EVERY DAY FOR FOUR WEEKS.

Can't do that? I can't help you. You need to talk to a psychologist, preferably one who works with salespeople. Call Hemsley. Call Dr. Ted Kurtz, the sales psychologist from Cold Spring Harbor, NY, who writes for *Registered Representative* magazine. Or call the Chapter of the American Psychological Association in your city — or in the state capital, if there's no chapter nearby — and get them to refer you to somebody. But get some help. It's out there. This is the '90s. There's nothing shameful in asking for help. The shame — and sadness, and depression — are in *not asking.* Believe me.

REWARDING YOUR ACTIVITY

This is the *crucial* element in the system — and the most difficult — because we've been trained to think of success only in terms of closed sales. But rewarding the activity is where we actually change the way we keep score.

Start by identifying some things you like to do. Then make doing them *conditional* on performing your managed money prospecting activity.

For instance, suppose you consider reading the *Wall Street Journal* important at the beginning of each business day. How about making reading the *Journal* dependent on picking up the phone and trying to make an appointment with someone about planning for his retirement?

You're performing an activity that will lead to change, and lead, in turn, to success. Didn't get the appointment? No matter. Now you can read the *Journal* with a clear conscience, because now it's a reward for the positive act of prospecting.

You can use any activity as a reward for any potentially productive behavior. You can use your morning cup of coffee. When you arrive at the office, fix yourself a cup ... *after* you present a managed money idea. Once again, the outcome of the call is immaterial. The point is to create an immediate reward for a positive behavior.

Next, logically, comes lunch. Want to go to lunch? Well, fine (as long as you're not going with another salesperson/planner, which is the *ultimate* avoidance behavior). But ... you guessed it ... first you have to make another managed money call. You know you can feel pretty crummy when you go to lunch after a wasted, unproductive morning. So, here's a way to feel going to lunch is a great reward for a new prospecting behavior.

And look: The day is only half over, and you've already made your three approaches. Can you make more this afternoon? I'll bet you can. But if you can't, that's OK. What's essential is that you do your three approaches (Hemsley calls the target your "baseline") every day for four weeks. That's how you know it's sustainable, that three really *is* your baseline.

You can create many other reward systems to accomplish the same behavior modification. (Aaron Hemsley's workshops and tape series help you learn the ones which most closely suit your style, and I urge you to become familiar with them.) One I particularly like, the "performance contract," is based on the profound psychological truth that we can often work better in concert with other people with similar goals — especially if added incentives are involved.

Suppose two of you in the office have established a baseline of three managed money approaches a day. You can contract to pay each other $10 for every approach you don't make on any day. These performance contracts can become a very powerful added stimulus, especially when you start raising your performance targets.

RAISING YOUR ACTIVITY

Let's say you've found your "baseline" number of managed money calls by making the same number of approaches every day for four weeks. Because the only lasting change is gradual change, we're going to raise the ante *just a little bit*, so that our rejection-sensitive unconscious won't feel the difference.

Suppose you established a "baseline" of three approaches — *Journal*, coffee and lunch. You made those three approaches every day for four weeks. Your little notebook is filled with a blizzard of checkmarks. What next? Of course ...

ADD ONE MORE DAILY CALL
FOR THE NEXT FOUR WEEKS.

Think you'll feel the strain of the increased activity? Of course not. You're in training. You've been running every day for a month. You can increase the distance just a bit without caving in.

You'll need a fourth reward, of course. Like to watch PBS' *Nightly Business Report* or the local news on TV when you get home? Me, too. This is gonna be easy: no fourth call, no TV news.

You can see that any ordinarily pleasurable activity (going to your favorite restaurant, watching Monday Night Football, or whatever) can be turned instantly into a reward system.

MAKE A GAME OUT OF PROSPECTING CALLS.

These seven words are among the best advice ever on selling. Because, after all, our approval-hungry unconscious is kind of childlike to begin with. And kids love games. (Ever notice how the top people in your office *always* win the sales contests, almost regardless of what the contest is about?)

Once again, does this prospecting system have anything to do with how the prospect responded? Nothing at all. Why? Because **you can't control the prospect's response; you can only control your behavior.**

And the more approaches you make, in the long run, the more successful you will surely be. Obviously, the only sane course of action is to reward the approaches, by conditioning the things you *like* to do upon performing the things you *have* to do. Stop trying so hard. Remember what Yoda says to Luke Skywalker in *Return of the Jedi*: "Try? There is no try ... there is only do and not do."

As they say in the Nike commercials: Just do it! But **make the rewards as clear, immediate and unequivocal as the rejection surely must be.** Then, there will be no stopping you.

Did you make four approaches a day for the second month? Magnificent. Don't look back now, because I don't want you to freak out on me, but you've now made 140 managed money approaches in the last two months.

Suppose you still don't fall off the wagon. In the third month, try five a day. Awesome! Five managed money approaches a day, and still you're functioning comfortably.

Or perhaps you're not. Let's say five turns out to be too much strain. Why? Who knows, and who cares? Sit around trying to figure out why and you'll immobilize yourself with self-recrimination. Snap out of it. You're in training. You went from half a mile in the first month to a mile in the second. Then you tried to go to a mile and a half in the third month, and found you couldn't do it. That's all.

"Why?" Who knows? Do you want to keep training, here, or do you want to take a couple of years off and study cardiovascular medicine so you'll understand why? Come to center. You're having an anxiety attack.

Forget why. Retreat to the last level of activity you could sustain, and go for another month. Then in the fourth month, try again to stretch sustainably to five. Chances are — if you haven't become impatient and gone back to denominating your success in closed sales — you'll be OK at five.

Now, let's cut to the chase. Suppose you follow this plan, starting with three approaches daily, but you need two months to sustain each increase in your "baseline." Here's the result: You wind up making ten approaches per day within fourteen months. (And, incidentally, if you can't think of ten rewards every day, then it's time you and I had a long heart-to-heart talk about sex.) You will make 1,440 prospecting calls in year one, and even if your activity level goes completely flat in the second year (but doesn't go down), you'll make about 2,400 approaches.

Without this program, if you start from where you are today and set a "goal" of 2,400 approaches in a year — any year — I guarantee you won't make it. But if, on the other hand, you make 2,400 approaches in a year, no matter how long it takes you to build up to them, then I guarantee you'll be in the top 1% of all managed money salespersons in America. No matter what you say ... and no matter what the 2,400 people say.

Because when you are comfortably talking to that many people — in a relaxed, concentrated, friendly way — you are going to learn, and grow ... and sell. You'll hear all the hopes, all the fears, all the dodges and stalls. And you will, in time, be able to deal with all of them.

So what's your hurry? Old Aesop, as usual, was right: I'll bet that tortoise is *still* running.

SUMMARY

- Goal-setting, as traditionally practiced, is a pernicious fraud, urged on us by sales managers who never made it as salespeople.

- If you like New Year's Resolutions, you'll just love goal-setting. If not, you'll be relieved to know there's a better way.

- Prospecting activity is like losing weight and running distances: You took a long time to get out of shape, and you'd better give yourself a long time to get back into shape.

- If you reward the activity that leads to change, you'll change. If you reward only the change itself — the five miles, the 30 pounds, the $100,000 order — you'll never get to your goals. Too many old, unconscious habits get in the way.

- Take it slow. The objective of a long-term prospecting program is simply to make the same number of approaches every day. And then, slowly, to increase the number. You're in training.

- Regulate the activity. Find out, in a relaxed and non-judgmental way, the level of activity you can comfortably sustain. Don't even think about results yet.

- Record the activity. Write it down, so it's real.

- Refine the activity. Flatten your experimental level of activity into a sustainable daily "baseline" of activity.

- Repeat the activity. Make your "baseline" number of approaches each day for a month.

- Reward the activity. Make each of the pleasurable activities of your day conditional on the performance of one "baseline" approach.

- Raise the activity. When you find a "baseline" number of managed money approaches you can sustain for four weeks, try adding one additional approach per day, for the next four weeks. If you make the new level of approaches, that's your new "baseline." If you can't, drop back and sustain the old "baseline" for a second month.

- Too slow? Too gradual? Sorry you feel that way. I'll bet that tortoise is *still* running.

6

Prospecting 2: Identifying And Approaching Your Natural Market

Anyone earning more than he is spending is a prospect for managed money. In fact, virtually all "net savers" own managed money — most people just haven't been taught to look at their financial holdings in terms of "managed money."

Take a guy whose employer is bought out and who turns up on your doorstep with a $180,000 lump sum from his pension plan termination. He may start turning blue when you talk about equity mutual funds, even though much of the company's retirement plan was invested in stocks and run by at least one money manager. Here's where the sales superstar and the washout instinctively differentiate themselves.

The washout whips out a tired old chart showing how the stock market never stops going up, through wars, depressions, recessions, assassinations, plunging necklines and rising hemlines. The superstar looks mildly surprised at the prospect's nervousness and asks, with perfect sincerity, "Don't like good common stocks? Gee, I'd be willing to bet that's where most of the $180,000 came from."

The prospect doesn't have the right perspective. So the superstar —in his own relaxed, confident way — simply clears up the misconception for the prospect. The washout spends hours and untold amounts of energy in a vain attempt to educate the guy. (And why is the attempt always vain? Right: Because the prospect doesn't care what you know ... until he knows that you care. How does an old, yellowing chart showing the market's imperviousness to disaster prove that you care? Right again: It doesn't.)

And if not from stocks, the $180,000 certainly came from bonds. Yet the prospect is seriously thinking of chucking it all into bank CDs. Once again, you have the option of trying to teach the guy all about the bond market ... or of asking him to continue doing what his bosses did, which was to put (at least) part of his money in a wonderfully diversified high-quality bond portfolio.

Even if a prospect's money is in a savings bank (heaven preserve us), it is pooled and invested in something — home mortgage loans, car loans, or whatever. The bank's managers are making portfolio decisions about the prospect's money every day ... and recent history indicates those decisions aren't always uniformly good. The banking crisis is, in fact, one of the best things that's happened to the financial planning/securities sales profession in decades. People finally see that, far from being a credible bastion of probity and strength, any private investment system which hides behind a government guarantee can't be either very smart or very good.

✳The point is: Not only is almost everybody a *candidate* for managed money, but nearly everybody is already a *consumer* of managed money ... they just haven't thought of it that way.

AVOID TARGET-MARKET DELUSION

Exhilarating as it may be to learn that everybody whose income exceeds expenditures is a prospect, it doesn't help sharpen your focus. But that's good, not bad. Because **all attempts to pre-select a clientele who will magically open up to you like a flower are avoidance behaviors.** Pre-selecting a clientele is a subtle way of saying, "I'm going to define my target audience so that a very large percentage accept me, and I won't have to endure a lot of rejection." This hope is, of course, a pipe dream.

Usually you'll see people in the grip of this particular self-delusion go from target market to target market about every six months. For each new target market, they'll spend a lot of time accumulating lists, joining new organizations, writing new prospecting letters, re-programming their PC's, and setting up new systems. Then, when they can't put it off any longer, they actually start calling people. And, of course, they suddenly discover a flaw in their carefully thought-out new marketing approach (i.e. people say no) that vitiates the whole exercise ... to the point where they have to find a new target market.

Relax...don't worry about pre-selecting a clientele. Your clientele is going to select itself. And, to a surprising extent, your clientele is going to consist of people like you. They may not be the same age or sex, or have the same marital status, religious or political affiliations, or tastes. But your natural clientele will be people who think the way you do about solving problems, choosing investments, using one's head, staying out of trouble, and so forth.

You can't disguise who you are, and you shouldn't try. (You should, however, carefully manage the image you project by working on the way you look and sound.) You have great strengths and attractive qualities that make your personality unique — and that make certain people more comfortable with you than with all the other planners/salespeople who are prospecting them. And, people become *real* clients — trusting, confiding, and showing you all their assets — only when they are comfortable with you.

You have to:

BE WHO YOU ARE;
SHOW PEOPLE THE GENUINE YOU;
AND SELL WHAT YOU LOVE.

You already know instinctively what kind of people you should be prospecting and what kinds of money management products you should be prospecting with. So before you make some elaborately specific prospecting plan (which is, in idealization and artificiality, only one step removed from "goal-setting"), stop and look inward, instead of outward. Take inventory, and ask yourself: "What have I learned so far about people, about myself, about money, and about investments? How can I synthesize the things I've learned into a consistent, natural, unforced and deeply felt prospecting approach — an approach that can take my practice to a whole new level, and beyond?... *an approach that I believe in strongly enough to stay the course* and not abandon at the first sign of resistance."

In other words, don't ask yourself who you should call, or what you should try to sell. Ask yourself: "Who am I?" Because, as in every aspect of life, you can only be successful *from the inside out.* You can attract prospective clients with externals, but you can only keep them by the force of who you are. So I vote for bagging the externals from the get-go, and concentrating on showing people the superb professional that is the *real* you.

To learn more about yourself and discover your natural market, read "The Book" — your account book.

**YOUR BOOK OF ACCOUNTS IS
YOUR PROFESSIONAL AUTOBIOGRAPHY,
AND THE ROSETTA STONE TO YOUR NATURAL MARKET.**

Look at the things you love to sell and the kinds of people you like to sell to. Go through the book of accounts you've accumulated so far, and see what you've been most successful selling over the past year or so —that's your natural market.

Suppose the common denominator you find in your account book is safety and income. Well, you've obviously learned some very important truths about people, about wealth, and now, about yourself.

You've discovered the bulk of people's net worth isn't "make-a-killing" money; it's "don't-get-killed" money. (Normally, we think of people as being risk averse. But that's a misnomer; they're *loss-averse* — a big difference.) And you've found out that you like working with "don't-get-killed" money, because the goal strikes a strong responsive chord in you. You don't much care for sticking your neck out — you prefer to sleep nights, like your clients. A nice mix of maturities, investment-grade paper, and don't forget your umbrella. Better safe than sorry.

FROM INDIVIDUAL SECURITIES TO MANAGED MONEY

But a number of things are starting to bother you about how you are accomplishing your clients' goals:

- People say they want safety, but you're beginning to think they really want a high coupon and the *illusion* of safety.

- People say they need income but then plow back all the income into the account.

Here's your evidence. If interest rates come down, people turn out to be addicted to last year's higher rates. They'll reduce investment quality, lengthen maturities ... anything to preserve yield. You're scared, quite properly, because when rates turn up again, lower quality, longer maturity debt portfolios will get their clocks cleaned.

After a while, people try to outguess the market by forecasting interest rates. The mere fact that nobody has ever been able to do so consistently doesn't stop people from trying.

About here, you start to figure out you could do a lot more to help people — and a lot more business — by taking the managed money approach. You really love and are tuned in to the debt markets. But you find you can insulate people from their own foibles through fixed-income money management — better for the client, and you'll be left with a lot more energy for your real work ... prospecting.

Alternatively, let's suppose you take inventory of yourself and your natural market and find your one true belief is in capital growth. The great goals of life — education and retirement — can only be achieved through growth. College costs have been growing at a significant premium to inflation, so a fixed-income strategy that only keeps you even after taxes and inflation is a non-starter. And, because people are living much longer, even very mild inflation will jeopardize their standard of living in retirement. So, clients must make a serious commitment to the equity markets.

But, once again, when you look at the practical pitfalls in selling with conviction the goal of growth, a lot of things make you queasy and drain your energy:

- You want people exposed to stocks, but you never seem to have a good handle on the market yourself. So, you have trouble advising people with warmth and conviction.

- As markets grow increasingly volatile, extremes of euphoria or panic become even more injurious to financial health. The media is always there to exacerbate this schizophrenia, of course. (For example, *USA Today* ran a column on the joys of short selling less than fifteen trading days from the bottom of the stock market in 1990.)

- People overtrade, underdiversify, take small profits while letting losses run, get-even-and-get-out, listen to tips and rumors, and more — all of which promote underperformance.

- If you fight 'em, they go someplace else. And if you don't fight 'em, you build up a lot of internal conflict ... and the people even blame you for not saving them from themselves.

Don't let your deeply felt commitment to a growth strategy founder on the flawed ways the strategy is implemented. This is your natural market, and the professional managed money approach will let you access it in an anxiety-free way. (Keep a little trading money on the side for fun if you wish. In the long run, the performance of the trading account will serve a very useful purpose — reminding the client, and you, how right you were to put the bulk of the money someplace where neither of you could touch it.)

GET ON WITH THE NUMBERS GAME

So, now, you've confirmed your instinctively correct idea as to the people you should prospect and the kinds of money management products you should prospect with. Stop worrying about the bewildering variety of mutual funds and other vehicles out there. You have to be who you are and talk about the investments you love. Obsessing about the infinite individual subtleties of client needs and worrying you haven't mastered every approach to solving those needs are excuses to avoid getting started. So start here and now, using the behavior-rewarding system outlined in the last chapter.

The proper mind-set lets you **stop caring about any individual call**, because you make a (numbers) game out of prospecting. When you stop worrying about each call, the most amazing result occurs: **You immediately become more effective, simply because you're more relaxed**. Your relaxation comes through to the client as confidence. And money management, as we've agreed, is the ultimate "confidence" sale.

When you're relaxed, you are also far more creative. You think more quickly and clearly, and you handle questions and objections more smoothly. Your answers are more interesting, even thought-provoking. **You project a genuine feeling of imperturbability** because you know you're making a "successful" presentation, regardless of the outcome. You know you're getting better with every call. And, across the desk or at the other end of the phone, the prospect starts feeling good about you, because you so clearly feel good about yourself.

IRAs: THE MUTUAL FUND "BOOT CAMP"

Suppose you accept everything in the last chapter and so far in this one, but you'd like to find a way to try this system on without upsetting your emotional apple cart or blowing lots of good prospects with a funky new approach that sounds good, but might not work in practice.

Well, try chatting with everybody in your "baseline" about their IRA. Remember IRAs? Everybody has one, and almost nobody contributes anymore because the contribution usually isn't tax deductible. With a little help from you, a lot of people just might wake up and notice the conventional wisdom about IRAs doesn't make sense — and you'll be the source of their enlightenment.

The main benefit of the IRA wasn't necessarily the tax deduction for the contribution. The bigger benefit is the years of tax-deferred compounding until retirement. (See Figure 6-1 below.) Never forget the words of the immortal Albert Einstein. Asked by a fatuous reporter to name the single greatest invention in human history, Einstein unhesitatingly replied, "compound interest."

You can't deduct the contribution. So what? In a 30% tax bracket, the deduction saves 30 cents on the dollar. The other seventy cents would still come out of your own pocket, right?

So right now you have tens of millions of Americans not funding IRAs every year — giving up a chance to buy ten, twenty or even thirty years of tax-deferred compounding — because to do so would cost them 100 cents on the dollar *instead of only 70*! Is this nuts, or is this nuts?

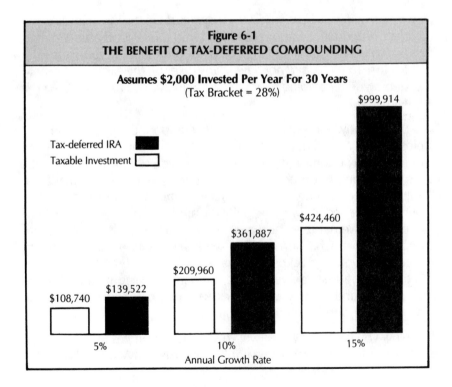

Figure 6-1
THE BENEFIT OF TAX-DEFERRED COMPOUNDING

Assumes $2,000 Invested Per Year For 30 Years
(Tax Bracket = 28%)

Tax-deferred IRA
Taxable Investment

$999,914
$424,460
$361,887
$209,960
$139,522
$108,740

5%   10%   15%
Annual Growth Rate

What's the approach? Easy. Just say, "Oh, by the way, you still contribute to your IRA every year, don't you?" Who do you suppose you can't say this to? Right: nobody. **The IRA gambit is an easy way to start your "baseline" program in a non-threatening, non-anxiety-producing way.**

Naturally, the person you approach will say "No," because you can't deduct the contribution anymore. You can, quite properly, look mildly amazed, and say, "Who cares about the tax deduction? The big benefit is the years and years of tax-deferred compounding of your savings, until you're ready to retire."

Then you might add one of two tags:

> "Why, if you'd just put $2,000 in your IRA in the five years since the tax deduction vaporized, and invested in a good portfolio of stocks, you'd already have another $12,000 to $14,000 saved for retirement... and those haven't been five great years for stocks, by any means."

> *- OR -*

> "Why, if you'd just put $2,000 in your IRA in the five years since the tax deduction vaporized, and invested in a good portfolio of high-grade corporate bonds, you'd be compounding your money at close to 9%... and not paying any taxes on the earnings. Every dime would be going right back to work for you as soon as you earned it."

(Yes, I know the phrases "you'd be compounding your money at close to 9% ... and not paying any taxes on the earnings," and "every dime would be going right back to work for you as soon as you earn it," are redundant. But nothing in my contract says I can only make the killer sales point once. Stated the first way, the sales point is correct — but stated the second way, the point is graphic, grabbing, emotional and energizing. Remember, the way you say what you say is infinitely more important than what you say. The spark that excites your client has to come from you; don't expect spontaneous combustion. And if you can't get excited about tax-deferred compounding of ordinarily taxable corporate bond yields, you'd better ask the doctor to step up the dosage on your anti-depressant medication.)

Now you can say, "When will you have five minutes to learn how to do this?" Or — even more powerfully, if it's true — "When will you have five minutes to see how I'm doing this in my *own* IRA?" If the prospect can't commit right then and there, you'll hear a question or objection. One of the great benefits of owning the fund in your own IRA is that you can say, "You know, I thought about that question when I was looking at this fund for my own account. And I decided ...," and you go on to powder the objection as if it had been your concern all along.

Because, rest assured ...

OWNING EVEN A LITTLE OF THE FUND YOU'RE SELLING INCREASES YOUR EFFECTIVENESS 300%.

You have to be who you are and sell what you love. But think how much more conviction and power you bring to this process after you've also *bought* what you love. (This is just another reason why the excruciating, micro-managing process of trying to match exquisitely complicated products with incredibly subtle individual investor "needs" is such a pitiful abstraction to me.)

When the prospect gives you the five minutes, you'll make a spectacular, compressed, deeply-felt presentation of the fund you love. (I'll give you the script in the chapters on presentations.) Then just finish with, "Would you like to make your IRA start growing again right now, using (name the fund)?"

This is a complete and total win-win situation. Observe the two possible outcomes:

- **Outcome 1: The prospect buys into the concept and the fund.** Wonderful. You opened an account, did a little business, and demonstrated to yourself that this "baseline" business isn't some weird cult exercise ... Fantastic. But what really matters is **now you've grabbed this prospect's whole retirement planning process by the tail.** Don't look now, but you're the last person this prospect has talked to, and the last person with whom he's *acted*, about his single most important goal in life. This is like coming in to pitch in the seventh inning of a game where your team is ahead 7-0. You're now in control; it's your game to lose.

  Now, **pull on the tail.** When the confirmation of the fund purchase comes through, go see the client again. ("I just want to make sure all the information on the confirmation tallies with what we agreed ...") Then say:

  "By the way ... what's your old IRA invested in? ... Why

wouldn't you be better off in this fund?

And later:

"By the way ... the IRA is great, but where's your serious retirement money going? You know if you invest larger amounts over the next twelve months, you'd really start to see those shares pile up ..."

- **Outcome 2: The prospect doesn't buy into the concept; he says, "No tax deduction, no soap."** Terrific. Who cares about an IRA, anyway? I sure don't. I was just casting about for a way to get you talking to the guy. Let's cut right to the chase:

    "Well, if you're no longer funding your IRA, can I ask how you **are** *saving for retirement? Because I can be of serious help to you ... if you'll share your serious plans with me."*

Got it? Or shall I do for you what radio broadcaster Bob Murphy does at the end of every winning Mets game? ...

THE HAPPY RE-CAP

- Guy buys — you start talking to him about his serious retirement money.
- Guy doesn't buy — you start talking to him about his serious retirement money.

WIN-WIN.

All I'm trying to do is talk you into making a fairly large number of relatively anxiety-free presentations, the outcome of which you don't care that much about. You quickly and painlessly accumulate a great deal of presentation experience and a whole flock of checkmarks on your "baseline" prospecting scorecard.

Another major benefit of the process is you very quickly see just how few questions people ask about any particular money management product ... and how frequently the few questions recur. This takes away most "Q&A anxiety" and gives you an easy familiarity with the common questions and objections. In and of itself, facility with Q&A is one tremendous confidence builder. (Meanwhile, the budding washout is still sitting up in the darkened office, all by himself, thinking, "What if they ask me ...?")

Nobody's recommending the IRA route as a major revenue-producing breakthrough to the exciting life of the managed money sales superstar. Far from it. The IRA is the lowest common denominator — the entry level introduction to selling mutual funds (because tax-deferred compounding dovetails so beautifully with automatic dividend reinvestment). If your anxiety levels are high about starting to prospect systematically with mutual funds, the IRA approach will help. If you can't bring yourself to try even this, or some variation, again: It's time to talk to a professional psychologist.

The IRA approach also lets you stop obsessing so much about the quality of leads to which you have access. Nothing is more common in our profession than having a lead who is so great you never call him. He's so terrific, you're only going to get one or two shots at him ... and you haven't found the one perfect investment idea. (People with this psychology go out of the business leaving behind lead-card file boxes that are bonanzas ... if only someone would call the people up and strongly recommend something, anything!) At $2,000 a crack, who cares about lead quality? And, come to think of it, who is not a prospect? As Dr. Tom Stanley says in his classic book about marketing to the affluent, the best prospects turn up in the oddest places ... like your local dry cleaner.

THE GOOD, THE BAD, AND THE UGLY

Let's talk about lead generation. You know all "net savers" — people whose incomes exceed their expenditures — are prospects for managed money. But the salesperson/planner's psyche won't accept anything so simple.

Our belief system clings to the notion of "good leads" and "bad leads," "good lists" and "bad lists." Moreover, as Aaron Hemsley points out, we live in an elaborate system of "can'ts." You can talk to a client, but you "can't" talk to a prospect. You can make a cold call, but you "can't" ask for a referral. You can ask for a referral, but you "can't" make a cold call. You can talk to a business owner, but you "can't" talk to a lawyer (or an accountant, or a doctor). All of these phenomena are elaborate ways in which we systematize our fear of rejection. Nothing more, nothing less. The notion that talking to a few carefully selected "good leads" will let you escape the frustration and strain of talking to a lot of "bad leads" is simply an avoidance behavior — and a self-fulfilling prophecy.

The notion that who you're talking to is important robs you of all the effortless spontaneity which comes from not caring. And that's why this book keeps stressing you have to start slowly and build gradually, as your anxiety level about managed money goes down and your confidence level edges up.

Mailers and advertising are two other widely practiced avoidance behaviors. The notion here is that you can somehow pre-qualify good prospects and have them approach you, without the strain of starting a conversation with another human being. Mailers are a particularly seductive way to avoid the real work of prospecting, because they're so time-consuming and you think you're actually working.

On the other hand, you can at least manage the ineffectiveness of mailers by sending them to carefully selected, demographically upscale zip codes. That way you know your mailer will be thrown away with the L.L. Bean and the Sharper Image catalogs. In other words, it will go out with a nice class of garbage.

But nothing can ever prepare you for the thrill of getting back an advertising coupon filled out in purple crayon, or one typed out neatly with the return address of the maximum-security cell block at your friendly neighborhood federal penitentiary.

By all means, send out a few mailers or prospecting letters every day, *if* you're going to follow up each one with a phone call as part of your "baseline" program. I particularly like this approach because when you make your follow-up call and the secretary asks what your call is in reference to, you can truthfully say, "We've had some correspondence about his retirement plan."

I don't much care for bought mutual fund leads on a couple of counts. First, since nearly half the households in America with incomes over $50,000 have made some mutual fund investment, where's the target marketing? The lead services could be copying a reverse directory of nice neighborhoods and still have a 50/50 chance of being right. Second, someone who's invested a lot in mutual funds sounds to me like somebody who's probably happy with his fund and the people who are selling it to him. Where's the edge? You could, I suppose, call him up and ask if he's happy with the way his investments are being handled. But you can just as easily call people out of the yellow pages and ask them the same question. So, why do you need the bought lead? Right ... your unconscious is still playing "good list/bad list."

If you want to do some cold prospecting and are looking for lists, be creative. Look for trade and professional directories that are off the beaten track. (Try asking your clients which ones they're listed in — they'll be flattered to tell you.) Large public and university business school libraries accumulate directories in great abundance. Five minutes in the Brooklyn Business Library turned up these directories, all of which have individual names, addresses and phone numbers:

Leaders in Electronics
The Blue Book of Optometrists
International Robotics Industry Directory
Who's Who In Fashion
Directory of Iron and Steel Works (U.S. and Canada)
Who's Who In Engineering
National Directory of Minority and Woman-owned Businesses

The last one, by the way, is 1,600 pages long. Sixteen hundred pages of people trying to build a successful business, dreaming about giving their kids an education and enjoying a long, comfortable retirement. Sounds like a pretty interesting group of people to me — and not one that's going to show up on a list that somebody buys from Dun & Bradstreet once every seventeen seconds of every working day.

FRESH APPROACHES TO REFERRALS

Of course, the best lead is always a referred lead, or someone you already know. (I'm certainly not talking about relatives and close friends. And, indeed, the newer you are in the business, the more I urge you to steer clear of them.) But if you've bought a couple of cars from the same dealer in the last few years (or had a lot of work done at the same body shop, after your kids performed their own special magic on your cars), you've either got a prospect ... or an especially rigid system of "can'ts."

Make a list of every business you've spent $500 with in the last twelve months (not including the IRS and the supermarket checkout kid). You may be surprised at the number of names you come up with. If you're not willing to do anything else, how about asking them the IRA question?

The normal approach to referrals is seriously flawed by the vague, defeatist way most of us ask for them. The question, "Do you know anyone else who could make good use of the services I perform for you?" almost always produces the same response. The client gets a little uncomfortable, and says something like, "Well, no, not right offhand, but let me think about it." He never brings up the subject again, and neither do we.

Be creative. Suppose your client is Senior VP of a major company in your area. Next time you're in the neighborhood, take a Polaroid snapshot of the directory in the lobby of the building. Some of the people on your client's professional level — or above it — will be listed there. Then, you can call your client and say, "Do you know a guy in your company named Byron Brown?" Your client says, "Sure! Byron's Senior VP in charge of marketing." You say, "Great! Could you introduce me to him?"

Most of us aren't just asking our clients to give referrals, we're asking them to *find* referrals and then give them to us. Maybe that's asking a little too much. In the Polaroid gambit, you find the referral; then the client is easily able to give you the introduction.

Another approach to referrals stems from the essential truth that you're selling what you love. If you've gotten someone to invest in an equity mutual fund or a "wrap" account, you succeeded because of the depth of your commitment to, and belief in, the equity vehicle. You believed, so you were believed.

Try asking clients who've made the investment for referrals using this approach:

> "Mr. Brown, part of the reason I'm so enthusiastic about this investment is I'm very bullish on equities in the '90s. The end of the Cold War, globalizing capitalism and trade, and the deleveraging of American business are major long-term positives.
>
> I'm trying to put a minimum of $5 million of client assets under management with these people before the equity market really takes off... and I feel like I'm running out of time. Please help me. Who can you think of — somebody with the same kinds of goals and financial capabilities you have — who'd like to hear this story?"

Whether this approach produces a referral or not, you'll profoundly deepen the client's appreciation of how genuinely you believe in what you're selling.

Another interesting, offbeat approach is to ask your business-owning clients to identify their principal competitors and the firms' key executives. You can be sure a good businessman knows exactly who he's running up against. Be sensitive to the vibes, here — if your client hates the guy like poison, forget it. But if he speaks of the competition with respect, or even grudging admiration, perhaps you're onto an interesting prospect. You don't have to use your client's name when you approach the competitor. Just indicate — since it's true — that you do business with other entrepreneurs in this business and have some real experience with businessmen like him.

The point is that you don't have to look for referrals in the same tired way everybody else does. Go about your business in an intriguing, intelligent way, and you'll engage the attention of other intelligent people. Being creative is more than just a key to success, it makes our business fun. And when you clearly enjoy what you do, people enjoy doing business with you.

SUMMARY

- Everybody in the country who's earning more than he's spending is a prospective investor in managed money. And, in all probability, he's already a consumer of managed money ... he just may not know it yet.

- Trying to pre-select a high-acceptance, low-rejection clientele is a pipe dream. Concentrate instead on prospecting from your deepest beliefs and your true skills. You have to be who you are, and you have to sell what you love.

- Take an inventory of your account book. It is, after all, your professional autobiography. How's that book coming?

- No single call matters. Prospecting is the purest imaginable numbers game. And the numbers will never let you down.

- Looking for a low-anxiety way to approach just about anybody? Try reviving people's interest in their IRA. Tax-deferred compounding is what the IRA is all about. And automatic dividend reinvestment in mutual funds is a perfectly efficient engine of compounding.

SUMMARY *(continued)*

- Whether your IRA approach succeeds or doesn't, use it as a springboard to go for the prospect's serious retirement money.

- Owning even a little of the fund that you're selling increases your effectiveness 300%. Don't just sell what you love; sell what you bought yourself.

- There are no "good lists" or "bad lists" — there is only "the numbers."

- Mailers and advertising are two widely practiced avoidance behaviors. To systematically generate good new prospects, you must start conversations with other human beings.

- Interesting lists are available, if you look. Concentrate on lists most people are probably too lazy to find.

- Be creative when you go after referrals. Avoid open-ended requests where the client has to figure out who the referral might be, as well as give you the introduction. Give the client a name, or at least a very specific track to run on.

7

Prospecting 3:
Talking To The Great Money
Management Markets Of The '90s

The threshold issue in all financial selling is the number of people you talk to. The next issue is how quickly you can make people sense that you genuinely care about their deepest financial needs, and that you deal in high-quality managed investments that help people meet their goals.

"Needs selling" is not a technique, or even a style. It's an expression of your willingness and ability to reach people in the most profound way and to convince them that you, and the money management firms you represent, have the capacity to help accomplish their objectives.

Come to think of it, what other kind of selling is there? Oh, I suppose there's the transaction-oriented kind ("Buy this ... it'll go up, and you'll make money"). But what real need does the transaction satisfy? (Yes, I know: Inside every investor there's a speculator struggling to get out. But heaven help him if and when he does.) And **why would you expect anyone to expose his serious capital to a crapshoot?** ... or to the salesperson who purveys it?

Then there's what I call "commodity" selling. No, not frozen pork bellies or orange juice futures, but the kind of selling where *you* become a commodity. In commodity selling, your products or services aren't differentiated; you compete only on the issue of price. "Yes, I know the other guy is showing you the Secaucus Water and Sewer Authority 6-1/2% bonds of 2004 at a price of 99, but that's because he's tacking on a quarter of a point commission. I'll offer them to you at 98-7/8 — I'll work for an eighth of a point." (Guess what is the ultimate form of commodity selling? Of course: discount brokerage.)

The real professionals of the '90s will have one objective, and one only: to own the client ... to be the last financial advisor the client ever deals with, because he's found someone he can trust for the rest of his life, and who his heirs can trust when he's gone.

Prioritize your ultimate objective and you'll see the one great truth about the next stage of our business:

THE '80s WAS THE DECADE OF THE TRANSACTION ...
THE '90s WILL BE THE DECADE OF THE RELATIONSHIP.

The unprecedented proliferation of products gave you a different story to tell every day, and the wild bull market kept everybody excited. These phenomena have cyclically run their course. True, more people have more money to invest today than ever before. But, the great preponderance of investable net worth will be earmarked for the most serious of life's goals — college, retirement — and seriously invested. Right ... *managed money.*

Let's look at the five most important markets for managed money and how they will develop throughout the '90s. As you go through this exercise, think about your clients and prospects, and about how much of their serious assets you've captured or are even trying to capture. And, as you go into your "baseline" prospecting program, try to see how the people you talk to fit into the patterns we're about to explore.

1. THE WEALTH CROWD

The biggest and strongest market managed money has traditionally served is the population segment over 50 years old. This group constitutes 25% of the American population — more than 64 million people — and is growing at a much faster rate than the population as a whole. But their wealth characteristics, rather than sheer numbers, ought to rivet your attention. Because these wonderful folks:

- control 70% of all the net worth of U.S. households;
- own 77% of all the financial assets in private hands;
- have a combined personal income of more than $800 billion;
- own two-thirds of all money market accounts;
- are, without a doubt, the most affluent and powerful consumer group that has ever existed; and
- are the best educated, most knowledgeable generation of investors yet.

These numbers are — and ought to be — mind-blowing. But, like all abstract statistics, you have to get behind the facts to know what the people who make up the statistics *really feel*. How? By knowing as much as you can about their life experiences. Because a huge preponderance of our hopes, fears and expectations about the future are rooted in our past. We are, after all, the sum of our experiences. So ...

ALWAYS FIND OUT
THE PROSPECT'S AGE

(Better yet, find out his exact birthday so you can show the kind of person you are by sending a birthday card. We'll talk about this more in a later chapter.)

Let's say you're talking to a man who turned 50 in 1991. Look how much you already know about the guy, and what you can deduce about his life experiences:

- He was born in 1941. His parents' adolescence occurred during the Great Depression, and that scarred everybody for life. Already, you know some of his attitudes toward safety, investments and security because they stem from his parents.

- This prospect's conscious childhood, say ages five to ten, was informed by the golden years after the Second World War, when America settled down, went back to work, bought a house, got a TV set ... and saw the dawn of the thermonuclear age, live from the Nevada desert. Interestingly, too, this guy is part of the last generation raised on radio ... which means he *listens* better than people raised purely on TV.

- When the prospect was nine — in June, just as fourth grade ended — the Korean War broke out. He had air-raid drills a couple of times a week in school and lived under the threat of nuclear war for the next 40 years. This, too, shaped the way he thinks.

- He entered high school in 1954. Eisenhower was in his second term. The Supreme Court handed down its decision in *Brown v. Board of Education,* marking the beginning of the end of segregation. In someplace called Indochina, the French Army was inexplicably losing a battle in a valley called Dien Bien Phu. The prospect heard about it every night on the news, but he didn't understand what it meant. As it turned out, neither did anyone else.

- If he went to college, he was class of '62. In the fall of that year, when the client was in his first job, he spent a week wondering if the world was going to end as a result of the Cuban missile crisis. When you're that age, you think you're going to live forever. Suddenly he found out: Maybe you're not.

- He may be just old enough to remember — but he never really understood — the whole adult world stopping around him one day in 1945, when he was four. His parents tried to explain to him that the President was dead. On November 22, 1963, when he was 22, he suddenly found out how they felt. Young people, just starting out in life, would never hope in quite the same way again.

- Later in the 1960s he got married (find out when — how many people remember his anniversary?) and started a family.

From here, you can fill in some historical blanks — and establish a more personal feel between yourself and the prospect — with some questions about his family and career.

- *How old are your kids? Are they out of college yet? What are they doing?* People love to talk about their kids, and you can start to find out whether tuition is still draining him dry.

- *What's your career been like?* Which is another way of asking: Where has he built up equity … retirement benefits … potential IRA rollovers? Isn't this so much nicer than asking him where he's parked his money?

This sort of historical approach to the client's life story is a phenomenal relationship builder. (Particularly if you're a younger member of our profession, you now know why you'd better start reading some modern American history. I've provided a brief bibliography at the end of this book.) And now that you've looked at the prospect *retrospectively*, you're in great shape to do some *prospective* work.

1a. THE "GET-IN-GEAR" GROUP

The client above is part of the single most dynamic market for managed money today: the pre-retirement group. These people are planning — or hoping, at any rate — to retire earlier than any generation in history. Moreover, they will be the longest-lived generation yet. Put those two facts together, and you have an awful lot of retirement years to be provided for. Then add the fact that the client and his wife don't want to be a financial burden on their children as their lives draw to a close, and you have one very interesting prospect for managed money because …

AT AGE 50, PROSPECTS ARE MUCH TOO YOUNG TO GO TO GROUND … MUCH TOO OLD TO FOOL AROUND.

"Too young to go to ground" means that the client probably still has a long way to go to accumulate sufficient capital to provide an income he can't outlive. He needs to make significant additions to capital over the next ten years and to make sure his current capital grows at a healthy clip. He can't just bury the money in CDs or Treasuries, or even in high-quality municipal bonds, and expect to get anywhere after inflation and taxes.

At least intuitively, the pre-retiree knows he *really* has to get in gear. (He may not know what to *do* about it, but that's where you come in.) The other thing he knows is he's "too old to fool around." Chances are that in the ten years since he turned 40, he suffered some painful capital losses. The individual investor significantly underperformed the stock market in the 1980s — a combination of pretty consistently awful stock selection and a severe whipsaw in the bust-boom-bust of 1987-90.

Don't forget that during the 1980s he probably experimented with tax sheltered investments (in the earlier part of the decade) and other limited partnerships (in the latter part) — probably unhappy experiences. (Note, too, that with tax shelters cyclically if not permanently gone from the landscape, managed money today has less competition for the investor's dollar.)

So, all in all, this investor's got religion — he's ready to tread the straight and narrow path. And, once again, **you are the bridge.** Reach this person with your seriousness and with your empathy for the task he has before him. Tell him with warmth and conviction that you'll help him get where he needs to be if he will *let you* … and he's yours. **Put yourself inside his head.** Fact-finding is OK, but I'd rather you do *feeling-finding.* Remember: Feelings are to facts as nineteen is to one.

Here's an approach that puts feelings above facts:

"What serious pre-retirement planning are you doing? Are you happy with the way it's going? I know some pretty terrific people who manage money for investors with exactly your goals. I think you — especially from what I know about you — would be

really comfortable with these people. Could I buy you a cup of coffee one morning next week, and tell you the story? It'll take ten minutes tops, I promise you … funny, but the best investments are always the most straightforward, and easy to understand. How's Tuesday at 8:00?"

I hear, in that little approach: empathy, seriousness, you, the client, great money managers, understanding, shared goals, the promise of simplicity, and more understanding. I don't hear anything at all about stocks, bonds, mutual funds, wrap accounts, track records, rates of return, or what you know. I think it's a nifty approach. You sounded great, and *you* should think you sounded great, too. The prospect's answer does not matter — guy wants the cup of coffee, you get a checkmark on the old "baseline" scoreboard; guy doesn't want the cup of coffee, you still get the checkmark.

If a prospect can say no to such a gentle, empathic, richly professional and totally non-threatening approach, please have the plain common sense to know there's nothing wrong with you. There's something real wrong with *the prospect.* You were terrific; now go approach somebody else.

Here are some other interesting questions you can and should be asking pre-retirees:

- *When are you planning to retire?*
- *Where are you going to go?*
- *What are you going to do?* (Don't ever assume the answer is "nothing." When my son and I were on safari in Kenya a few years ago, we met a guy who'd just retired after 30 years with IBM. What was he going to do? … hike to the top of Mt. Kilimanjaro, go back to New Jersey, and start his own business!)
- *What kind of income do you think you'll need to support your lifestyle? Where do you think it will come from? How are you adjusting for inflation?*
- *What's your strategy? What kinds of investments are you making toward that goal? Are they working? Are you happy with the way you're going?*
- *What's your main concern? What are you most worried about?*
- *What's your single worst-performing investment? Why don't we get rid of it?* (Note the "we" in the sentence.)
- *Do you have any real feeling for what your whole portfolio is earning? Want me to help you figure it out?*

Close this book, take out a pen and paper, and I'll bet you can quickly write down another ten good questions to ask people. And you'll frame those questions in your own personal style rather than mine ... which can only make them better.

Ask anything and everything you can think of. *Assume nothing.* The only stupid question is the one you don't ask.

My favorite president, Harry S Truman, always said, "The only thing new under the sun is the history you don't know." (My corollary belief, incidentally, is that the only thing new under the investment sun is the cycle you haven't lived through — or, having lived through the cycle, you don't recognize it when it comes around again in another asset class. But I digress.) Know your prospective client's life history and you will already know a lot about how he thinks, what he needs, and what he's afraid of.

2. THE SLOW-AND-SURE SET

The other, older part of the 50+ population segment is people who have already retired. Once again, look at their life history before you start trying to figure out their wants, needs, and governing prejudices.

Let's take a prospect who turned 67 in 1991.

- He was born in 1924. He may be a first-generation American, because of the huge waves of young immigrants who reached our shores in the prior twenty years. (That was the assimilation generation — the kids who learned English in public school because it wasn't the language spoken at home.)

- The prospect is among the richest old folks ever. If the parents of today's 67-year-olds could be alive again for one moment to see how much money their children accumulated, they'd drop dead all over again.

- The prospect may not be that smart about investments, but he's done a lot of hard living. He probably didn't go to college, but had to drop out of high school to help support the family. One or more siblings may have died of tuberculosis.

- His conscious childhood (ages 5-10) coincided with the onset of the Great Depression to its nadir, 1929-34. The poverty and desperation of those years were Dickensian, and this generation's scars will never heal.

- If the prospect made it through high school, class of '42, he went straight into the service. And by that time, he was probably shipped out to fight the war in the Pacific. Your prospect's best buddy — the guy he double-dated with at the senior prom — may still be out there. The prospect can tell you exactly where he was when he heard the news that FDR died.

- But after the war, something wonderful may have happened: The prospect went to college on the GI Bill and became the first college graduate in his family. He married, went to work, bought a house in Levittown, and had a baby in 1949 — just in time to avoid being recalled to active duty when the Korean War broke out.

- He may have worked for the same company for the next thirty years or more. To this generation, a job was a precious thing, and you didn't turn your back on it lightly. The Vietnam War just broke this guy's heart, and so did Nixon ... because he supported both until right near the end.

- Perhaps he didn't accumulate a lot of capital by today's standards. But when you total up the boxcar numbers he received when he sold the family home, and add his savings and pension benefits, you've got a very comfortable client on your hands.

- Trouble is, he's as risk averse as any ten people you can name. But a day in a hospital now costs what his father earned in a month. And this client is starting to get *real worried* about outliving his income.

You have a couple of options with this client. You can waltz into his condo in Clearwater, Florida, start talking about a conservative stock fund, then look on in horror as the guy's head spins completely around six times and he spits up pea soup like in *The Exorcist* ... and you wonder what's going on.

Or you can have the plain common sense, as well as the instinctive relationship orientation, to get him to tell you his age and life experiences, so you'll really know who you're dealing with ... and how to deal with him. Like I said, **let the incipient washouts do fact-finding; you do feeling-finding and you'll be a superstar** ... all in good time.

Your feeling-finding with retirees will uncover a lot of fear, suspicion and negativity. That can be really maddening, and you may get very upset when you find you can't break suspicions down, no matter what you do.

Retirees are slow in making investment decisions. They have too much time on their hands, for one thing, and they find they can use up an awful lot of time obsessing about a decision you'd normally expect someone to make in an instant. But if a retiree makes a decision right away ... what's he going to do with the rest of the week? In a very real sense, there's just no percentage for the retiree in making up his mind.

Consumer studies have found that people's respect for (and reliance on) wirehouse brokers drops off a steep cliff after age 65. The broker needs to get an order, book a commission, and move on to the next ticket. The retiree needs to talk about it, think about it, read about it, chat with his friends about it, talk about it some more, remind you of the story about how his father's $490 nest egg disappeared when the bank in Asbury Park closed in 1932 ... etc., etc., etc. Do business with each other? Heck, it's a wonder the retiree and the wirehouse broker don't murder each other!

So here again, you can quickly see this is a market almost completely insensitive to what you know.

RETIREES INVEST WITH PEOPLE THEY TRUST ... PERIOD.

Gain their trust, and there's no limit to the business you'll do. Educate retirees, and they'll smile politely, offer you another cup of coffee, tell you for the ninth time how much you look like their niece or nephew, and tell you they'd like to "think about it." Then, they'll go down to see that nice young woman at the bank tomorrow, and she'll roll over all their CDs for another year. And, she'll keep this old person filling out forms for an hour, just like they want her to.

The keys to dealing with retirees are:

- **Have Patience.**
- **Have a genuine interest in the retiree and his life experiences.**
- **Get to their concerns and fears.** This is very important and very difficult, because people don't talk easily about their deepest fears. And when they do, they may talk about fears euphemistically, in ways that throw you off the track. For instance, we all learn early in our careers that when an older client says, "I don't want that bond because the maturity is too long," he means "I'm afraid I'll die still owning the damned thing."
- **Use gradualness.** When you look at a retired person's assets, comment first on something you like. Make him feel good about

an investment he's made. He doesn't want to feel criticized. Then, find something that's not appropriate on his list, but comment only on how it's *not working anymore.* Try to make small, incremental changes in the portfolio so that the client doesn't feel threatened.

- **Stress service.** Retirees sometimes feel a lot less connected to life than when they were working. Service from you — a note about the progress of one of their investments, a reminder that something in their portfolio is maturing — helps people feel connected, involved ... and leads to more business.

- **Show leadership.** There's a big difference between genuine respect for a client's concerns and pandering to his whims. People don't respect you if you involve yourself in their own game-playing; you have to communicate, gently but firmly, the fact that you're keeping them headed in the right direction. Once in a while you'll lose an account by leading. Consider it the best account you ever lost, because the client either already was, or was about to become, more trouble than he was worth.

Here are some interesting questions you can ask retirees:

- *Are your investments generating enough income?* This is a particularly provocative question that gets people talking, if only because almost nobody instinctively feels he's getting enough income.

- *How old are your children? What are they doing?* These questions often lead in very interesting directions you couldn't have anticipated.

- *Do you have grandchildren? How old are they?* People love to be asked these questions. They lead into whether, and to what extent, the retiree wants to help with his grandchildren's education. Helping one's grandchildren in a tangible way to graduate college is, psychologically, a way for the retiree to stay alive, even though he won't be there to attend graduation. Remember: feelings, not facts.

- *Are you concerned about inflation? What do you think it's going to do over the next ten years? How will your investments keep pace?*

- *Do any of your investments particularly bother you? Are any not really working? Why don't we get rid of them?*

- *Do you like managing your own investments? Is it something you're comfortable doing?*

When you ask these kinds of questions you're saying: "I'm interested in you. You matter to me. Your opinions have weight and validity." You'd be surprised how few people make retirees feel this way ... and how much you can accomplish by just tapping into their feelings.

3. THE BOTTOM-LINE BUNCH

An even greater market is poised in the starting blocks behind the 50+ crowd — the baby boomers, who are just now coming toward the end of their peak spending years and entering their peak saving years.

The baby boom exploded after the Second World War —generally from 1945 to 1950. In the mid-1990s, this huge population segment will hit 45 to 50 years old. And, their children will be finishing college —an occurrence which releases a lot of cash flow that you can channel into the serious business of saving for retirement. Indeed, many polls confirm that boomers will sharply increase savings rates in the 1990s.

A survey conducted for *Rolling Stone* magazine (no kidding) to determine the attitudes of the 18 to 44 age group found money was the second most important concern — trailing only health:

- 44% were worried about not having enough money for retirement;
- 41% were worried about being able to send their children to college; and surprisingly,
- only 22% believed that Social Security would be there when they retired.

The boomers, therefore, have a keen sense of the need to accumulate capital for later years. They're also very busy with their careers and extremely well-educated. Boomers are used to being challenged to make decisions — their mindset is very much one of "let's get on with it." You can and should, therefore, come at them in a crisp, businesslike way.

The boomers' life histories tend to be marked by disillusionment and distrust of institutions — their college and young adult years were scarred by Vietnam and Watergate — so they're sensitive to the risk of being conned. Boomers perceive themselves as extremely bottom-line oriented. So, they respond particularly strongly to simplicity, directness and professionalism.

Here are some good questions for boomers:

- *When would you like to retire, and when do you really think you'll be able to retire?*

- *At the rate you're going, exactly what will your firm's retirement plan pay you? How can we find out?*

- *Do you know exactly what you can plan on getting from Social Security? There's a form you can send in, and the Social Security Administration will send you an estimate of your benefits at various retirement dates. Want me to have one sent to you? Just give me your address and Social Security number.*

- *What are your investments like? Are they really geared toward capital accumulation for retirement?*

- *You've probably built up a fair-sized IRA account. Are you still funding it? How's it invested? Are you happy with it?*

- *If retirement planning were a baseball game, what base would you say you're on? What do you think it'll take to get you home?*

- *I know this isn't much fun, and you're busy, but you need to stop and take a good hard look at where you stand financially in terms of your retirement goals. I can really be helpful to you on that, and I'll accommodate myself to your schedule. What's a good time?*

Busy professionals need to know they're dealing with other busy professionals. You'll have trouble getting boomers to sit still long enough for a serious discussion about retirement, not least because they're afraid of what they'll find out. (And, usually, they're right to be afraid.) So, you have to take the bull by the horns with this crowd.

Shrinking violets definitely don't cut it. But neither do boors. Boomers want to deal with smart, savvy, self-confident people. But, engage them in an overt contest of wills and you'll usually lose. Don't argue, but don't be deterred, either. The client — when he becomes a client — will thank you later for keeping him focused. He, and the people he eventually refers you to, will be putting away some very serious money over the next ten years. And they won't take all day to make up their minds about it, either — they simply haven't got the time. It's a conundrum, and it doesn't make life any easier for you, but ...

**THE BEST PROSPECT
IS OFTEN THE PERSON WHO HAS
THE LEAST TIME TO SEE YOU.**

Stay on them. They're worth it.

4. SCHOLASTIC ACCUMULATION TARGETS

Yet another great market for managed money in the 1990s will be the college planning market. In the past, college planning was a fertile field because there were so many kids. But, in the last ten years, even as birth rates went south, the cost of college went completely into the stratosphere. Just when a competitive college education went from being a luxury to being an absolute necessity, look at what happened to costs (see Table 7-1 below).

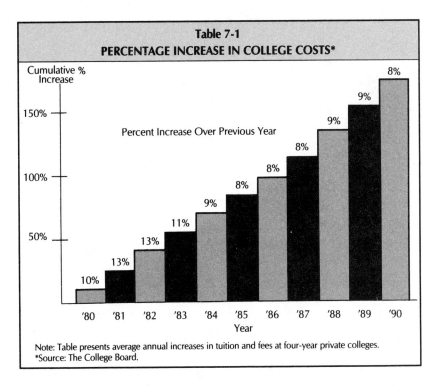

Table 7-1
PERCENTAGE INCREASE IN COLLEGE COSTS*

Note: Table presents average annual increases in tuition and fees at four-year private colleges.
*Source: The College Board.

Throughout the 1980s, the rate of cost increase was well in excess of inflation — almost twice the CPI. The good news is that the rate of increase in college costs will probably moderate in the 1990s. The bad news, however, is twofold. First, cost *increases* may moderate, but costs certainly will not go down. Second, the really good colleges and universities — where people really want their kids to go — are still going to have many times more applicants than available places. So, these schools will never really be price-sensitive. They'll charge whatever is necessary to maintain the infrastructure and faculty to keep on top … and people will gladly pay the freight.

Say your clients are thinking about state schools. Assume the annual cost is $7,500 today, and rises only 6% a year from here on out — far less than the recent past. Take a look at what the client is up against (see Table 7-2). Figure the better private schools are going to cost at least twice as much.

Table 7-2 PROJECTED COLLEGE COSTS			
Child's Age	Total Cost of 4-Year Education	Child's Age	Total Cost of 4-Year Education
1	$88,349	10	$52,293
2	83,349	11	49,333
3	78,631	12	46,541
4	74,180	13	43,907
5	69,981	14	41,422
6	66,019	15	39,078
7	62,282	16	36,866
8	58,756	17	34,779
9	55,430	18	32,810

The picture is not pretty. But you see why college planning is a bigger market than ever, and why mutual funds, where you have the double-barreled effects of dollar-cost-averaging and automatic dividend reinvestment, are ideal instruments. The math also shows that unless you have *some* exposure to equities, you're guaranteed to lose the race.

You may never become rich selling monthly accumulation plans and dollar-cost-averaging. But what a great way to prospect, simply because everyone you run across with a child under college age is a potential buyer. And you don't have to think up any fancy strategies for approaching people, either. All you have to say is:

"How are you planning to pay for your children's college education? Can I have ten minutes to show you an exceptionally smart way to accumulate the capital you'll need?"

(Or, if it's true:)

"Can I have ten minutes to show you how I'm doing it?"

Be creative. Go to local schools and PTAs. Know the local high schools' college guidance counselors. Pick their brains; let them see your genuine interest in this market. Suggest you participate in regular meetings with parents to provide a purely generic seminar on college costs. (People who want more information can fill out and hand in response cards at the end of the meeting.) Heck, you're performing a public service — be proud of it.

A lot of schools publish a list of class mothers. Call a class mother and see if she'd like to round up some of the other parents to hear your generic college-cost speech over coffee one morning. Finish up by telling the attendees you'll be glad to meet privately, *with spouses*, to discuss specific funding strategies. (Never present anything to anyone unless you're sure all decision-makers are in the room.)

Become known as the college planning expert in town. Invest in the better source books of college information, so that you can talk knowledgeably about costs. (The classic, *Comparative Guide to American Colleges*, by James Cass and Max Birnbaum, is updated and published each year by Harper & Row.) At least one fund company offers a diskette for your PC, giving current and projected costs at just about every school based on the child's age and the inflation rate you pick. Discussing college costs generically is abstract. But having people tell you the schools they'd like their kids to attend, and then cranking up the PC and showing exactly what those schools cost — that's reality. (Using Cass & Birnbaum's Guide, you can also answer other questions parents may not have focused on yet — acceptance rates, extent of financial aid, etc. No wonder people will want to talk with you: You are value added.)

As you become better versed in the whole issue of college costs, you will be correctly perceived as a real specialist. People will, in time, come to regard the specific fund recommendations you make as an afterthought — exactly as it should be in all segments of marketing managed money.

- Isolate the need.
- Empathize.
- Offer your help and support.
- Make people know that their goals become your goals when they become your client.
- Then sell the solution you love (where possible, the solution you yourself use).

Soon, you will own the account. You will be the family's financial adviser and friend. When they needed you — even if they didn't at first realize how much they needed you — you were the bridge.

5. THE INSTI-VIDUAL MARKET

Another great, booming money management market for the 1990s (if Congress doesn't decide otherwise on a whim someday) is the 401(k) plan market. Between 1983 and 1988, the number of workers eligible for 401(k) plans grew from 7 million to 27.5 million — a whopping 300% increase. And after the Tax Reform Act of 1986, almost 28 million people became ineligible to take the IRA tax deduction. So, the 401(k) fills a tremendous void. In fact, since 1986 401(k) assets have grown 500% to over $150 billion at the end of 1990. Many observers believe 401(k) assets will zoom to between $400 and $600 billion by the year 2000. Why? Lots of reasons.

- **401(k)s remove employers from ERISA's strictures about fiduciary obligation.** Since the passage in 1974 of the Employee Retirement Income Security Act, the trustees of qualified pension and profit sharing plans have been subject to a "prudent man" rule. Employers ask attorneys what the rule means, exactly. The answer is always the same: The judge will tell you at the end of your trial. The answer isn't acceptable to a lot of employers — can you blame them? So, they are very interested in a plan which transfers the fiduciary responsibility to the planholder.

- **401(k)s fix the employer's costs.** In a defined benefit pension plan, if the investments don't perform the employer has to pony up the difference. In a 401(k), the employer says to his employees, in effect: "Here's a menu of investment options. I'll match your contribution up to a point (if that's how the plan is set up). Pick your investment option, and good luck to you."

- **Administratively, 401(k)s are a no-brainer.** A variety of independent administrators offer "turnkey" packages, which provide at relatively modest fees: investment management, plan record-keeping, and communication with employees.

- **In terms of visibility and good will among employees, 401(k)s load a lot of bang into the employer's buck.** Say an employer only wants to match 20% of his employees' 401(k) contributions. The employee is looking at an immediate 20% "return" on his investment — even before the contribution itself starts earning anything. And a guy earning $75,000 a year and socking away the full tax-deductible amount he's eligible to contribute — about $8,300, at this writing — suddenly finds that his retirement nest egg went up over $10,000 in a year. And he is one happy camper. In fact, people with higher incomes will accumulate more in three or four years with the 401(k) than they have in their IRAs since 1974! If you're the salesperson/planner who helps put the 401(k) plan in, you'll make a lot of friends.

For you ...

MAKING A LOT OF FRIENDS
IN A HIGHLY LEVERAGED WAY
IS WHAT 401(k)s ARE ALL ABOUT.

The 401(k) is an "insti-vidual" sale. You sell the corporate decisionmaker on the plan, then you meet with all those nice folks who are covered by the plan, and who look to you for education on the various investment options. Of course, you appear bathed in the glow of the employer's approval, giving you lots of credibility. And, when you think about it, you're not trying to *sell* anything. You're there to help the employees understand options and choose wisely, given their goals and risk tolerances. Are the employees — and their bosses — going to become your clients? Well, if you're as smart as I think you are — and as genuinely committed to education, service and follow-up — I'm betting you have a lock.

You can approach this market lots of ways:

- **Offer to do a talk for local service organizations and chamber of commerce groups.** Call your talk *"401(k): The Rich Man's IRA,"* or *"401(k): The Last Real Tax Shelter."* Or how about *"Keep Your Key Employees (and yourself) Happy With A 401(k) Plan."*

- **Call local companies and ask for the name of the employee benefits manager.** Send him a great letter outlining the benefits of a 401(k). (The wholesaler of your favorite fund can provide a text.) Then, try to see him.

- **Ask people you know if they have a 401(k) plan at work.** If not, tell them they're missing a great bet on a tax-sheltered retirement plan, possibly because the employer doesn't know about it. Then ask for an introduction to the key individual at your friend's company.

- **When companies you prospect already have a plan, tell them you may have ways to improve the investment performance or lower the administrative costs.** You won't need more than a half-hour meeting to find out if you can help.

401(k) is one of the really smart markets for managed money in the 1990s. But don't neglect your basic business by going on some kind of quest for the Holy Grail of 401(k) superstardom. 401(k)s are a long, slow process, taking patience, wholesaler support, and the courage to prospect big people.

SUMMARY

- **"Needs selling" isn't a technique, it's a belief system. Needs selling helps you reach people where they really live — where the important investment decisions are made.**

- **The 1980s was the decade of the transaction, just as the 1970s was the decade of the product. But, the 1990s will be the decade of the relationship.**

- **The most fertile field for sowing managed money relationships is the 50-and-older set. They have the needs and the money.**

- **Study a client by his life history. You'll know — or quickly find out — about his hopes and fears. And, by showing a genuine interest in his life experiences, rather than by just studying his portfolio ... you'll make a friend, as well.**

- **From age 50 on, your prospect senses he's "much too young to go to ground, and much too old to fool around." Forget fact-finding; do some serious feeling-finding.**

SUMMARY *(continued)*

- The 50+ group may have made a lot of money during the 1980s, but took some major investment portfolio hits, too. Help the client be serious, because he's coming into the home stretch. First and foremost, ask great questions, then really listen to the answers. Assume nothing.

- The post-retiree is fretful, indecisive, suspicious, and phenomenally risk-averse (though his definition of risk may be seriously flawed). Take it easy on him; his life history will tell you he's been through a lot.

- The key things to practice with retirees are: patience, genuine empathy and interest, discovering concerns and fears, gradualness, service ... and real leadership.

- The next great money management market will be the baby boomers, who will pass from peak spending years to their peak savings years in this decade. Boomers are eager to get on with it and will respond strongly to simplicity, directness and professionalism. They need answers, not hand-holding.

- With boomers, discipline yourself to respect the conundrum that the best prospect is often the person who has the least time to see you. But don't let yourself be humiliated, either. No prospect is worth it.

- College planning will continue to be a great market for managed money in the 1990s, because costs have gone wild. Entry into this market is about as simple as seeing someone holding a kid's hand and being willing to approach him.

- Be known as the college expert in your area. Invest in the sourcebooks and the software. Put yourself in front of the parents ... and then, when they start planning, ask for referrals to the grandparents.

- The 401(k) will be the great "insti-vidual" market of the 1990s. 401(k)s are easier and lower risk for the employer than ERISA plans, and probably lower cost, as well. People can put relatively large sums away (compared to an IRA). And best of all, you do the individual selling. You can make a lot of new friends in a hurry, if you're patient and professional in selling the employer.

8

Prospecting 4: Leveraging Up

Once you have a "baseline" prospecting program taking shape, you can begin to raise your sights above making your daily calls and start seriously leveraging off the many resources now available to you in managed money.

If you're seriously committed to selling managed money you're a great asset to fund sponsors. And, the resources and support from fund sponsors are only going to grow. Why? Because the focus of the mutual fund industry is now moving from developing new products to creating better distribution.

Look at the progression of events. During the 1980s, spurred on by the phenomenal growth of money market funds, managed money went from a rarity to a staple in the individual investor's portfolio. In fact, the money market fund, more than everything else, turned us from a nation of savers into a nation of investors. The number of accounts in other types of open-end funds quintupled in the decade; assets grew seven-fold.

Today, assets in mutual funds equal three-quarters of those of life insurance companies and nearly half the deposits in commercial banks. A 1977 study of the 25 largest money managers in *Institutional Investor* magazine found only two were mutual fund companies. By 1989, seven of the top 27 were fund sponsors.

The 1980s were also a period of great product proliferation, from sector funds to country funds to global debt and equity funds. Then, toward decade's end, came the phenomenally successful "wrap fee" accounts. Nearly every logical product niche is now filled, if not actually crowded, with great depth of product.

Product proliferation is largely over — all the available product shelves are stocked and overstocked. What, then, will the critical issue of the 1990s be? Of course, from here on out ...

THE SPONSOR'S MAJOR GOAL WILL BE PENETRATION. SO, THE CRITICAL VARIABLE NOW IS YOU, AND THE PRODUCTS YOU'LL CHOOSE.

This news is about the best a fledgling managed money superstar could hear. The sponsors are all competing for *your* time, attention, energy and goodwill. **You're holding all the cards**; let's talk about some intelligent ways you can play them.

You can call on three essential tools to help leverage yourself to the front rank of money management producers in the 1990s: the wholesaler; networking; and seminars.

USING THE WHOLESALER

Once you've identified a money management product (or at least a type) you can love that fits your natural market, pull the fire alarm ... call for help.

As you start your "baseline" program, enlist the aid of *at least* two people: your firm's internal wholesaler or product manager and the "outside" wholesaler who helps people in your area market the product you've chosen.

Take it from an old, battle-hardened veteran: Salespeople and planners don't begin to use all the staff help that's available in managed money. Maybe that's natural because your essential decency makes you think, "Gee, I've never done a lot of business for these guys, and they're probably out there running around closing cases for the heavy hitters. They probably haven't time for a rookie like me."

Fageddaboudit! (That's how people in the neighborhood where I grew up said, "Forget about it.") The heavy hitters are out there comfortably flying solo and closing their own cases. The wholesaler, for your information, is at this moment slogging from desk to desk in the Sioux Falls, South Dakota office, watching each producer's eyes glaze over as he pleadingly tries to interest them in his mutual fund. And he is silently praying, "Please, Lord, let me find just *one* person today who's seriously, excitedly interested in learning to sell my fund. I don't care if he couldn't spell mutual fund if you spotted him the m, the f, and all three u's. Just find me somebody who *wants to work the product,* and I'll never ask for anything else again!"

I made this point, in almost the same words, in my book *Shared Perceptions,* which is about selling real estate investments. Ever since, I've rarely had a speaking engagement, or attended a large industry meeting, where a wholesaler didn't come up to me and say a heartfelt "Amen" to this observation.

Money management wholesalers are practically bumping into each other looking for the next superstar. This is no time for modesty. Find a good wholesaler, and chain him to your desk.

WHOLESALERS ARE THE ULTIMATE LEVERAGE.

Don't reinvent the wheel. If you picked a product on which you will make a few hundred "baseline" approaches over the next few months, you need — and you richly deserve — all the help you can get. Wholesalers will help you refine and sharpen your presentation. They'll predict the twenty most common questions/objections and give you *killer responses.* They'll scout up some leads, maybe some orphaned accounts (which can be great fun to work), invite you to sales conferences, and help out in other ways you don't now dream of.

If you're not using the wholesaler, you can be sure someone else is. And at the same moment you're trying and failing to close a sale without the wholesaler, the producer using the wholesaler is writing a ticket.

If all else fails, maintain your perspective by remembering one thing: The wholesaler is paid an override on sales made in his territory. When you close a $25,000 sale with the wholesaler's help, he makes an override. And when you close a $25,000 sale without the wholesaler's help ... *he makes the same override!*

Before leaving the issue of the wholesaler, let's make one other observation. Forget the size, the history, the great name and the track record of the money management product you want to sell. In your town and among your prospects ...

THE WHOLESALER IS THE PRODUCT.
BECAUSE, EXCEPT FOR A FEW GLOSSY PIECES OF PAPER,
HE IS ALL YOUR CLIENTS (AND YOU)
ARE GOING TO SEE.

Murray's Third Law of Wholesaling Justice states that all money management organizations end up with the wholesalers they deserve. The Los Angeles Raiders' cheerleaders do not work for Mother Theresa. Birds of a feather most assuredly do flock together. What you see *is* what you get, not an aberration or a unique personnel mistake.

If you're falling in love with a good-looking money management product, but find the representative in your area is a weird dude, take my advice: Isolate on the weird dude. Trust your instincts: The critical variable is the bozo, not the "mountain chart" that goes up like the south face of Mt. Everest. Find another product to love. Fast.

HOW TO BUILD A NETWORK

Once you've decided to build your money management prospecting skills by showing a particular product, have the internal and external wholesalers help you establish a network of other planners/salespeople who are working the same product.

The network is not just another way to avoid reinventing the wheel. Your production will someday be at levels qualifying you routinely to meet your colleagues and money management company personnel at regional and national meetings. Networking may now be the only way for you to reach outside your office.

Suppose the wholesaler can identify five other producers besides you actively working his product. Imagine how a half-hour weekly conference call would accelerate all six of you up the learning curve. You hear (and improve on) each others' sales ideas, prospecting techniques, presentation skills, Q&A/objections handling and war stories. To be reminded regularly that others are going through exactly what you're going through means a lot. A "support group" can take the sting (not to mention the loneliness) out of the frustration and disappointment you feel when you hit the occasional dry spell.

You can also use your network to create the "performance contract" mentioned in Chapter 5. If you are trying to make four money management approaches a day, ask if somebody in your group is working at the same level. If so, you can agree to pay each other, say, $10 for every call you don't complete. You can settle up at the end of each week ... but my guess is that neither of you will have to. Because a friendly competitive buddy system tends to keep both parties percolating.

Plan a weekly conference call with your network. To make this call a focused, effective exchange and not just a telephone bull session, follow these guidelines:

- **Limit the group's size.** Seven is the limit to have everybody participating in the call. Also, more than seven makes the telephone arrangements unwieldy.

- **Limit the call to 30 minutes, no matter what.** Any more probably isn't worth doing anyway and can wait until next week.

- **Have an agenda, or at least a regular format.** Every couple of months, review the format to make sure everybody still feels it's working.

- **Agenda items can include:** each member's best answer to a key objection; one member making his presentation each week so the group can learn and/or critique; a pot every week for the biggest order (or most orders) that week, etc. Be creative; make it *fun.*

- **A member who misses three calls in a row is excused from the group.** (He clearly wanted out anyway, and just didn't know how to tell you — or maybe himself.)

- **Hostility, excessive competitiveness and/or a negative attitude are grounds for being excused from the group.** The weekly call only works if the call is a real "up."

The late Napoleon Hill (whose book *Think And Grow Rich* is to the literature of motivation/self-help what the book of Genesis is to the Bible) called such arrangements "Master Mind Groups." Aaron Hemsley calls them "Performance Groups." Regardless of what it's called, **networking is an organized, relentlessly positive way to make each member better and smarter.** The whole turns out to be much more than the sum of the parts. Your managed money learning curve becomes shorter and less steep, which helps you produce more sales sooner. And networking may acquaint you with colleagues and friends who can leverage each other's careers for years to come.

LEVERAGE WITH SEMINARS

Now, let's assume you accept the notion that your best approach early in a prospecting program is to leverage off the wholesaler (the sponsor's or your firm's). Once you establish a comfortable relationship with a wholesaler, you are ready for high gear ... in addition to doing your "baseline" presentations, you can start planning a seminar. And then another. Since managed money is essentially a "confidence" sale, **nothing builds a prospect's confidence faster than seeing a room full of people listening to, and liking, a professionally organized seminar.**

The advantages are manifold. First, and most important, the wholesaler makes the presentation, not you. And, almost equally important, the wholesaler pays for the seminar.

You watch a professional, who has practiced hundreds of times, make a superbly organized presentation. And you see what people react to ... what I call the Nod Factor. Watch closely to see when the audience nods. Notice which sales points caused the nod. And after the presentation, you watch the audience lob questions and objections at the wholesaler (not you) and listen to how he handles them.

Managed money is a totally relationship-oriented sale, not a transaction-oriented sale like the purchase of 100 shares of stock. The relationship-oriented sale is a face-to-face event. Therefore, promoting a regular, easy, comfortable coming-together of planners/salespeople and clients — which seminars do peerlessly — is preferred over any other kind of indirect client contact.

Yet seminars are only a tool, not a panacea. Seminars work well only in the proper context, and they must be properly organized to be effective.

You and your colleagues have to agree on the kind of seminar you're going to run. You have to work *backward* from the number of people you want to talk to, and where you'll hold the seminar, and what subject matter you want to discuss. Many variations can work — fifty people in a nice local hotel meeting room, or twenty businessmen at a buffet breakfast in your office's conference room, or whatever.

Let's start with the people you want to talk to. A seminar will only work when you, and the other salespeople in your office with whom you're organizing the seminar, **build and control the audience.** Sending out 4,000 letters and putting an ad in the *Des Moines Register* isn't the way to organize a seminar.

Shotgun invitations simply will not work, and you wouldn't want them to because you have no control over the audience. With your luck, you'd pull in 120 people — a good crowd. But, the second the wholesaler was finished, a 72-year-old guy would stagger to his feet, waving his cane, and shout, "Oh, yeah? Well, I'll tell you about mutual funds. In 1968, I invested my life's savings in Enterprise Fund, because *Forbes* said it was the best-performing mutual fund of the year. And in 1969, it went down 60%. Now, what do you say to *that,* Mr. Big Shot?"

Or, even worse, you'll have a hotel room set up for 150 people, and 18 very nice, qualified prospects show up. They'll look at you, at the empty chairs and the wholesaler, and think, "How could I be so dumb?" People will do business with you for lots of reasons, but pity isn't one of them.

The best way to build the audience is to **specify a seminar topic that speaks very directly to the concerns of the people you're trying to attract.** But don't forget the purpose. A seminar should be designed to do only one thing — to communicate, in the clearest, most cogent way possible, the facts about an investment. Generic content sets the stage, articulates the concept, and establishes a need. But **a specific investment must be presented in the seminar.**

One additional word of caution about seminar content: Never, never show more than one money management product at any seminar. You will lose the ability to stand on the beautifully conceptual fit between one product and the investor need targeted as the seminar's theme. And you'll end up provoking long, wrangling, counterproductive comparisons. (You certainly can do seminars that show managed money as part of an investment approach. For instance, if you're doing a pension investing seminar, you might want to show zero-coupon Treasuries and a good corporate-bond mutual fund. But that's it.)

Lots of creative methods are available to build seminar audiences within the "natural markets" which already exist in your office's account books. Here are some examples:

● **Municipal bond buyers** — Take a survey of every account in the office that's bought $25,000 of municipal bonds in the last twelve months. Mail the master list a personal, hand-written, stamped (not postage-metered) envelope. The nicely printed invitation announces a seminar on *"A Professional Manager's Approach To Investing In Municipal Bonds,"* or *"Municipal Bonds In A Falling Interest Rate Market: What Should You Do Now?"*

● **Pension plan accounts** — Hold a seminar for all the pension, profit-sharing, IRA, Keogh and 401(k) plans in the office. Offer this topic: *"Long-term Growth For Long Term Goals: Investing For Retirement In The Nineties."*

• **The "Progress Report"** — As your office starts to build a position in a particular product, or a family of funds, you'll want to establish the "Progress Report" seminar, say, four times a year. The object is to build a regular audience that looks forward to the event, and steadily increases. Encourage attendees to bring friends, colleagues, and other interested parties.

The "progress report" meeting is easily the most productive. This seminar can keep clients from bailing out in tough markets ("Let's just stay calm; our progress report seminar is coming up, and we can talk to the sponsor then about…"). And when people really like what they hear at the seminar, they can always find some new money to add to the account.

• **Dinner with the sponsor** — Perhaps the strongest approach (and one you can bring off when you've sold a lot of someone's product) is a sit-down dinner with a very senior executive of the sponsor, or even with the portfolio manager, as the featured speaker. All your clients who invest with this sponsor are invited to the dinner *provided* they each bring a friend who hasn't previously invested.

• **"Participatory Democracy" approach** — If you find yourself scratching your head about the whole issue of seminars (if, in other words, you and your colleagues have no idea what kind of seminar would work best), *ask your clients.* Have a little note printed up like the one shown on the following page.

If you have enough response, of course, you can schedule seminars for virtually all the times that a cluster of people check. Or you can fall back on the notion that the ideal speaker for the occasion couldn't come in on a Wednesday night … would Thursday be OK?

The "participatory democracy" approach to seminar planning has another benefit. The person who specified a Tuesday breakfast feels a certain moral responsibility to show up for it.

Once you've defined the topic and audience, you need to attend to some important details. Four days after you send out the invitations, *each salesperson should call his invitees and start building an audience.* Each invitee, whether he's coming or not, is offered the

SEMINAR SCHEDULING LETTER

Dear _____:

The accelerating pace of change around the world — and the response of the stock and bond markets — dictate a major reassessment of the traditional ways in which we all invest. We here in the Wichita Falls office of Millbrook Securities are committed to identifying changing trends and specific opportunities.

To keep you up to date, we plan to offer a series of one-hour group meetings with our clients. And we'd particularly appreciate your personal participation in one or more of these meetings.

Will you please tell us which one of the meeting topics and times listed below would best suit your schedule. Thanks for your consideration.

Sincerely,

_____

Topics of interest:

_____ Retirement Planning
_____ Tax-Free Income
_____ College Tuition Funding
_____ Other: Please indicate a topic
      of interest _____

_____

Times:

_____ Breakfast   8:00 a.m. - 9:00 a.m.
_____ Luncheon   12:00 p.m. - 1:00 p.m.
_____ Late Afternoon   5:15 p.m. - 6:15 p.m.
_____ Evening   7:45 p.m. - 8:45 p.m.

Preferred Day of Week: _____

opportunity to recommend one acquaintance not currently a client of your firm (only one, because seating is, after all, limited).

On the day of the seminar, have a secretary call each person who's accepted the invitation. This reconfirming call assures the audience. On the day of the seminar, *you need a registration desk at the door,* so you're sure you have a name, address and phone number for everyone who attended.

By process of elimination, the list also tells you who accepted the invitation but didn't show up. Now, you have the opportunity to call the no-shows and say, "I'm sorry you weren't able to come to our seminar last night; I really missed seeing you. The speaker gave us some insight into a rather unique way of investing for retirement. I'd like to share it with you. Could you stop in for coffee tomorrow morning?"

One final, but vital, reminder: *The seminar is not the end — the seminar is the means.* The seminar is the presentation, never the close. When the seminar ends, the host should clearly tell the audience they will be called to determine what specific investment decisions the information in the seminar may have prompted.

The work of a seminar is not done until all the attendees are called back and asked what investment action they would like to take.

SUMMARY

- Wholesalers are your first source of "leverage" — don't be shy enlisting their aid. They need you.

- Wholesalers are paid an override for your sales whether they help you or not. When you're not using them, someone else is.

- "Networking" improves your chance of success and reinforces behavior. Keep it organized, small, exclusive and positive.

- Seminars are the ultimate expression of relationship-oriented prospecting.

- Build the seminar audience from the topic backwards.

- Never present more than one money management product at a seminar, although you may present, carefully, more than one investment medium to reach an investment objective.

- The purpose of a seminar is to sell product. The seminar is the presentation, not the close. Your work is not done until all attendees are given follow-up calls.

9

Prospecting 5:
Verbal Skills And "Attitude Aerobics"

As you begin to make more and better prospecting calls, you should start thinking about the issue of *tone* in the prospecting and sales process. Tone — *how* you say what you say — takes on a great deal of importance. When you are cold calling, the prospect doesn't know you well and isn't used to hearing you talk about managed money. Instead, he is listening to the *way* you are saying what you say. Your tone is critical because no one ever achieved money management superstardom without recognizing the fact that ...

**THE WAY YOU SAY WHAT YOU SAY
IS MORE IMPORTANT THAN WHAT YOU SAY.**

Think about it. People invest in a program of managed money only when they perceive you are a caring professional who is genuinely looking after their most serious financial interests. That's why **people don't, as a rule, buy managed money from people they understand; they buy from people they believe in.**

And if, in fact, the client ends up making an act of faith in the communicator/salesperson, then the tone and feeling of the presentation is the central issue — not the pure, intellectual truth and beauty of your product knowledge.

The client is listening for a combination of confidence, genuine enthusiasm for a transaction, and a real sense of concern for his needs. He knows you can't prove the program is going to work, any more than you can *prove* a stock will go up. The client wants to hear how you feel.

If this is getting a little too abstract for you, let's go back a few pages to the investor who said he was coming to your seminar and did not show.

Without getting too grotesque, here is how the average transaction-oriented salesperson sounds when (or if) he calls the client the next day:

"Gee, I thought you said you were coming to the seminar last night. What happened? Well, anyway, our firm is coming out with this mutual fund, and I think you ought to buy some. I'm going to send you the prospectus. Take a look at it, OK?"

What is this salesperson trying to do, give his client a guilt trip? Who cares what happened? (Suppose the client says, "My dog died"?)

Next, our boy uses the deathless phrase "coming out with," which should be banned altogether from the salesperson's lexicon. He thinks his client "ought to buy some." Any particular reason? ... other than Mr. Personality is having a slow month? He's "going to send out a prospectus." Why? To guarantee the sale never takes place? Would any sane salesperson put a 50-page prospectus in someone's hands before giving him a conceptual story?

This salesperson is really saying, "I wanted to get you to the meeting so the wholesaler could close you, because I sure as hell can't. But I'll keep going through the motions. Who knows? Even though you'll never figure out what this investment is, you may like it."

Now, look again at the phraseology we suggested earlier:

"I'm sorry you weren't able to come to our seminar last night; I really missed seeing you. The speaker gave us some insight into a rather unique way of investing for retirement, and I'd like to share it with you. Could you stop in for coffee tomorrow morning?"

Now, what does the client hear? First of all, he knows he stood you up. But you're not making him fabricate a story about why he wasn't there; you're being genuinely gracious, even going so far as to say *he was missed*. Next he hears the speaker had a great idea about investing for retirement. (Maybe now he really is sorry he wasn't there.) But, wait, you're still offering to *share the idea* with him ... and you'd like to buy him a cup of coffee in the bargain.

The no-show will probably give you the courtesy of a hearing if he's a real prospect. If he won't, he's told you (though not in so many words) he's not going to invest with you right now. You can take this conclusion to the bank. Don't bang your head against the wall. You have to let prospects disqualify themselves, if that's what they are determined to do.

Was there much substantive difference between the two call-backs? *There wasn't any.* Was there a difference between what the two salespeople wanted to accomplish? *There wasn't any.*

Then why is the effect of the two approaches so radically different? *Tone.* (Well, 90% tone, anyway. The other 10% was tactical: sending out the bloody prospectus versus inviting the prospect in to hear the story.)

THE CAPITAL CRIME

Thinking about tone will help you guard against one of the most distasteful and destructive habits a nervous new planner/salesperson can fall into: the use of jargon. The dangers of jargon are both stylistic and substantive. Using jargon offers a number of different ways to destroy the relationship with a potentially good client even before you reach first base.

Everybody hates it when a professional from another discipline lays jargon on them that they can't understand. (This instant generation of hostility is the opposite of what the sales process is all about.) Picture lying in the hospital. The doctor is saying an arrhythmic condition in your left ventricle is aggravated by a streptococcus infection. The resulting fluid build-up in your lungs is placing an additional strain on your aorta ... You're thinking, "Shut up, stupid, and *tell me if I'm going to live!*" To which Dr. Hippocrates muses, "Well, we'll just have to wait and see."

When you're standing in the service station on a summer Friday, and the mechanic is trying to explain the relationship between your starter, the battery, your carburetor and the transmission, all you want to know is: "*When can I drive my car to the beach?*"

Same thing with managed money. Your prospective client is only too aware of how little he understands about the stock and bond markets, so the very last thing he wants to hear out of you is anything that sounds even remotely like:

p/e ratio;
inverted yield curve;
floating exchange rates;
debt service coverage;
Dow theory non-confirmation;
12(b)1;

and any other half-baked technical term you can think of.

Using jargon will only make the prospect mad, because that's the way the person on the receiving end of jargon always reacts — the same way a doctor, lawyer, mechanic or engineer makes you mad when he doesn't care enough about you to speak to you in terms you can understand.

If you're lucky, the prospect is merely annoyed. If your luck doesn't hold, he won't just sit there stewing — he'll start asking you what all the terms mean, and that's where the substantive damage is done.

SALESPERSON: *Now, the great thing about this fund is that it invests in small cap, high tech, out of favor growth companies ...*

PROSPECT: *What's a small cap, high tech, out of favor growth company?*

SALESPERSON: (Eight minutes of halting, rambling "white noise," clearly showing you are a technology-illiterate, hiding inside an empty suit.)

PROSPECT: *If they're small, how do they get the money to grow? What if their inventions don't work? What if IBM makes the same gizmo cheaper, and puts them out of business? If they're out of favor, who wants them? I'm confused ...*

SALESPERSON: (Makes low, moaning noises as the conceptual logic of the investment vanishes into the air like dewdrops in the sunlight of an August morning ...)

Contrast the comic opera above with the following:

SUPERSTAR: *Over time, the stocks of good smaller companies always outperform stocks of bigger companies. That's because most important innovations come from small, aggressive, visionary companies, and not from established, conservative giants. IBM is the greatest computer company in the world, for instance. But it never occurred to them that everyone could have his own computer at his desk in the office and in his den at home. Then two guys nobody ever heard of started something called Apple Computer. Do you see what I mean?*

PROSPECT: *Of course.*

SUPERSTAR: *Well, the potential rewards of this kind of investing are outstanding. But a tremendous amount of research must go into understanding these companies, choosing the right ones ... and, if you're wrong, knowing when something's not working. In other words, it's not a kind of investing that you and I can do ourselves. You need a full-time professional manager who does nothing but screen these kinds of companies. And, for safety's sake, you have to own a portfolio of them; you can't bet the ranch on one potential high-flyer. That makes sense, too, doesn't it?*

PROSPECT: *Yup.*

SUPERSTAR: *Well, my friends at the Gronsky Group have a small mutual fund, the Gronsky Special Equity Fund, with a portfolio of 60 or so of these kinds of emerging, innovative companies. The portfolio is managed by a fellow named Axel Sprocket, Ph.D., who's made a career out of just this kind of research. I think that by diverting 10% to 15% of your equity portfolio into Gronsky Special Equity, you could achieve a significantly higher overall return. Because when this kind of investing works, you can really see the difference. Sound OK to you?*

PROSPECT: *Actually, it sounds perfect.*

The idea that you can meaningfully change the effect you have on people by adjustments in your "tone" is a major theme in subsequent chapters. In the meantime, start thinking and assessing where you stand with respect to "tone" right away.

TAKE YOUR TONE TEMPERATURE

The single most effective way to take your own "tone temperature" instantaneously is to:

START TAPING YOUR PHONE
CALLS AND PRESENTATIONS.

Hearing a tape of yourself speaking for the first time can be a jarring experience. We can't really hear what we sound like when we're talking. That's a physiological fact as well as a psychological reality. (Please understand that I'm only recommending audiotaping here. Going straight to videotape, first crack out of the box, might be too traumatic. Still, videotape is ultimately a very worthwhile exercise, particularly in small groups where you can critique each other and compare styles.)

Taping telephone conversations with clients and prospects is the surest, fastest way to start figuring out the adjustments you need. Record five conversations of a sales or service nature with your clients every day for a month. The subject of the call doesn't matter. In fact, the more different topics you cover, the more rounded and accurate a picture of what your clients and prospects are hearing. You can easily spot any common, recurrent rough spots in your tone.

SHAPE UP WITH "ATTITUDE AEROBICS"

If you think your "tone" is an important determinant, just imagine how much more critical your attitude is. Yet most of the advice we get about attitude turns out to be pretty vapid. "Have a positive mental attitude," they tell you. But do they tell you how?

"Positive mental attitude" is to psychology as voodoo is to neurosurgery. But you can do a number of genuinely effective things to affect your attitude. And the one thing they all have in common is: They're all things you do for other people. I'm convinced that there's a psychological or attitudinal equivalent to Newton's law — that every action produces an equal reaction. I think every kind, thoughtful, positive thing you say or do to someone else washes right back over you. And every unkind, unflattering, dismissive, impatient or condescending thing you say or do immediately corrodes you, in proportion to your intensity.

Suppose you walk into an appointment, and the prospect's receptionist says he's running twenty minutes late. You can signal in many ways your annoyance, impatience and low regard for her boss because he didn't stay on schedule or call you. The thing is, she may not even notice — but you will. When you finally get in to see the guy, your unconscious will carry a residue of emotional toxicity, because you feel a little shabby for taking it out on the receptionist. That's going to come through — entirely non-verbally, of course. And something about you is going to bother him, somehow.

Rewind. Suppose you'd just grinned when she told you her boss was running late, and you said the truth: "That's OK; I could use a few extra minutes. I had a little trouble finding the building, and for a while I thought I was going to be late. So I'm glad things worked out this way."

She may not respond positively. But, you still feel better just for having been easy-going and truthful. When you are inside, the guy may find himself liking you, just because you like yourself. That's how it works.

Then again, like most human beings, the receptionist may respond with some warmth to your genuineness. Next thing, she's getting you a cup of coffee and making sure the boss knows you're waiting. When she shows you in, and you thank her (by name, of course), something tells the boss that she approves of you. And since he thinks she's pretty good at sizing people up quickly, he's already looking at you with renewed interest. And you haven't even said a word yet.

What did it take? Only the right *attitude*. And you can systematically acquire the right approach (if you don't already have it) in exactly the same way you build up your "baseline" prospecting habits. You start with three basic perceptions about people:

(1) Nobody's life is particularly easy.
(2) Nobody is suffering from an excess of kindness heaped upon him by his fellow man.
(3) Everyone is vitally interested in himself, and wishes everyone else were more interested in him, too.

You have the capacity to touch effortlessly the lives of almost everyone you come in contact with. In most cases, the cost is zero. In all cases, the psychic income to you — in the way you feel about yourself, in the way people respond to you — exceeds the cost by a factor of infinity.

BIRTHDAY CARDS

The simple act of finding out someone's birthday and sending a fifty-cent birthday card has the power to alter completely your relationship. Nobody gets "too many" birthday cards, any more than anyone gets "too much" love. If you don't know and observe the birthday of everyone in your business or personal life who means anything to you, you're leaving some emotional capital on the table. And you may be leaving some money (in lost business) on the table, as well.

If this idea feels false or sentimental to you, and you shy away, I can cure you instantly:

JUST IMAGINE YOURSELF ON THE RECEIVING END.

Say somebody you buy something from took the trouble to find out your birthday and sent you a card. And you know it's basically to keep his business relationship with you in good repair. Do you care? Do you think any less of him? No. At worst you think he's smart, in a nice way. And at best, you're genuinely touched. (The approach does not work with Christmas cards, or other major holiday cards. Everybody knows it's Christmas, but not enough people know it's your birthday.)

I'll bet 95% of the adult population gets fewer than a dozen birthday cards. Do you have any idea what it means to somebody who, after 50 years of living, only receives six birthday cards, and then opens a seventh one from you? From then on, you're a friend … somebody who matters. If you don't really know much about international bond funds, I'm betting this guy will forgive you. (Are you beginning to see what I mean by saying success isn't about what you know, but about who you are?)

SEE WHAT PEOPLE CARE ABOUT

If you have any eye at all, you can see clues that tell you what a prospect cares about in your first two minutes in his home or office. I'm not talking about that tired old shabby tactic of complimenting furniture, a tie, or a newly shampooed rug. People hate that as an empty gesture. Emerson was right, as always: "What is done for effect is seen to be done for effect, and what is done for love is felt to be done for love."

But if I walk into a guy's office and see a fish mounted on the wall, I want to know everything about the fish. Think the guy's interior decorator put that fish up there? Heck, no. There's a story connected with the fish, a story the guy loves. And while he's telling me the story, I'll find out more about him — about what he's really like — than I could in an hour of conventional "fact-finding." And when this guy's next birthday rolls around, I'll stop into Orvis Brothers and buy one beautiful trout fly, stick it in a birthday card, and send it to him. Total cost: $6 and ten minutes. Total return? I'm not even sure I can count that high.

Let's say you go into the prospect's office, and there's a plaque on the wall from the United Way which says, "In Appreciation …," but you can't make out the rest of it. You think he put the plaque there to cover a hole in the wall? What's your next best guess?

The plaque is there because it's a testimonial to something he's proud of. He *wants* you to see it ... and he's dying to talk about it. So ask. Get up, walk right up to the plaque so you can read it. Stand there, and *ask.* Five minutes later, when he finally stops talking about the fund-raising record they set the year he ran the drive, tell him he ought to be proud. And, if the spirit moves you, tell him next time he's collecting, you'd like to help out in a small way with a little donation. (The last part is voluntary; the rest is mandatory.)

Will you get the order you want, right then and there? Maybe yes, maybe no. But you honored the prospect for something he cares deeply about. And I guarantee that's going to come back to you, sometime, some way. The Beatles weren't kidding, you know: In the end, the love you take *is* equal to the love you make.

ASK ABOUT PEOPLE'S KIDS, REMEMBER WHAT YOU HEAR

If you have children, you care about them. So, what do you think your prospect feels?

One day in late 1974, two years into a horrendous bear market, I called on an account I inherited. The client ran a family-owned electrical contracting business and had done a couple of fair-sized trades with my predecessor. When I walked into his office, he was seated at his desk with a credenza behind him. On the credenza were a few mementos and one picture — a 5x7, nicely framed, of a little girl in a ballet costume who looked about twelve years old. Without really thinking, I asked, "Is that your daughter?"

I didn't get a word in edgewise for about ten minutes. Turned out the kid was a ballet prodigy. Every Christmas, George Balanchine picked a few promising young dancers from an open audition and put them in a production of *The Nutcracker* at Lincoln Center. The client told me his daughter won a place in the show the previous year. Clearly, the event was the high point in her — and, I thought, his — life.

A few months later, one of the great Russian ballet companies came to New York. I went to the box office and bought two tickets. (I can never forget the cost, $17.50 each, because after two years of a bear market, $35 was money to me.) I sent the tickets to the client with a note saying I thought he and his daughter might like to go.

Whereupon the guy turned into what I call the Rasputin Account: Nothing I did could kill him. Didn't matter if my stock recommendations went down. In fact, nothing mattered. He was mine, even after I went out of full-time production. When my firm stopped letting staff guys above a certain level produce, I finally succeeded in giving the account to another broker ... but only after the account made both of us promise I'd still get the commissions somehow.

You literally can't imagine — any more than I could — what your genuine interest in people's kids means to them. (Incidentally, the observation goes double for grandchildren.) The operative word in all of this is "genuine."

THANK YOU NOTES

In the age of the telephone, people don't write to each other much anymore. There's a great line in the film *Absence of Malice*. When Paul Newman goes to Sally Field's apartment, he finds Field sitting there, typing. Newman asks her what she's doing, and she says she's writing to her father. Newman says, "Most people phone these days." And Field says, "I could call, I guess. But then what've you got?"

One of the most surprising and delightful things you can do for anyone (and, as we've seen, for your own attitude) is write a short note thanking a person for something he did — anything, no matter how small.

Take the receptionist we met a couple of pages ago — the one who was nice to you (because you were nice to her). She knows her job is never going to affect the course of human history. But she tries to do her job efficiently and effectively.

In all probability, she doesn't think anybody really notices the way she does her job. And, for the most part, she's right. Thirty or forty people come in every day, tell her who they want to see, and sit down. They go in and out again. Some may take a second to say good-bye to her; some don't even bother.

But suppose, in a couple of days, she receives a note in the mail from you:

Dear Ms. Jones,

   I enjoyed meeting you the other day, and I appreciate your taking care of me the way you did.

As I said, I had some trouble finding your office. And I was getting a little worried, because my appointment with Mr. Boss was important to me. I appreciated the coffee and having a few minutes to collect my thoughts.

It's always fun to meet someone who's really good at her job. I look forward to seeing you next time I visit with Mr. Boss.

Sincerely,

I don't care how slowly you write, or how deliberately you seal the envelope and lick the stamp, this effort cannot take more than five minutes. Chances are no one has ever done anything remotely like this for her. And just imagine what the effect is. You will almost always be able to see Mr. Boss when you want to. And you certainly know who to call to find out his birthday.

But, I'd rather you focus on just how good sending the note makes you feel about *yourself,* which really blows some fresh air through your attitude. Because you took a few minutes to perform a very elementary act of kindness, you feel different. Just for a moment, you treated someone the way you'd like people to treat you. And that always feels great. (Now, I was born and raised in New York City. And, for nearly a quarter of a century, I've been in a business that breeds cynicism. So you know I'd *never* be cornball enough to mention the Golden Rule, or anything like it. But you can take a hint, right?)

American Airlines, for my money, is a company that uses its head more than all its competitors, combined. Every few months, American sends the top 2% to 3% of its frequent flyers (of whom, regrettably, I am one) a package of little, wallet-sized "You're Someone Special" forms. The idea is that you give one to an American employee who does a really good job for you. The employee turns in the form for free mileage for personal travel.

By this method, American has a constant survey of its best customers' attitudes and spots winners in its work force at the same time. And I have a chance to really brighten someone's day, which feels great. Every so often, I'll be in an airport, and some gate agent will be knocking himself out to rearrange my schedule or get me a seat where I can write more easily. So I sneak off and fill out the "You're Someone Special" slip, go back and lay it on 'em. People light up like kids on Christmas morning! (And, in my heart, I know other frequent flyers get those slips in the mail and throw them away!)

But American is the exception to the rule by giving you the medium through which to say thank you. If you want to get into the habit of saying thank you, you have to take the law into your own hands, so to speak. I recommend you write at least one thank you note every day.

If you can't see even one person who is really trying every day, I'm afraid you're getting closed off, emotionally. Wake up; look around. The fitness instructor at your health club gave a great class this morning; wouldn't she love her boss to get a note from you about it? Somebody wrote a great article in a magazine you read; how about a note to the editor? The woman in the fish market just cut you some fresh tuna steaks. She could as easily have sold you the steaks left on display, but she extended herself. Isn't that noteworthy? (This one happened to me in real life; the note I wrote is still up on the wall of the store.)

Not long ago, I was sitting in first class (to which I upgrade on my own nickel, thank you) on a flight to California. I particularly liked the wine they served with lunch. I asked the flight attendant to show me the bottle. The winery was new, and passengers liked it.

Well, I got the name of the winery and sent the owner a little note. You would not believe the return letter; the guy was beside himself. He told me how much it meant to him and his family ... told me the American Airlines contract was their first big break, and that he'd sent my note on to the catering people and received a very positive response ... hoped I'd visit the Napa Valley soon and bring my family as their guests, of course ... and on and on. I felt like a million bucks. Try it on sometime.

When you get the hang of this, you'll find yourself looking each day for somebody to send the day's note to. In other words, **get in the habit of saying thank you and you'll be hoping for and expecting positive things to happen to you every day.**

Gotcha! That's real "positive mental attitude." And it can only come from what you do, not just from what you think. Like all permanent change, this one comes about one day at a time, four or five minutes a day. Sounds a lot like your "baseline" prospecting program? You bet it does! And why? Because that's what works.

You and I know that our profession has more than enough frustration and pain. And, if we let it, the resultant anger could end up taking over our lives. We can't allow that outcome. We have to really open up to people if we're going to induce them to be open to us. My suggestion: "attitude aerobics." It oxygenates your soul. "We are what we repeatedly do," Aristotle said. "Excellence then is not an act, but a habit."

SUMMARY

- Once again (but certainly not for the last time): The way you say what you say is infinitely more important than what you say.

- Using jargon is a capital crime. Jargon alienates the daylights out of the prospect, and only serves to demonstrate how insecure you are.

- Taping your presentations is a painful but very productive way to improve your tone.

- "Positive mental attitude" is to psychology what voodoo is to neurosurgery. You can't change the way you think by *thinking* anything. But you can very effectively change your attitude by what you do: "attitude aerobics."

- The primary effect of the nice things (and the nasty things) you say and do is on you, not on the other person.

- Nobody's life is particularly easy; no one is suffering from an overdose of kindness; and everyone wishes people were more interested in them. You have much greater power to intervene in people's lives than you suspect.

- Some (but by no means all) "attitude aerobics":
  - Birthday cards.
  - See what people care about and then be genuinely interested.
  - Ask about people's kids; remember and act upon what you hear.
  - Send somebody a nice note every day.

- "Attitude aerobics" oxygenates your soul by offsetting the everyday pain and frustration of our profession.

10

Presentations 1:
The Universal Five-Point
Managed Money Presentation

One of the great, vanished institutions that made New York unique in years gone by was the used bookstore. Before the real estate boom of the 1980s sank them, the major used bookstores were huge, cavernous, multi-storied, and open at all hours. Picture Grand Central Station with floor-to-ceiling bookcases on every inch of wall space, ladders running up and down everywhere, and waist-high tables, piled with books, covering all but the narrowest aisles.

Everything about the stores was old. The books, of course, but also the turn-of-the-century buildings, and especially the workers: gnomic, ancient, irascible men and women, with unimaginable life stories, who seemed to know instantly whether the store had the book you were looking for, and where to find it. How? Part of the magic: You could never figure out the system, and the keepers of the catacombs sure weren't about to tell you.

One rainy Saturday afternoon about twenty years ago, early in my career as a stockbroker, I was just browsing in one of these places with no purpose in mind. My career was proceeding, at that point, by what might charitably be called "trial and error."

I was thinking about the way I presented investments to people. I had tried proving the stock was going to go up with a barrage of facts and numbers. That approach hadn't worked particularly well — either people didn't buy the stocks or the stocks didn't go up. Then I wondered what would happen if I just told what I loved about the stock, and why I thought the prospect would love it. Trouble was, I assumed the more I could think of to love, the more effective the story. But that approach wasn't working out too well, either.

As the rain beat down outside the old bookstore, and my young mind danced over my career, some benevolent muse guided me to a shelf full of biographies. In front was Mark Van Doren's biography of Benjamin Franklin — the original 1938 edition (which I have here next to me as I write). I took the book off the shelf without thinking, flipped open randomly (to page 529, as it happened), and read the following:

> *"One of the firmest and boldest of the delegates, Franklin was one of the most silent. Jefferson said long afterwards, 'I served with General Washington in the legislature of Virginia before the Revolution, and during it with Dr. Franklin in Congress. **I never heard either of them speak ten minutes at a time, nor to any but the main point that was to decide the question. They laid their shoulders to the great points, knowing that the little ones would follow of themselves.'**"*

The last two sentences hit me right between the eyes — as I hope they do you. And I thanked whatever fates had led me to the page, the book, and the store on that day. Because I knew that quote was destined to change my career and my life. And to this day, those words express my whole philosophy of presenting investments.

Think about everything you've seen or heard people do supremely well: Spencer Tracy's acting; Joe Montana marching the 49ers downfield; Navratilova at the net; Frank Sinatra in his prime, or Ella Fitzgerald in hers; your best high school teacher; Joe DiMaggio's or Ted Williams' swing (if you're old enough and lucky enough to have seen them — Rod Carew's, if you're not). Or, think about the most deceptively simple works of art: a Robert Frost poem; a Cole Porter lyric; Cary Grant's comic timing, or Gracie Allen's (don't forget that before he was America's funniest nonagenarian, George Burns was Gracie's straight man); the incredible use of silence in the oratory of Winston Churchill, President Kennedy and Dr. King.

How do you instinctively describe all these people? Of course:

THEY MAKE IT LOOK EASY.

No matter what the activity, the truly great practitioners:

(1) appear to be performing effortlessly and with great economy;
(2) act simply and directly; and
(3) transcend "technique" — their performance is a perfect expression of themselves.

And yet, you know this impression is an illusion. You know the years of study and practice, and the stupendous energy and drive expended to reach this level of skill.

Presenting managed investments well is an art. And, **the starting point in learning to present is the perception that less is more.**

THE PURSUIT OF SIMPLICITY

To become a truly great salesperson of managed money you can't rely just on what you know. To reach people where they really live and induce them to respond to you at the deepest levels, you have to let go of, and go beyond, what you know.

The great cellist Pablo Casals gave a "master class" near his home in Puerto Rico during the last years of his life. A "master class" is for artists who have studied an instrument all their lives at the finest music schools with the best teachers, and who are ready to take their places in the very top ranks of musicians in the world. Their training is completed with one of the greatest living masters.

On the first morning of class Casals always said, "Now, we must please forget the notes." He was saying, of course, "You know the music; you have all the technical proficiency you need or you wouldn't be here. Now, if you're to become *artists,* you have to go beyond the obvious."

Well, even if you don't have all the technical proficiency yet, the principle is the same. Because ...

TO BECOME A GREAT COMMUNICATOR/SALESPERSON YOU MUST LEARN TO TRANSCEND THE FACTS.

And while I'm trashing facts, let me also say an unkind word or two about "technique." "Technique" (particularly as used in the phrase "closing technique") is another persistent illusion dear to the hearts of budding washouts. As nearly as I can make out, it is a belief in some magical combination of words and phrases which have the power to hypnotize people into buying what you are selling. (I shouldn't be too mean. I'm the first to acknowledge the childlike qualities in a salesperson's emotional makeup. And, after all, children believe very strongly in magic.) The illusion of "technique" is especially prevalent in those books suggesting you'll encounter only four (or five, or three) basic personality types, and if you learn how to interact with each, you'll close everybody.

I find this notion about technique unutterably sad. There are as many personality types as there are people, and trying to jam everyone into a few pigeonholes blinds you to the variety and richness of humanity. What's more, the idea that you have to change your personality to press the buttons of different types of people is the antithesis of my belief that *you have to be who you are*. Because being who you are is where your real strength, conviction and energy come from.

"Technique" is for rookies — a track you run on until you blaze your own trail. This book will give you very specific ways to make presentations and to answer questions and objections. But don't mistake these ideas for "techniques." They are deep channels through which can flow the most genuine communication. In summary ...

"TECHNIQUE" IS WHAT YOU DO WHILE YOU'RE WAITING FOR YOUR PERSONAL STYLE AND YOUR SELLING STYLE TO BECOME IDENTICAL.

You must go past "technique." In Satchel Paige's words, "It ain't restful."

THE TROUBLE WITH MANAGED MONEY

From the standpoint of developing a presentation, the real difficulty with managed money is its simplicity. It's too obvious. Everybody needs managed money and can easily see why. The products themselves are almost painfully simple. For instance, what's a mutual fund?

> *"People with similar goals put their money together. Somebody smart manages the money, trying to move in the direction the investors want. You can put any amount into the fund, whenever you want. And you can take out any amount you want, whenever you want. When you sell, the fund will either be worth more or less than your cost."*

Makes you nervous just reading it, doesn't it? *Nothing* can be that simple. Where's the *nuance*? Where's the *subtlety*? Where's the *romance*?

Well, mutual funds have plenty of nuances, subleties and romance.

But those are refinements. And just because you are all hot and bothered about them does not mean the client appreciates, understands, cares much, or would even recognize the subleties if they ran up and bit him on the ankle. (There you go again, obsessing about the facts, when all the client wants is the truth.)

Salespeople find the pristine simplicity of most money management vehicles highly anxiety producing. And we respond by creating crazy-quilt presentations full of all the extraneous material we're immersed in daily — the piles of literature and assaults of wholesalers and sales managers trying to differentiate their products and gain our attention.

Our mistake is turning around and laying all that intellectual truth and beauty on the poor investing public. They can't and don't care to understand any of it, because their concerns are far more basic:

- Am I going to have enough to retire on?
- Am I going to outlive my income?
- Am I going to be able to send my kids to college?
- Can I trust you? Are you trying to sell me something that's good for you but not for me?
- Am I paying a fair price for this investment, or could I buy it for less, or no, cost?
- Am I investing with experienced, reliable people? Is someone else doing a better job?
- Is it going to be all right?

Pablo was right: Hurry up and forget the notes. Managed investments speak to people's deepest financial and emotional needs. So if you're ever to become an artist, you should realize — and organize everything you say in the light of — the startling fact that ...

THE DEEPEST HUMAN NEEDS ARE ALSO
THE SIMPLEST HUMAN NEEDS.

Needs aren't subtle, complex, or nuanced. They are simple, stark, life-or-death issues. Never think you're dealing with people's intellects when real needs are the issues on the table. You need to talk right into their hearts. If you're not, you might as well be talking to a wall. **Your head/intellect is an AC appliance, but your clients' hearts are only wired for DC.**

So, if the investments are basically simple, and the clients' needs are even simpler ... why would you ever think of making a long, complex, and detailed presentation? Right: You wouldn't — unless you are anxious, nervous, or worried about something.

Unfortunately, your emotional state, and not the words you say, comes through most clearly to the client. The washout "tries" harder and harder — the more nervous he is, the more he talks, but he has less and less success because he's beaming his distress and anxiety at the client. Even successful salespersons have this problem. Most of us are pretty verbal to begin with. And verbal people talk too much when nervous.

To make matters worse, we have a subconscious dread that if we stop talking, the client is going to ask questions we can't answer. So we try to anticipate all the possible questions and pack all the answers into our presentation. The result: We talk almost interminably. After which the prospect still thinks of a different question to ask (not even a real question, as we'll see in a later chapter). The prospect has gotten such a megadose of bad vibes from the washout, he'll ask *anything* just to put up barriers to hide behind. So relax. Take a few deep breaths; forget the notes.

THE GREAT LAW OF PRESENTATIONS

Here are four more axioms about presentations you may not necessarily like:

(1) Presentations are a necessary evil, to be dispensed with quickly so you can get to what really matters, which is Q&A.

(2) During feeling-finding, you discover a prospect's hopes. During the presentation, you show him something you believe accomplishes his hopes.

(3) Then comes Q&A. *These are his fears.* The sale takes place only when you thoroughly calm the prospect's fears. (Note: I didn't say "when you answer his objections." *It ain't the same thing.*)

(4) Your chance of learning your prospect's deepest fears while *you* are talking is zero.

Don't hurry past these points. Stop. Read them over, as often as you like. You must understand and accept them. They are the immutable truths building up to Murray's Great Law of Presentations, which, as you may already anticipate, is:

THE QUALITY OF A MONEY MANAGEMENT PRESENTATION IS AN INVERSE FUNCTION OF ITS LENGTH.

The longest presentation is the worst, no matter how many great points you include. The prospect can't understand what you are saying. He doesn't understand why you seem so anxious. Above all, if the investment is so good, he wonders why you are selling so hard.

The shortest presentation is the best. The optimum presentation would be total silence. You'd just smile, and hold out the application and a pen to the prospect. (Think of this one as a Zen presentation.)

You'll have to start out somewhere in between. So I'm about to offer you The Universal Five-Point Managed Money Presentation. Why five points? Easy:

- No prospect alive can absorb and retain more than five important ideas in one sitting. His circuits overload, and you lose him.
- The sun has never shone on a managed investment which has more than five supremely important issues in it.
- It's my book.

The object of this chapter is to have you sit down with your prospect and make the best presentation you ever made — in the quietest, most direct and least complicated way. All I can do, though, is to prepare you for the presentation itself ... nothing can prepare you for the surprise and delight with which prospects respond to simple clarity.

Look at the process from the prospect's viewpoint. Your prospect is daunted and a little on guard, because he realizes he doesn't understand all the intricacies of managed investments. He'll be intensely grateful to you for purifying the critical factors to a precious, comprehensible few.

The other major benefit of the Universal Five-Point Presentation is that you can use it, with virtually no changes, to present *any* managed investment. Universality. No more going back to ground zero and reinventing the wheel every time you find a new product you like, or that fits a particular client's needs. The Universal Five Point Presentation is fueled and ready to fly at all times.

ROLLING OUT THE FIVE KEY POINTS

What five universal points will make you a superstar? In the end, only you can answer that. You've got to let the points flow naturally from your personal style, and from the real, natural superiority of the managed investment that you fall in love with. No rigid formula from this or any other book will work, unless it sounds and feels like *you*.

Having said that, I do think there are five points inside which every managed investment fits and every salesperson/planner can learn to function easily and comfortably:

1. **THE CONCEPT;**
2. **THE PEOPLE;**
3. **THE INVESTMENT AND WHAT IT DOES FOR YOU;**
4. **HOW THE INVESTMENT WORKS; and**
5. **THE RISKS/LIMITATIONS.**

Point #1: THE CONCEPT — THE CONCEPT is an opening statement defining the client's core financial need. As you define the need, you should describe some of the emotions "we all feel" about the need — making common cause between your feelings and the client's. THE CONCEPT ends with a generic statement of how a particular kind of investing has historically satisfied the need *when managed by real professionals*.

Articulating THE CONCEPT is the one critical, indispensable way to begin any financial services presentation. The client's reaction will instantly tell you if you're on the right track. He nods, he concurs ... and already you have him agreeing with you. You haven't said a word about product yet, nor should you. (Observe, however, the hallmark of the washout is immediately talking about the product. Even if he's right, he's dead ... because he's evoked no agreement yet on THE CONCEPT.)

When the client agrees with you about the need (let's say the growth of a retirement nest egg), you can touch on the things "we're all concerned about" — staying ahead of inflation, not subjecting our capital to a lot of risk. More nods; more affirmation.

Then you go on to a style of investing, say blue chip common stocks that over time grow earnings and increase dividends. "But investing even in great blue chip companies is not a do-it-yourself hobby anymore — we absolutely have to have the highest quality professional managers. Does that make sense so far?" Of course it does; more affirmation, and you're done with THE CONCEPT.

In the following chapters, I'll suggest a precisely worded concept presentation for each major type of managed investment. For now, just remember that Point #1 of your Universal Five-Point Presentation will *always* be THE CONCEPT: a short summary of your understanding of the client's major goal, together with the matching goals of a particular form of money management product. Because, at the outset, a prospect will find money management a fairly abstract notion, unless you've first touched on the beautifully conceptual fit of blue chip stocks (or high-grade corporate bonds, or whatever) with his stated goals. In this light, perhaps you can more clearly see what I meant, several chapters ago, when I suggested that **THE CONCEPT is the solution to the client's problem. The product is just the box the solution comes in.**

Point #2: THE PEOPLE — The second presentation point is a strong statement about the people who will run the money, and about your and your firm's relationship with them. The identity, character, business acumen and staying power of the management company are the critical issues that will determine the long-term success of the investment.

So, management is what your client is buying — the critical ingredient of your plan for the client's financial health. Management is why you're recommending the investment — as opposed to the prospect running his own money or the money being run by some other manager. So, selling management is the logical thing to do, and the superstar does it to a fare-thee-well.

The superstar knows, on the deepest level, people relate best to other people who care about them ... not to lists of stocks or bonds; not to "value" versus "growth"; and not, God help us, to "beta" or "quartiles." So stress the quality and longevity — and only after that, the skills — of the management company and their people.

In particular, **stress the extent to which you have personally been exposed to the management and watched their funds perform,** and the fact that (if it's true) you personally invest with them. Any special aspect of investment management at which the managers are particularly skilled is also fair game.

Always watch your time and never lapse into jargon. Remember, you are simply feeding the prospect some general confidence-building ideas. You are letting the prospect sense your commitment to, and depth of feeling for, the managers. And you are giving him a sense of your enthusiasm for the manager's uniqueness.

Observe two cautions. First, don't hide behind words like "biggest" and "best." The prospect usually feels he's being hyped, and you aren't really giving him a feeling for why you like this particular manager. The investor knows that "big" can work for or against him, and that large or small managers can concentrate on one investment strategy supremely well. "Best" is immeasurable, a subjective value judgment. The issue is tone, again. Do you want to sound like someone who brings good people together, or do you want to sound like a car salesman?

Second, making a big point of the manager's track record, oddly enough, is fairly dangerous. All selling that hides behind numbers is essentially weak. Selling track record is particularly weak. **Winners sell opportunity and relationships; losers sell "proof"** — or, more accurately, try and fail to sell "proof."

Offering proof is the wrong way to appeal to a prospect. You should be inducing your prospect to invest his confidence in you, and, through you, in the manager. Talk about the key executives of the manager whom you know. Talk about your firm's relationship with them. Talk about how comfortable your other clients are who own the same fund. It goes without saying you and your firm wouldn't select a manager with an inferior record. And you never would invest your own money with an also-ran. Track record is the answer to a question nobody's asked you yet. Hold the mountain chart in reserve. Don't initially duck behind a chart of essentially incomprehensible, cold numbers you probably don't understand anyway.

The real danger lies in all the suspicions and questions emphasizing the track record seems to unleash. Just count the number of absolute show-stoppers you may provoke if you say, "And here you can clearly see this fund is best because the average total return is 18.62% for the last ten years."

   (1) What's total return?
   (2) Yeah, but what if I bought in the middle of the year? What if I was only in for five years?
   (3) What did they do in the fourth quarter of '87? The third quarter of '90?
   (4) Before or after the commission?
   (5) How much of that was dividends?
   (6) Yeah, but that was the '80s. A wild bull market, takeovers, junk bonds ... The '90s are going to be awful.
   (7) My girl friend Shirley's stockbroker guarantees her 25% a year.
   (8) Yeah, but what if you had to take money out to pay the taxes?

(9) How do you know the record will continue?

(10) So, if they're so smart, how come they need me?

(11) Let's see, that's about three times the return I'm getting on my municipal bonds. I guess this fund is three times more risky than muni's, right?

Don't break up the conceptual beauty and logic of the Universal Five-Point Presentation by firing the track record gun right in the middle of it. With your luck, you'll shoot yourself in the foot. You may want to make a glancing, gentle reference to superior performance in your presentation. But, for a detailed discussion of the record, my advice is: Wait until you're asked. If the prospect doesn't ask, you never have to tap-dance into the quagmire at all.

Point #3: THE INVESTMENT AND WHAT IT DOES FOR YOU —This critical juncture never fails to distinguish the superstar from the washout. The washout, unable to restrain himself any longer, starts explaining to the prospect what the recommended investment *is*. That's like trying to run up the side of a glacier wearing tennis shoes: a furious amount of activity, but no traction, and thus no forward progress. Why? Because no one in the history of mankind ever bought anything — a mutual fund, a vacuum cleaner, a set of pots and pans — because of what the object *is*.

The superstar only sketches, in his own naturally artistic way, the barest outlines of the investment. Instead, he spends real time and energy on what the investment will *do* for the client. Of course the investment is good — but, oh, how many wonderful things the investment *does*: you sleep nights, knowing your money is in the hands of smart people who care; you never have to worry about changing investments, clipping coupons, keeping records, or any similar headaches, ever again; you can put money in and take it out whenever you want; you're totally liquid; you can receive the income; you can reinvest the income (always without another commission); you can change your mind any time you want; and on and on.

This investment does so many wonderful things, the prospect is going to be so happy with it. You've owned the fund yourself for years, and all it does is grow, every time you turn around. More in some years, less in others — who can figure the market — but long term? Just keeps going up.

Forget the dozen points you learned in the office sales meeting. The purpose of that meeting was to convince you to sell Fund X instead of Fund Y. Those points are not germane here.

Make absolutely no estimate of the investment's value in five years, ten years, or when the prospect retires. You can't; you don't know. But that's OK, because nobody else knows either. Stand on the issues of diversification; smart, caring professional management; and your own personal conviction that, at the end of the day, the prospect will look at this decision as one of the half dozen best investment decisions he ever made. And, if you believe that, *tell him*! Don't you realize that's what he really cares about?

The great advantage of making the presentation in this manner is you **presume acceptance by the prospect.** In a simple, understated way you're saying: "We agree on your need, and we agree a program of managed money can help. My fund is the obvious choice. I won't bore you with the details."

Most presentations do the opposite. Salespeople think, "I love this fund, and I know it's right for this prospect," but they don't say so. They concentrate on stating all the right facts to convince the prospect how good the fund is ... without laying the conceptual foundation first.

The superstar says, "I love this prospect. I understand exactly what my prospect is trying to accomplish. And, boy, is this managed investment perfect for him. It's as plain as the nose on your face. God, I love this job."

In other words, the superstar gives his prospect one of the two possible impressions all salespeople/planners always make:

- **The Superstar Impression:** "This guy is trying to make something wonderful happen to me, and to the people I love."

- **The Washout Impression:** "This guy is trying to sell me something."

Say what you will. Talk as long or as little as you like; face-to-face or on the phone; in your office or in the prospect's home. It doesn't matter — you're inevitably going to create one of those two impressions. You decide which one you want to create. Tell prospects all the wonderful benefits the investment will bring, and you have a chance to create the first impression. Tell them what the investment is — no matter how really great the truth — and I can virtually guarantee, with the best heart in the world, you'll create the second impression.

Point #4: HOW THE INVESTMENT WORKS — You have very clearly established what the investment does for people — how beautifully the investment meshes with their most important needs and goals. *Now* you can tell them a little bit about how it works ... and if you like, cite examples in the prospectus.

Go very carefully here, because **the primary risk is giving the prospect a lot more information than he wants or needs.** But, used properly, the fourth step in the presentation allows you to show your prospect two potentially interesting points, in ascending order of importance:

(1) the investment has a particularly intelligent, well-thought-out and consistent investment strategy; and

(2) *you understand the strategy.*

In other words, Point Four lets you remind the client you understand his needs and you deliberately picked this investment because the investment's strategy dovetails so neatly with his needs.

"Now, I said the fund's objective is serious long-term growth of capital. But the fund is also designed for people like us who can't afford to take a lot of risk. So, the fund's managers concentrate their investments in the highest quality growth companies in America. If you scan the portfolio, you can see for yourself: names like General Electric, IBM, Pfizer, PepsiCo, Phillip Morris. Great growth companies you'd love to own, because they're constantly increasing earnings and dividends."

What a warm and comforting statement, which takes all of forty seconds. And you effortlessly shot down two of the great objections to equity funds — volatility and risk — before they ever cleared the launching pad. Nothing in this presentation is coincidental or unplanned, but it sounds as effortless, casual and spontaneous as any conversation with a friend.

Avoid one thing when highlighting a fund's investment strategy. **Never state the attributes in terms of what the investment is not.** For instance, you'd never say, ... "great growth companies, *not speculative flyers.*" And most particularly, you'd never say anything like "quality growth companies, which means the portfolio is *less volatile* than other funds." Saying a prospect's portfolio is "less volatile" is like telling him he's going to be shot with a smaller caliber bullet. Inarguably, a .22 puts a much smaller hole in you than a .45. But, the prospect really has his heart set on not being shot at all.

You simply can never sell managed money by negative comparison. Say to a prospect he doesn't have to worry about volatility, and I can guarantee you he will *instantly* start worrying about volatility. People have enough to worry about. Your recommendation has more wonderful attributes than you can possibly cover in a short presentation. So just concentrate on a few of them, and don't try to make your idea look good in relation to something inferior or scary.

The trademarks of the superstar are economy of dialogue, simplicity in presentation, and the presumption of the ability to generate understanding and to succeed. Don't worry. If you leave something out your prospect wants to know about, he'll ask you.

Point #5: RISKS/LIMITATIONS — Always refer to the risks and limitations of the investment as you're closing the presentation. Doing so is extremely disarming and genuinely comforting to an intelligent investor. Your prospect sees you are not just another salesperson, painting an unreasonably rosy picture to make a sale.

The planner/salesperson who makes some cogent reference to risks/limitations *without being asked* scores twice. First, the prospect sees your approach is realistic and professional. He knows any investment has some risk and that maximizing one benefit (say, income) limits the potential for another benefit (growth). Second, you can point out how the investment manager takes steps to handle the risk, which loops your prospect's attention back to the great strengths of the manager.

No reasonable investor thinks any investment is without risk. He wants to know how risks are recognized and dealt with effectively. **The superstar always goes on the offensive in raising the issue of risk.** He can only gain his prospect's respect, and he never exposes himself to being in a defensive posture when asked, as he inevitably will be, "What are the risks?"

PERFECTING THE APPROACH

Whatever managed investment you choose can be presented with this simple, effective, generic, universally adaptable approach. Simply work up a clear, logical, compelling arrangement of the points ... and then *start practicing.* Tape your presentation again and again. Role-play with the wholesalers; role-play with your networking group (incidentally, what are their five points?). Grind it, polish it, and just make the presentation as tight and seamless as you can. Because ...

THE ACT OF PERFECTING A SALES PRESENTATION IS MORE BENEFICIAL THAN ALL THE PRODUCT-KNOWLEDGE SESSIONS IN THE WORLD.

Well, sure it is. You know that the fifth or tenth time you hear a story, you are able to chip away at it, to find holes and formulate questions the presentation just doesn't answer. Practicing so that you can spot the flaws prompts you to tighten the presentation even further. (As you begin to approach superstardom, you may even consciously decide to leave some rough spots in the presentation because you'll know exactly what questions they provoke. And, you'll know just how terrific your answers are!)

Your objective is to get so good you can be shaken out of a sound sleep and be making the presentation, with the utmost warmth and conviction, before your feet hit the floor.

When you get that good, you can actually begin to detach yourself from the presentation, let the force of painstakingly acquired habit take over, and **devote your real attention to watching the prospect's reactions.** Remember the Nod Factor? I said that, during a seminar, you can observe which points in the wholesaler's presentation the audience is reacting to. Well, the next step in your presentation progress is to be able to observe the client's reactions to what you're saying. (A pro can read and adjust to those reactions, even while speaking.)

The seamless beauty of your presentation can, after all, only take you so far. In the end, what you say doesn't matter, only how the client reacts to what you say. But having a perfectly rehearsed presentation enables you to tune yourself out, and start watching the prospect's reactions.

SUMMARY

- Simplicity, economy, directness, and natural expression are the hallmarks of all great presentations.

- No one ever became a great communicator/salesperson of anything until he learned to transcend the facts.

- "Technique" is what you do while you're waiting for your personal style and your selling style to fuse. When you're selling from deep conviction, with confidence that you can reach your prospect where he really lives, "technique" withers away, and your craft at last becomes an art.

- The trouble with managed money: It's too simple. We overcompensate by trying to overload the prospect with facts, numbers, subtleties and shadings that he neither understands nor cares about.

- Managed investments address people's deepest needs. The deepest needs are also the simplest needs. So keep your presentation simple. Your head is an AC appliance, but the prospect's heart is only wired for DC.

- The great preponderance of your communication is non-verbal. So you need a presentation that lets you turn off your mind and watch what you're making the prospect feel.

- The quality of a money management presentation is an inverse function of its length. Less is more.

- The act of perfecting a sales presentation is more beneficial than all the product-knowledge sessions in the world.

- The Universal Five-Point Presentation consists of:
  1. THE CONCEPT;
  2. THE PEOPLE;
  3. THE INVESTMENT AND WHAT IT DOES FOR YOU;
  4. HOW THE INVESTMENT WORKS; and
  5. RISKS/LIMITATIONS.

- Operate on the presumption of success. Things generally turn out the way you really believe they will.

11

Presentations 2: Retaining Control

Economizing your presentation down to five stated points (spoken over no more than about five minutes) isn't easy. When you've accomplished the feat, you'll be so proud of the way you can lay out the logic of any managed investment you may be genuinely surprised, and somewhat put off, if your prospect interrupts with a question.

If you've worked as hard as you should on refining your presentation down to its clear and most logical essence, you really don't *deserve* to be interrupted. You'll feel, with a lot of justification, that the prospect should keep still and let you set out the logic the way you want to. He won't have to wait that long for Q&A, because your presentation is so short. You are convinced he'll quickly see the logic in its completeness. If he'll let you finish, he'll be over the hump and on the downhill side of the decision-making process.

The trouble is you can't tell the prospect not to interrupt. You can't explain to him the best course of action is to hold his questions so you can give him the whole story in one clip. He's not ready for that.

It's human nature, after all, to ask a question when one occurs to you. And the more successful, accomplished and intense your prospect is, the more incapable he may be of sitting back and letting you unfold your presentation at your own practiced pace. Hence, he may break in at any time with a question clearly requiring you to comment.

I suggest you resort to a little diplomatic delaying tactic. When your prospect can no longer contain himself and breaks in with a question, hold up a hand, nod very acceptingly, and say:

"I'm coming to that."

If you *are* coming to that (if he's raising an issue which genuinely appears later on in your presentation), so much the better. More often, however, you won't be coming to his specific point in your initial presentation. So, using the phrase "I'm coming to that" takes on a gentle air of subterfuge — subterfuge in a good cause, mind you, that will ultimately be very useful to you *and* the client. But subterfuge nonetheless. And that demands a momentary digression.

You've just read the first and last recommendation in this book that you employ anything but the most sincere, direct and honest statements and tactics. Salespeople who feel they have to slant the facts, or overweigh the positive versus the negatives, or not state the negatives at all, or manipulate their clients in any way, end up very unhappy people (if they're not already). And they leave a fair amount of human and financial damage in their wake.

The worst part of manipulative selling, though, is that *you* end up hurt. Elbert Hubbard said it best: "Men are not so much punished *for* their sins as *by* them." You carry the results of being less than honest around with you, and the cumulative effect, consciously or unconsciously, will really shrivel you up.

Do you say, "Well, I had to overstate because that's the only way I could ever get this jerk to make up his mind?" Well, clearly you don't like the client. What's worse, you don't believe in your own capacity to reach him honestly. Stop calling him. He's hurting you by making you dislike both himself *and* yourself.

Salespeople who accumulate a book of accounts they don't like, or even respect, are really piling up a lot of psychological conflict. What's worse, they're constructing a world of associates for whom they feel hostility and disdain. But, as Emerson tells us, "People seem not to see that their opinion of the world is also a confession of character." Try to remember: You are how you feel about your clients. (OK, OK, end of sermon.)

You've just said "I'm coming to that" primarily to hold your prospect still for the few more minutes you'll take to finish your presentation. And he can't (or at least in most instances, won't) argue with that. So using "I'm coming to that" lets you get through your presentation without having the pace and the conceptual logic chopped up.

But that's not all. If, in fact, you do not return to the question your prospect asked, then:

"I'M COMING TO THAT" WILL TELL YOU, WITH UNERRING ACCURACY, WHETHER OR NOT THE PROSPECT REALLY CARES ABOUT THE QUESTION.

How? Simple. If the question is really bothering the prospect and you don't return to it, he'll ask you the question again. Then, and only then, do you treat the issue as serious.

Most of the time you'll never hear the question again, which says about the prospect:

• he figured out the answer; or
• he grasped the overriding conceptual logic of why you love this managed investment for him, so he stopped caring about his question; or
• his question never mattered in the first place. He was just constitutionally incapable of sitting there, in his plush, intimidating office, letting *you* control the agenda. That's human nature. And you handled the situation in a *very* nice way.

Let's spend another minute on the issue of control. Remember, after you've settled in with your client, gotten your coffee and come to the business at hand ...

THE PERIOD OF YOUR GREATEST CONTROL OVER THE PROSPECT'S IMPRESSIONS OF YOU AND YOUR PRODUCT IS DURING YOUR PRESENTATION.

While you're making your presentation, you're beaming a steady impression of confidence, which is the essential element in the sale. Sometime during the presentation, you must have the prospect realize, "Hey, this salesperson believes in what he's selling just as much as I believe in what I do. I may not accept what he's saying yet (I may still have a lot of questions) but this guy is no peddler, he's no lightweight, and he's sincere. Hmmm ..."

What is the prospect listening to at that moment? You guessed it: He's listening to the *way* you're saying what you're saying more than he's listening to what you're saying. Heard that before? While you have control, you have to accomplish as much as you can.

Your presentation is your cleanest, best shot; because in a moment, you'll have to start giving up control as the interview moves on to Q&A. The sale can't begin until the customer starts asking questions. You have to accept that Q&A is where the rubber meets the road. Make the very best opening statement you can in order to condition the prospect's mind as favorably as possible.

The stronger, surer and more concise your presentation, the more you can be certain that you've shaken up the prospect's thinking. That way, he may see beyond the relatively unimportant issue of the product you're presenting to the paramount issue of the kind of professional you are (because, first and foremost, you're selling yourself).

REACTING TO REJECTION

What if, after your best and most deeply felt presentation, the prospect turns a deaf ear not just to the investment but to *you?* If you're prospecting right, rejection will happen less and less. If you can actually talk your way into a prospect's office and you're not finding any common ground on which to do business, you are not qualifying your prospects well enough. You should never have to work terribly hard to get to see someone, only to have him signal that he'll never do business with you. But, **you have to let prospects disqualify themselves if that's what they've made up their minds to do.**

A slow form of suicide is the act of trying desperately to sell somebody when he clearly and steadfastly is refusing to be sold. Life is too short; your reserves of sales energy are not limitless. Control your reaction and spend your energy generating new, more reasonable prospects rather than desperately clutching at a few marginal ones, just because they are the prospects you have.

TO ACHIEVE MONEY MANAGEMENT STARDOM YOU MUST REALIZE, AND FULLY ACCEPT, THAT YOUR SERVICES ARE THE BEST THING THAT HAS HAPPENED TO YOUR CLIENTS IN YEARS.

Alfred North Whitehead put it another way, and his version is chiseled into the cornerstone of the Columbia University School of Business: "A great society is one whose men of business think greatly of their functions." That's it. Unless you have a firmly fixed conviction that you're doing a terrific job finding sensible money management solutions to clients' needs, you aren't going to make it. If, deep down, you feel you're just another journeyman salesperson trying for a share of the managed money sales pie like everybody else, forget it. Either sell investments that you really love, or ... try another profession.

That's why it's so sad to hear salespeople ask, "What's the number of times you make a presentation to a prospect before you give up?" The answer, of course, is that you never "give up." You "go on" to a more deserving prospect. The salesperson who's looking objectively for a correct number of times to call a prospect doesn't know how to communicate with people or hear what they're really saying to him.

Face facts: If you've been in sales for any length of time, you should be able to tell in ten minutes whether a prospect is accepting your style of doing business. If you can't, either you should get out of sales or you are ignoring the basic fact that sales is a numbers game. You are desperately spending time talking to someone who's inflicting pain on you rather than hanging up (or walking away) and prospecting someone else.

In plain fact, salespeople put up with about as much rejection as they think they deserve. The salesperson who, in Whitehead's words, "thinks greatly of his functions" will instantly and painlessly turn away from rejection and forge ahead in search of someone who accepts him for the fine professional he is. If you do otherwise, you internalize the rejection by accepting that a prospect's negative reaction to you and your sales approach is somehow correct. That's a terribly sad way to live your life. No superstar behaves that way.

The superstar has unshakable faith in three things:

(1) himself;
(2) his product; and
(3) the numbers.

SUMMARY

- Use "I'm coming to that" so you can make your presentation in one piece. You need to control the interview throughout the presentation.

- "I'm coming to that" filters out unimportant questions and leaves only substantive concerns.

- Your period of greatest control over your client's impressions of you and the product is during the presentation.

- Beam constantly at your prospect your belief in what a truly great job you're trying to do for him.

- Don't spend a lot of time prospecting people you don't like, or who don't seem to like you.

- Let prospects disqualify themselves, if that's what they insist on doing. Even if you can strong-arm a prospect into making an investment, he will never forgive you for it, and he'll figure out a way to make your life hell. Do business with people who want to do business with you. You'll live longer.

- Respect yourself and your function, or your clients won't.

12

How To Present
Equity Mutual Funds — Part I

Let's set the stage for developing our equity mutual fund presentation by agreeing on where equities fit into a portfolio. Simply stated, equities are the only financial asset that provides maintenance of purchasing power and growth of capital. Certainly, bonds can help diversify a portfolio and stabilize return. But the great goals of long-term investing — education and retirement — cannot be met solely with fixed-income securities. In the long run, equities are in a class by themselves, as Table 12-1 demonstrates.

The table doesn't just show you the outcome of a sixty-five year, five-horse race. The implications are far more profound. Yes, the return on stocks is around twice long-term corporate or government bonds, and over two-and-a-half times Treasury bills (whose return is like CD's). The point is the real return on high-quality debt is minimal if you back out inflation and taxes.

Table 12-1 SUMMARY OF ANNUAL RETURNS 1926 - 1990	
Common Stocks	10.1%
Long-Term Corporate Bonds	5.2%
Long-Term Government Bonds	4.5%
U.S. Treasury Bills	3.7%
Inflation	3.2%
Source: *Stocks, Bonds, Bills and Inflation 1991 Yearbook,*™ Ibbotson Associates, Chicago.	

And, when you think about it, really superior returns *should* come from ownership of successful companies. After all, where does the real wealth of the world come from? *Capitalism.* For forty years, the United States and the Soviet Union faced off in the ultimate struggle for world supremacy. Today, the U.S. is the only true global power, while the Soviet system is in ruin. In a matchup of democratic capitalism versus totalitarian socialism, the good guys won.

Americans should take pride in the genius of the capitalist system. And, aided by the knowledge conveyed in the table above, U.S. investors surely must have increased their common stock ownership, both in personal and retirement plan portfolios. Right? *Wrong.* American portfolios are, at this writing, historically underweighted in equities. And the level and intensity of risk-aversion in investor psychology is pandemic. (When a noticeable percentage of the population has a disease, it's epidemic. When damn near everybody has it, it's pandemic.)

The result: Equity mutual funds are among the most under-owned financial assets in the spectrum of investments. And there's good reason to suspect they will turn out to be the "sleeper" asset of the 1990s. To build a compelling presentation (and to handle Q&A), you need to understand why equities are so under-owned and what your role is in curing the problem.

CONFRONTING IRRATIONAL FEARS

The fear of equities seems more characteristic of a depression economy than an era where capitalism is breaking out all over the globe. So your first premise has to be that risk-aversion to equities is profoundly irrational. Please don't mistake this for condescension or name-calling; this is a drop-dead, *critical point.*

The key reason planners and salespeople get such a tremendous sense of futility from trying to reason people out of equity risk-aversion is simply that the aversion is deeply rooted in the investor's unconscious. On that level, people don't reason, they feel. **No amount of reasoning can ever change the way a person feels.**

**THE ONLY WAY TO CHANGE
HOW A PROSPECT FEELS ABOUT
ANY EMOTIONALLY CHARGED INVESTMENT
IS BY INDUCING HIM
TO PUT HIS TRUST IN YOU.**

People don't change the way they feel based on superior reasoning. People change by letting go of fears, which only happens in the sales/planning process when people accept:

- that you genuinely care about and understand their deepest financial needs; and

- that you know what you're doing, even if they don't yet completely understand everything you're saying.

Here again, for the umpty-umpth time, is the reality that prospects don't care what you know until they know that you care, and why facts are a quagmire.

One of the better regional brokerage firms recently surveyed clients to determine the most important characteristics of a broker. Not surprisingly, a whopping 81% rated "concern for client's welfare" as most important. "Understanding client's objectives/needs" finished a strong second with 68% of respondents saying it was a most important factor.

Straggling along on the outside, "making money" finished a poor third, with only 59% saying it was "most important." Yet the washout still wanders around in the dark, extolling track record and wondering why he isn't convincing anybody!

Say you step in an elevator in a tall downtown building. The only other person on the elevator is crouching in a corner, drawn up into a nearly fetal position. He is wide-eyed, frothing at the mouth, and moaning over and over that the elevator is about to fall. So you go over, hunker down next to him, and whip out a chart that shows elevators in downtown buildings constructed since 1946 within a one mile radius have only fallen once every 170 trillion round trips.

Not going to get much of a response from the guy, are you? Well, I may be stretching the point a bit, but keep this analogy in mind next time you run into a prospect who is outwardly calm, nattily attired, and speaks in tones of sweet reason, but says "stocks are cancer/give me something guaranteed ..." And know what you're dealing with is not far from the panic of the guy crouched in the corner of the elevator.

SOURCES OF EQUITY PSYCHOSIS

If we can appreciate how the equity psychosis grew to its current pandemic proportions, perhaps we can build a presentation which functions like a series of antibiotic injections.

People caught the disease of equity risk aversion four main ways.

1. Life History — Let's say you're talking to a 60-year-old. Remember, he was born in 1931, so his mind was formed in the Great Depression. Experiences of the Depression are unimaginable to later generations. But, in counseling and selling, you fail to consider those feelings at your own peril. The thought of having come this far, and then losing it all, is probably the 60-year-old's greatest living nightmare. (Outliving his income should be his greatest concern, but isn't — because we fear what we've been through in childhood more than we fear something we haven't experienced.)

This prospect probably misperceives the true nature of risk. The risks in today's world are not the risks of the first 35 years of this person's life, when everything he learned about economics is summed up in the phrase "sound as a dollar." The dollar was the fixed star in this guy's economic universe. (If he thought about other currencies at all, they were like the Italian lira, which used to inflate about 100% a year, whether it needed to or not.)

Inflation was a low-level abstraction to this prospect. In 1962, the steel companies double-crossed the President by raising prices after Kennedy had the unions stand still on wages. Kennedy went on national TV and darkly warned that if the steel companies didn't roll back prices, *inflation would be 4% next year!* The country erupted in a firestorm of rage, and the steel companies folded. Today, we assume inflation below 4% went out with Coolidge. This investor lived without inflation more than half his life. Not until 1966, when President Johnson tried to pay for the Great Society and the Vietnam War with the same money, did our investor get his first real whiff of inflation.

Moreover, our prospect was past age 40 before Nixon took the dollar off the gold standard and let foreign exchange rates float. And the prospect is still trying to forget the economic nightmare that followed, with soaring inflation and astronomical interest rates. (And you wonder why this generation loved Reagan so much.)

So, the prospect thinks he's OK if he puts $100,000 into something that's "guaranteed" to return his $100,000 in three years, plus some stated rate of interest, and that he can roll over for another three years, and then another ... "Who is this guy ... Rabbitson? ... Ibbotson? — and why are you waving that chart in my face?"

The fact that everything the prospect buys will cost half again as much in nine years doesn't enter into his thinking, *because he won't let it.* He still wants and needs to believe that (a) a dollar is a dollar, and (b) he's got enough dollars and doesn't need to "risk" any of them trying to make more. To him, risk is synonymous with variability. Your risk/reward ratio is this guy's risk/risk ratio.

By extension, this prospect has no concept of real versus nominal rates of return. Ten years ago, when his money market fund was paying 18%, he was actually getting a *negative* real return, after inflation and taxes. Today, at 7%, his real return is positive. But I would pay money to watch you try to explain to this guy how 7% is more than 18%.

Try to reason the historical return of equities to this generation, never mind people ten years older, and you're digging yourself a big hole. So how do you sell them? **Sell growth of income** ... *that* they can relate to. Show them how the income from a good income-stock fund grew over the last ten years versus how the income from CDs went down, and you're into where they live.

Keep the explanation real: A postage stamp went up this much; your local newspaper went up that much; your phone bill went up so much ... and the income from $100,000 in Gronsky Equity Income Fund went up from $8,050 to $12,200! (Always speak in dollars; never in percentages.) Then let the prospect show *you* what's happened to the net asset value. ("Oh, sure ...," says the superstar, as if the 80% increase in N.A.V. almost goes without saying.) **You conquer anxiety with specificity, not with countervailing abstractions.** Just know, and respect, your prospect's life history...and select your specifics accordingly.

2. Underperformance In The 1980s — The individual investor significantly underperformed the stock market during the 1980s, and he is not the least bit happy about it. He consistently selected against himself throughout the decade, so he has nobody to blame but himself. (But the individual investor always needs to blame someone else ... if he didn't, everybody in our industry would be working for Charles Schwab.)

To illustrate what happened, look at Piper Jaffray's index of 3,400 stocks from 1983 through 1990. This index, on an unweighted basis, actually went down a total of 3%. The same index, *weighted for market capitalization,* went up 104%.

Here's the message. The kind of higher-capitalization, higher-priced stocks the individual investor never buys (IBM, Merck, Coca-Cola, GE, etc.) performed superbly well. While the smaller-cap, lower-priced stocks the individual does buy performed badly. (And not just relatively badly, either — absolutely badly.)

So the great bull market of the 1980s was, to the individual investor, a largely mythological beast ... until the decade was nearly over. At which point, the individual investor walked into ...

3. The Great Whipsaw of 1987-90 — The investor stumbled into the idea that a bull market was going on a mere four years after it started ... about par for the course. So, from Autumn of 1986, the Dow Jones Industrial Average went straight up 1000 points and didn't stop until Messrs. Dow and Jones were sure everybody was in. Then the market staged the largest, fastest decline of all time in October 1987, and blew everybody out again. With everybody hiding out in CDs, the market proceeded to soar in 1988 and three quarters of 1989. When everybody was back in, the mini-crash of Friday the 13th; October 1989 blew everybody out again. Sucked 'em back into the "bull-trap" which culminated in almost-but-not-quite-Dow-3000; then eviscerated 'em again in the invasion/recession massacre.

The denouement of the Great Whipsaw of 1987-90 actually didn't happen until January 1991. Then, a huge public consensus — along with an unprecedented amount of cash — built up around the conviction the market would take a fast 200 to 300 point hit if and when war broke out. So, right on schedule, war broke out — and the market scored its biggest one-week gain in history.

Somewhere in this sequence, nearly everybody gave up, especially if he paid any attention to ...

4. Journalism (or "Earth Collides With Sun; All Life Destroyed; Film At 11, Right After The Game") — Journalism reports today's "facts" and then extrapolates. As in June 1990: "Oil fell to $17 a barrel today; experts say it could go as low as $10." And forty days later: "Jolted by the crisis in the Gulf, oil hit $40 today, as experts predicted it could go as high as $100 in the event of war." (My all-time favorite: "Surprise snowstorm dumps eighteen inches on city; experts see more snow on the way.")

Particularly in the role of the Great Extrapolator, journalism is the mortal enemy of the investment truth that all economic phenomena run in cycles. For instance, on August 13, 1979, after six years of stagflation, *Business Week* put out the classic cover story "The Death of Equities." It will warm and cheer you no end, as it does me, to reflect that the DJIA closed at 875.26 that day. And, while I'm taking cheap anecdotal shots at journalism, let us not forget Dan Dorfman's *USA Today* column on the wonderfulness of short-selling ... about 15 trading days before the panic bottom of October 11, 1990.

I'll have more to say about the appalling effect of headlines on investor decision-making when we reach Q&A/objections handling. In the present context, the way journalism reported (and extrapolated) each jagged leg of the Great Whipsaw contributed enormously to the current fear and loathing of equities.

NOW FOR THE GOOD NEWS

As formidable and deep-seated as today's risk aversion is, you can find two major silver linings. You need to keep both in mind if your equity fund presentation is to be a real heat-seeking missile which hits the target, despite the target's deep camouflage and heavy fortification.

● **Silver Lining #1: Time is very much on your side.** Every generation of investors is smarter, better educated and richer than the last. As this decade progresses, the biggest and smartest generation ever seen — the baby boomers — will pass from peak spending years to peak savings years. Boomers plan on retiring earlier and living longer than anyone ever has.

And, after more than a decade of college costs rising at over twice the rate of CPI increases, parents are realizing that fixed income investments are a non-starter. If your investments are, after inflation and the "kiddie tax," just barely holding your purchasing power, but your target (tuition) is receding into the distance at twice that rate ... you're not just failing to gain ground, you're fading fast. This realization will trigger a major shift into equity funds.

The boomers will also know, almost instinctively, the greatest enemy they'll face in retirement is the erosion of purchasing power. So they'll know — or can at least be shown, without major brain damage — only equities preserve purchasing power. Boomers will be, I promise you, massive consumers of equity mutual funds — through you or through someone else.

● **Silver Lining #2: Get down on your knees and thank heaven for the mass hysteria of risk aversion — it's the proof you're right to love equities.**

Do you know where the Dow Jones Industrial Average was on the first birthday of our sixty-year-old pal born in 1931? — about 40. On his 59th birthday, the DJIA hit 3000. The stock market has been going pretty much straight up for this guy's whole life. *And his whole generation regards equities as a carcinogen!* — proving conclusively equity risk-aversion is a mass psychosis. When a huge, deeply felt consensus builds up around any asset class, the consensus is about to be wildly, spectacularly, and almost incalculably wrong. So, give thanks to the fates, for they are smiling on you. You're trying to sell equity mutual funds when the great consensus fears them like the plague. Rest assured where there is no fear, there is no value.

Remember who told you this: Go to bed every night from now on in dread that you will wake up tomorrow and find everyone agrees with the wisdom of investing in equity mutual funds. On that day, only your own discipline and dollar-cost-averaging can save you. For even if there's a foot of snow on the ground and you're in a 28-day month that starts with the letter F... the day will be like August 1987. (Or, as Yogi Berra said, "it's deja vu all over again.") And those who haven't learned from history will, as Santayana promised, be doomed to repeat it.

I'll leave this point by postulating:

MURRAY'S LAW OF THE IMMUTABLE PERSPICACITY OF TEN INVESTORS

Present An Investment Idea To Ten Investors ...

● **If no one will buy, the investment is about to quintuple.**
● **If one of the ten investors buys, you'll have a triple.**
● **If three buy, a mere double.**

-and-

● **If (God help you) six buy, the price will immediately halve.**

Gentlemen (and ladies), I give you a toast: to pandemic equity risk-aversion, and having the universal fear hang on for a little while longer — so we, and all the investors who trust us, will be rich.

SUMMARY

- You can not maintain purchasing power — and certainly not grow your capital — without investing in equity common stocks. Equities are to bonds as Corvettes are to Clydesdales.

- Equity mutual funds are the most under-owned financial asset in American portfolios. And they may turn out to be the "sleeper" asset of the 1990s, as more and more people need more and more growth.

- The DJIA went from 40 to 3000 in 58 years. And everybody who lived through that ascent is equity risk-averse. You are therefore dealing with mass hysteria, here. Facts and charts won't get you where you want to go. Do the prospect's life-history work, and you may see why — he's working off a completely different set of assumptions about economic reality than you are.

- The individual investor completely fell on his sword in the stock market during the 1980s; and now, journalistic shortsightedness and volatility phobia are immobilizing him.

- Live with it. Remember, if the consensus thinks equities are carcinogenic, stocks just may be about to go to the moon, long-term.

13

How To Present
Equity Mutual Funds — Part II

Develop your specific five-point equity presentation from the perspective that it's your prospect's best shot at a nontechnical, simple, comprehensible explanation. Then you can proceed to strip away the details and technicalities and go straight to the heart of the investment. That way, you can be confident your explanation of the managed investment gives the prospect the best chance to understand and to see your honest enthusiasm.

You may not be willing to accept that **all your prospect really wants is a simple explanation.** But simplifying does serve your prospects' purposes, not your own, because **your presentation skills are the only possible bridge between the perceived complexities of managed money and the prospect's needs.** Seen this way, presentation skills are indispensable, critical communication tools, not a way of glossing over realities to manipulate the prospect.

In setting up a standardized approach to presenting a specific managed investment, use the previously established format and build out from THE CONCEPT. In formulating THE CONCEPT, restate the investor's goals. Then speak generically about how a particular type of investing accomplishes the goal, before saying anything about the particular investment product.

The object is simply to have the investor say "yes" a minimum of two times before he hears a specific recommendation. All great salespeople know the chances of closing the sale are in direct proportion to the number of times the client says "yes" during a presentation. That's not manipulation, just plain old common sense.

POINT #1: THE CONCEPT

For the investor who needs growth of capital, here's one version of THE CONCEPT:

SUPERSTAR: *You know, you and I have very similar investment goals. Now that our kids are moving through college, we've got to set our sights on accumulating some serious capital for retirement if we can. Isn't that one of your main financial goals?*

PROSPECT: *One of my main goals? Man, it's the Super Bowl of my financial life! And I'm not at all sure I've covered the point spread yet, either.* (Also, the prospect is intrigued by your identifying your objectives with his. Obviously, you can't always do this, but when you can the phraseology is *very* powerful.)

SUPERSTAR: *Well, for the last year or so, I've been shopping around for an equity money manager to manage my own serious retirement dollars. I enjoy matching wits with the market on individual stocks now and again, but I can't afford to take those kinds of chances with my core retirement dollars. I decided to hire a manager who'd actually won the Super Bowl a couple of times, you know?*

PROSPECT: (Now really interested) *You're coming in loud and clear.*

SUPERSTAR: *I read Barrons's and Forbes and all the other compilers of "ten best" lists, but I couldn't get comfortable: everybody's criteria and ratings systems are different. Nobody's favorite manager is the same as anyone else's. And six months later, the standings all change anyway. I finally gave up and went to the senior investment people in my firm to see if they could recommend a serious, consistent long-term player who runs money for people like us. They introduced me to some really outstanding people, and* (only if true, of course) *I've been investing with them ever since. Want to hear about them?*

PROSPECT: *You bet I do.*

(Speaking time with prospect responses: 1-1/2 minutes)

Now, let's take a time-out and look at what you accomplished in just ninety seconds. First you didn't try to pass yourself off as "The Expert." Far from it; in fact, you may even feel this presentation goes too far in the other direction.

Notice how very simply, comfortably and conceptually you pulled up alongside somebody in your "natural market" and laid the concept of equity money management on him in a totally nontechnical, nonthreatening way. This presentation makes absolutely no pretense to a lot of knowledge of markets, timing, or investments.

The presentation says you started looking at money managers a short while ago. You checked with your firm to see if they could recommend a good one. They did. You put some money with the manager your firm recommended. You're happy. Now, maybe your client would like to have a look. That's all. Who can get mad at you for that? Nobody. And, in fact, when you open in a low-key, conversational way very few people will say, "No, I don't want to hear about it."

The "I'm-not-the-expert-all-I-do-is-love-this-thing" approach also tends to limit the prospect's inclination to hit you with a barrage of super-sharp questioning. He senses you like the investment because of the fit with your financial objectives and the recommendation by people in your firm who are paid to know about money managers.

In that minute and a half the client agreed with you two important times and then said "yes" a third time when you asked him if he'd like to hear the story. You implanted the basic concept (a professionally managed equity portfolio stressing upside), before you even named the product. You said: Here's something that I really like because it's good for people like you and me. (You have to be who you are, and you have to sell what you love.)

Perhaps you feel confident enough to come at the situation more strongly and to take a more authoritative approach to your initial presentation. Fine. That's a commentary on your style and on the way you see your relationship to your natural market. The same process is valid. Only the tone differs. Try this on for size:

SUPERSTAR: *I imagine we're both alike, in that our first choice for growth investing for retirement is common stocks. But, even though the market is about three times higher than it was ten years ago, we've been battered and whipsawed by the sharp market gyrations. Hasn't that been your experience?*

PROSPECT: *You know it, bubba.*

SUPERSTAR: *Well, I know the growth potential of common stocks is something I can't turn my back on. Just because I got shaken up on a play doesn't mean they postpone the Super Bowl. You know what I mean?*

PROSPECT: *Yes, no matter how bad we get racked up, the game goes on.*

SUPERSTAR: *So I decided to bench myself in favor of an All-Pro money manager. And I've been putting all my retirement money with him since then. I think you should consider doing the same thing. How does that sound to you?*

PROSPECT: *The concept sounds OK. What specifically are you recommending?*

What is the substantive difference between the two presentations? Right: There's *no difference.* There were some not-particularly-subtle stylistic variations, but that's about the size of it. One presentation had a kind of "we're-all-in-the-same-boat-neighbor" quality, while the other was a stronger statement of what you want the client to do. Neither is more right, except to the extent your personal style or situation make one better.

The words don't matter. Here's the principle:

CREATE ANY OPENING STATEMENT THAT SAYS:

- **I'VE BEEN THINKING ABOUT WHAT YOU NEED.**
- **YOU NEED MANAGED CAPITAL GROWTH.**
- **I KNOW GOOD QUALITY PEOPLE WHO CAN ACCOMPLISH THIS GOAL FOR YOU.**
-and always-
- **GIVE THE PROSPECT AMPLE OPPORTUNITY TO AGREE AS YOU GO ALONG.**

All that matters is generating, with empathy, a shared perception of financial need and a general notion that equities (specifically, *managed* equities) meet the need. Trust your instincts. The Universal Five-Point Presentation is a track to run on, not a straitjacket. Play around with it. The presentation is right when it sounds like *you.*

POINT #2: THE PEOPLE

Now you're through your conceptual opening statement. It was light, confident, punchy and presumptive (not presumptuous, mind you;

there's an enormous difference). You're *presuming* agreement on the basic logic: pre-retirement investing means long-term growth; which means common stocks; which means this is the Super Bowl, not amateur night; which means you better hire the best manager money can buy; which implies you get what you pay for; which shoots the "load" objection right between the eyes, before it even goes for its gun — but I'm getting ahead of myself.)

Now, before you launch into the second presentation point, The People, pause for one perceptible moment. (This may subliminally suggest to the prospect that you are actually thinking and not just talking. Prospects find this refreshing, since most financial salespeople/ planners give the impression that, for them, thinking and talking are mutually exclusive.) In the moment of silence, I'd like you to perform a quick but brutally honest "Binary Impression Test" on yourself. Ask: *"Does this guy think I may be trying to make something wonderful happen to him, or does he think I'm trying to sell him something?"*

Adjust your tone accordingly. Or, if you don't need to, draw renewed strength from the realization of how beautifully you're communicating. Now, on to The People.

"My firm has a very close relationship with the Gronsky Group, a large, well-known money management firm that manages four billion dollars for institutions as well as for people like us.

Of course, we can refer clients to a lot of money managers, but we've always been especially comfortable with the Gronsky people, because ..."

Now, plug in three very specific, very attention-grabbing attributes of the manager and the fund you're recommending. For example:

(a) *They're classic growth investors. They focus on earnings momentum and growth rates, and nothing else.*
(b) *Their management technique is one of extreme defensiveness. They buy only blue-chip, high quality stocks.*
(c) *During the past decade, they've not had a single down year.*
(d) *They focus almost exclusively on a company's cash flow, particularly excess cash flow. The managers, Lewis and Clark, believe they're buying part of a business, not just a stock.*
(e) *Their management technique is forward looking: They're always on the lookout for the next big emerging industry.*
(f) *They focus on three high-growth industries: cellular*

communications, cable TV, and pollution control.

(g) They tend to "buy and hold" the very best company in any given industry, so they have an incredibly low turnover rate.

(h) They're value buyers, and they'll tend to own a stock for many years. Some of their equities now throw off dividends that are greater than the price they paid for the stock!

(i) Over the past ten years, they've taken $10,000 and turned it into $61,900! And that's the kind of growth potential you deserve to be exposed to.

(j) They concentrate only on the largest, best-known, most stable companies. Their average stock is 40% larger than the average stock in the S&P 500!

(k) Their portfolio manager, Harry Callahan, is willing to do the kind of research on promising smaller companies where you get your hands dirty ... research that other fund managers are either too busy or too lazy to bother with.

(l) During the last five years, they've paid out an average of 7.4% in current income — which is about as much as you'd have gotten from CDs. But the value of the shares more than doubled!

Take another quick time-out, and look at what you've accomplished. Point #1 of your five-point presentation was THE CONCEPT. Point #2 was THE PEOPLE. Please look at the terms in which the management company was presented, and try to feel the effect of the key words and phrases. The first few ideas are constant — you'll use them all the time, in the same way — and the others are the variables.

CONSTANTS

- *My firm has a very close relationship with ...*
  MESSAGE: I'm not flying solo here. This manager was very carefully selected. And we're very happily married to these people for the long term.

- *... a large, well-known money management firm ...*
  MESSAGE: Who said anything about a mutual fund? Have you even heard the phrase mutual fund in this presentation yet? No, because it's a detail. The people — their strength, reputation and size — are what we care about. The managers are your birthday present; "mutual fund" is the box your present comes in.

- *... that manages four billion dollars for institutions as well as for people like us ...*

MESSAGE: Lots of big money believes in, and trusts, these guys. And this is not something we flog just to retail investors. Big institutions like them, too.

- *... we refer clients to a lot of money managers ...*
  MESSAGE: There were many intelligent, beautiful and inspiring ladies at the party. This is the one we really wanted to dance with.

- *... we've always been especially comfortable ...*
  MESSAGE: Relax. When you get used to this, you're really going to like it.

VARIABLES

(Note: The variables suggested below obviously don't all go with each other. We're just sampling a menu of short, pithy attributes that give flavor and feeling to why we love these people.)

- *... classic growth investors ... earnings momentum ...*
  MESSAGE: There's a classic, well-known, well-accepted, pure strategy at work here ... this isn't just a big, stupid basket of stocks.

- *... extreme defensiveness ... blue chip ... high quality ...*
  MESSAGE: I know you're scared; these guys are scared, too. They handle your money just like you would. No big risks.

- *... not a single down year ...*
  MESSAGE: Losing money in stocks is for losers. It's simply not a factor here.

- *... cash flow ... buying part of a business ...*
  MESSAGE: People lie. Statistics lie. Cash flow never lies. Serious investors buy businesses, they don't speculate in stocks.

- *... forward looking ... next big emerging industry ...*
  MESSAGE: What you dreamed of doing all your investing life, these guys do every day.

Are you starting to see how this works? If you sense risk-aversion and defensiveness, throw a clip of three defensive, blue chip, serious attributes in your gun, and fire away. Sense some closet aggressiveness and a long-suppressed desire to swing for the fences? Throw in that last one — "next big emerging industry," or "classic growth investors." (Incidentally, by my definition, "turned $10,000 into ..." is *not* a track record point, it's a whiff of excitement. Track record selling is when you laboriously go through a long discussion of the record, particularly compared to the S&P 500 or other funds. By the same logic, "paid out an average of 7.4%" isn't a track record point either. It's a large caliber, soft-nosed bullet fired into the head of the CD objection ... at very close range, so as to kill instantaneously but painlessly.)

Where do these beautiful silver bullets come from? Well, if your internal and sponsor wholesalers are sharp, they should be the source. Call your internal marketing person, as well as the sponsor's wholesaler, and ask:

> *"What five points would you have me tell my clients, to the exclusion of all others, to induce them correctly to make this investment?"*

When they recover from the shock of being asked so intelligent and pointed a question, they'll probably have some extremely interesting things to say. They may even, in a burst of creativity, work up a multitude of "essential" elements proving the superiority of the product. Don't permit it. Discipline your resources, as you're prepared to discipline yourself. Have them think through the basic, irreducible logic of the investment and come up with the *key* points — say five.

You can mine these nuggets from a couple of other wonderful sources. One is *Mutual Fund Values* published by Morningstar (800-876-5005). After years of mind-numbing, purely statistical coverage of funds, along came Morningstar, with beautifully written, subtle, incisive and extremely perceptive short discussions of such things as management style, portfolio strategies, and a real flesh-and-blood feel for the personalties of the managers. Morningstar reports are a joy to read and a rich source of zingers for Point #2: The People.

Another good source is a paperback called *The 100 Best Mutual Funds You Can Buy*, written by Gordon K. Williamson and published by Bob Adams, Inc., Holbrook, Massachusetts. (The book is available in most bookstores for $12.95.) If you're looking at a fund (or funds) covered in the book, chances are the wholesaler will have given you copies of the relevant pages. But I recommend you go through the whole book anyway, just to absorb different ways to think about — and talk about — funds.

SHIFTING GEARS

Before we go on to Point #3, I'd like to point out something that may have slipped by you unnoticed. THE CONCEPT, even adding in time for the prospect to chime agreement a couple of times, is a minute and a half long. The "constant" section of Point #2 — before you get to the "variables" — takes a bit less than thirty seconds.

You've been talking to the prospect — slowly, confidently, persuasively and warmly — for two full minutes. In those two minutes of heavy eye contact, you've gotten a huge amount of non-verbal information from the prospect that tells you volumes about how he's reacting to you. Even when he's trying to be polite or keep his feelings to himself, you can read what he's really thinking.

Why is this important? Glad you asked: **You haven't told the prospect which of the Gronsky funds you want him to buy yet.** So, based on the wealth of non-verbal data he's transmitted to you in the last 120 seconds ... **you still have time to change gears!**

Contrast this with the poor, benighted washout, who has spent the first two minutes rhapsodizing about the Gronsky Special Equity Fund — a small-cap, aggressive growth stock fund — when suddenly he notices the prospect is sitting there looking like he just swallowed a hairbrush. The washout looks down at his feet and sees that he's tap-danced into the middle of a minefield. Now he'll have to try to tiptoe back out again. Personally, I don't think he has a chance to get out alive. Do you?

The superstar empathized, conceptualized, and postulated the equation: growth = stocks. So far, the prospect hasn't run screaming from the room, but he doesn't look too enraptured either. So the superstar spends another half a minute pledging his firm's undying love for the Gronsky people. The prospect nods, but still looks very guarded and apprehensive.

And suddenly, the superstar's finely tuned unconscious mind (which is the officer of the deck, because his conscious mind can literally make the Five-Point Presentation in its sleep) yells, "Mayday! Iceberg of risk-aversion dead ahead! All engines back full; 45° right rudder!"

The superstar went in planning to present the Gronsky Special Equity Fund, too. But he instinctively sees the product will elicit a single, high-pitched scream from the prospect. So instead of firing off the "variables": "look out for emerging industries"; "focus on high growth industries"; and "research smaller companies" — he segues seamlessly into "extreme defensiveness," "value buyers," and "pay out current income." Then, without a flutter, he goes on to present Gronsky Equity

Income ... with the prospect starting to breathe normally again, and none the wiser. (Forgive me, but I just have to ask: *Don't you love it?*)

Flexibility is a hallmark of the relaxed and confident superstar. He leaves himself room to maneuver based on his ability to read the client's unspoken but very clear signals.

The concept of non-verbal communication deserves some amplification. I've said half a dozen times that *the way you say what you say* is much more important than *what you say*. But non-verbal communication is more important than both put together. To be precise, psychologists have demonstrated conclusively what the listener responds to in any conversation.

SOURCES OF "WHAT GETS THROUGH" IN A CONVERSATION	
Words	7%
The way you say what you say (The white coats call that "paralinguistics." See? Don't you hate jargon?)	38%
Non-verbal cues	55%

If nothing else, this breakdown tells you why I think all fact-based, number-based selling is such a complete waste of time and energy.

POINT #3: THE INVESTMENT AND WHAT IT DOES FOR YOU

You are now two-and-a-half minutes into the presentation, and you are on the downhill side, filling in some of the details on the investment and what the investment does for the prospect.

SUPERSTAR: *The Gronsky Group manages several different kinds of portfolios, including a money market fund. And, of course, you can switch back and forth among these different portfolios whenever you want, as often as you want, at absolutely no cost. This is really beside the point, but **total liquidity and total flexibility** are essential, I think, and Gronsky provides you with both.*

The portfolio you want, though, is Gronsky Equity Income Fund. This is their flagship fund — started back in 1957 — and if you handed them $10,000 when they opened the shop and then plowed back the dividends … well, you'd be sitting on about $590,000 right now. And that's what you'd expect, really: blue chip stocks, smart, disciplined managers and a long-term perspective … that's always been the formula for success, and it always will be.

So what the investment does for you, of course, is grow your capital in a conservative way until you retire … and then we can switch, entirely without cost, to a bond portfolio, so you can live on the income. Can you see how that would work?

(Speaking time: 1 minute, 20 seconds)

Once again, stop, take a deep breath … and look at all you've accomplished in the last 80 seconds. You told your prospect:

- he will always enjoy total flexibility and total liquidity;
- which portfolio he wants — not which one you want to sell him, but the one *he* wants;
- the fund has been around since Eisenhower's second term and has been making people rich ever since;
- the fund's strategy is a no-lose proposition which will always work if you give it time — a welcome thought to the risk-averse, *USA Today*/six o'clock news junkie who needs reassurance;
- a mind-blowing perspective-restorer about costs. (Yes, he may pay some small percentage of $100,000 to buy now. But then he can sell a couple or three hundred thousand dollars in stocks when he retires, and buy the same amount of bonds, at no cost. What a bargain!);
- plenty of growth now … plenty of income later … (God, I love this job!).

POINT #4: HOW THE INVESTMENT WORKS

I should confess something I didn't have the heart to tell you earlier in the chapter:

POINT FOUR IS OPTIONAL.

I threw in Point Four because I know you *need* to keep talking during the presentation. I guess I was afraid if I said you could present any mutual fund ever made in just four points, spoken in far less than five minutes, you'd have been upset and thrown this book in the fireplace.

I don't want to be dogmatic. Take your prospect's emotional temperature, non-verbally, of course. If he's the kind of person who says, "If these guys could multiply somebody's money 600% in 30 years, I don't want to know how they do it, *just sign me up ...*," well, I'm gonna fold and take the order. I make a point never to argue with people at times like this — it's not polite.

If, on the other hand, I sense this prospect is a subscriber to *Popular Mechanics*, or something, I'll roll in Point Four:

SUPERSTAR: *How do they do it? Well, like all great ideas, it's basically simple once you understand it. You see,* **blue chip companies tend to raise the dividend a little bit every year,** *as the earnings grow. So, over time, people bid the stock up because of the larger dividend. That's about it. Find a great company whose earnings and dividends keep going up, and you've probably found a stock that keeps going up. That's what the Gronsky Group has been doing, all day every day, since 1957. That's how they got $4 billion to manage.* **Everybody who invests with them loves 'em.** *Just like I do. And just like you will.*

(Speaking time: 45 seconds)

You can start to see how certain words and phrases look very conversational and descriptive in a low-key way, but turn out to be very forceful statements of your belief in the power of equities and in this manager's class and distinctions.

See, too, the power of being presumptive. You're making some very important statements here about how great companies' earnings, dividends and stock prices always go up over time. And you're making them in a very relaxed, matter-of-fact way. They're not arguments. Far from it; the way you say these words and phrases makes it sound as if you are just touching briefly on what must be *obvious* to the prospect. You're already holding the moral high ground of the greatness of long-term investing in equities. So the risk-aversion/volatility objection is obviously going to have a long uphill battle against your serene faith in equities ... if that objection ever surfaces at all. Your calm may have already killed it.

POINT #5: RISKS/LIMITATIONS

Another way to put objections in the ground before they get their guns out of the holsters is simply to shoot them while the prospect is waiting for you to finish your presentation. (Letting the bad guy draw first went out with the Lone Ranger.)

No investment is a panacea; no investment is without risk. Above all, every benefit an investment delivers is created at the expense of some other benefit. For example, real growth precludes a very high level of income, and the converse is also true.

People should know these truths. So if you make a presentation that is all sunshine and roses and a one-way ticket to the promised land, people instinctively know you're hyping them. The bridge of trust you were starting to build with the prospect can get dynamited to smithereens. And you've got nobody to blame but yourself.

So here's my vote: **Use the last few moments of the presentation to suggest some of the risks/limitations that the prospect is pretty sure to pounce on anyway.**

If you presented Gronsky Special Equity, you could probably say something like:

SUPERSTAR: *Don't look for a lot of current income, though, because these kinds of smaller companies tend to be plowing back every dime of earnings into future growth. And this isn't some hot trading idea, so don't expect instant gratification either. There's a long-term, patient strategy at work here, and you have to give it time.*

We all want to impart a sense of urgency to motivate our prospect to act, but creating the illusion the fund is going straight up from here is for washouts. Besides, an intelligent prospect will never believe it.

Or, if you were showing Gronsky Equity Income Fund, you would say:

SUPERSTAR: *Now, big companies that pay out large dividends — like the ones Gronsky owns in this portfolio — tend to be pretty stable and mature. Electric utilities, telephone companies, natural gas pipeline systems — those are the backbone of the American economy. They'll never be anybody's idea of exciting, and they're never going to quintuple in a year and make you the*

*hero of the cocktail party circuit. Slow and steady wins the race
... OK?*

People love that. They want to be reassured your approach is one of a steady, seasoned professional before they'll write out the really big check. So now just add:

SUPERSTAR: *Considering all that, would $ _____ be an appropriate amount for you to start with?*

... and you're done with the Universal Five-Point Presentation. Now if you'll go back and read the presentation straight through, picking any three of the "variable" silver bullets you like, here's what you'll find:

Point	Speaking Time
#1: THE CONCEPT	1 minute, 30 seconds
#2: THE PEOPLE	1 minute
#3: THE INVESTMENT AND WHAT IT DOES FOR YOU	1 minute, 20 seconds
#4: HOW IT WORKS	1 minute (tops)
#5: RISKS/LIMITATIONS (and a trial close)	30 seconds

Yup: just a shade over five minutes ... less, if you can do without optional Point Four. But even assuming you can't, aren't you just a little relieved? (The prospect is, I can assure you.) **Five basic points of really paramount importance, in just about as many minutes ... that's what it's all about.**

No jargon. No complicated investment strategies. No convoluted econometric formulas or stock market indicators. No numbers you can't prove. No estimates of how much money the prospect will make. No promise you might someday wish you had back. No hype. No sweat.

This presentation says: "I knew you'd love this investment as soon as you heard about it, the same way I did." (Even if you're investing in a different Gronsky portfolio from the one that suits the prospect, it's the people that count.) "This strategy is so clear, and so obviously successful, I just wanted to take you through the important, conceptual highlights. I'm not here to bury you in a lot of detail. I'm just here to solve the most important financial concerns you have. I don't even have to ask you whether you'd like to own this portfolio; I just want to know how much you feel is right for you."

Does your prospect still have a hundred questions? Great. Your attitude should be: "If he thinks the stuff I told him in the presentation was great, wait until he hears the terrific answers to all his tough questions." Not that you know all the answers, of course; we already warranted to you that you don't. But you've gone in with the attitude that all the tough questions have great answers. (As promised, in Chapter 20 we'll show you a great way to get all the answers, *right before your client's very eyes.*)

Knowing lots of great answers is not the point. The point is (and it's worth restating, because it's one of the hardest things for less experienced planners and salespeople to accept) ...

NO MATTER HOW MUCH LONGER YOU TALK
AND HOW MANY MORE THINGS YOU SAY,
YOUR CHANCES OF
NAILING YOUR PROSPECT'S DEEPEST FEARS DON'T EXIST.

You can't talk past people's real concerns; you have to let people verbalize them. So why postpone it? Make your best, simplest, most confident, most deeply felt presentation, ask for an order, and then *shut up.*

Short, generic, presumptive presentations speak of nothing but confidence, and managed money is the ultimate confidence sale. Long, detailed, technically specific, numbers-oriented presentations speak of nothing but fear. People do not invest their confidence in frightened salespeople.

TONE RE-VISITED: SHADINGS AND NUANCES

Once again, the point of this chapter is only partially how to present equity mutual funds. The larger issue is how you go about building the Universal Five-Point Presentation. In following chapters, you'll see a wide variety of money management products broken down and arranged into the same five points. The product changes, but THE PRESENTATION is THE PRESENTATION.

With that said, let's examine some of the shadings and nuances you can use to vary the tone and therefore the emotional impact of different kinds of equity fund presentations within the Universal Five-Point framework.

Even though the five points remain the same, you will stress different factors depending on the fund and the prospect. The aggressive, small-cap growth stock fund you present to a 40-year-old is going to sound a lot different from the income-stock fund you present to a 60-year-old. The washout will unfailingly isolate on, and obsess about, the differences — confusing and frightening the prospect. The superstar will focus instead on the deep channel of truth the Universal Presentation opens up with his prospect. And he will enjoy, and soon excel at, the subtle navigational variations you use to reach different prospects through the same presentational channel. Let's line three basic equity fund types up side by side, and see how the presentational shadings take effect. (See the table on the next page.)

Your ability to make the distinctions inexpressibly rich is limited only by (a) your love for the product you're selling, and (b) your willingness to practice and practice your presentation until it is a seamless, effortless work of art.

FINE TUNING THE FIVE-POINT PRESENTATION FOR VARIOUS EQUITY FUND TYPES

	Aggressive/Small Cap	Growth	Income-Stock
THE CONCEPT	Above-average long-term growth of capital with concomitant — but carefully managed — risk. Use a small part of your growth capital to make a potentially large impact on your overall portfolio return. Smaller stocks simply outperform larger stocks, because big breakthroughs mean quantum leaps for small outfits over long time frames.	Meaningful long-term growth of capital. Own a managed portfolio of quality companies growing at a substantially greater rate than the economy. Companies with new products, new markets, new managements.	Growth of income. Your living expenses are not fixed, so fixed income investing is a treadmill to oblivion. If you have years of inflation to face, growth of income is the only safety. Dividend growth carries stock prices slowly but surely higher.
THE PEOPLE ("Variables")	Stress: smarts; forward thinking; sophistication; special research skills; ability of managers to anticipate and exploit change.	Stress: experience; ability to spot the megatrends; understanding of the cycle; ability to spot undervaluation; ownership of great companies as investors in a business, not stock pickers; trends, not fads.	Stress: longevity; size; reputation; conservatism; prudence; risk-aversion; defensiveness; caution; quality.
THE INVESTMENT, AND WHAT IT DOES FOR YOU	Cite fund's participation in specific high-growth industries (biotech, cellular), show how average capitalization in the fund is a small fraction of S&P 500 companies; size and flexibility of fund, quickness, staying in front of the curve.	Large portfolio, broad diversification; exposure to many growth industries; high-cap, high quality well-known specific names; opportunism (buying great stocks cheap in down markets); disciplined strategy with a long-term perspective.	Largest, highest-quality, blue chip, mature companies in mature industries; don't look at the price every day, look at the check every quarter, see how the checks just grow and grow.
HOW IT WORKS	Controlled-risk aggressiveness	Quality and consistency	Pure, blue-chip dividend growth
RISKS/ LIMITATIONS	Will go down more in down markets, just as it goes up more in up markets (great for dollar-cost-averaging). No income ("plowing it all back ... for more growth").	Less growth (but more income); risk of short-term market dives. (But: great growth stocks may go down, but they don't stay down — if you're diversified.)	Can't make a killing, but can't get killed.

SUMMARY

- Simplify your presentation for the prospect's sake, not your own. Give the poor guy a chance to really understand the wonderful thing you're trying to do for him.

- Get the prospect in the habit of nodding and agreeing with you the way the Boston Irish used to vote: early and often.

- Point #1: THE CONCEPT is: You have to have growth (of capital, of income), and you have to have great professional management. Don't even think of trying to do it yourself; the stakes are too high.

- Point #2: THE PEOPLE stresses that the critical variable is who's managing — not what's being managed. People make acts of faith in other people, not in lists of stocks. Tell your prospect *why* the people are terrific, not just *that* they are.

- Point #3: THE INVESTMENT AND WHAT IT DOES FOR YOU doesn't show up until the presentation is 40% over. That way, there's still time to switch gears if you see you initially misread the client.

- Point #4: HOW IT WORKS is optional. A lot of people only care about what an investment does for them, not how it works.

- Point #5: RISKS/LIMITATIONS tells the prospect you're a balanced, steady, seasoned professional, not a carnival barker. Also, you blast a few obvious objections right out of the saddle before they can go for their guns.

- You're home and dry, and ready for Q&A, in five minutes. If you think you're relieved, imagine how relieved the prospect is.

- You move THE PRESENTATION around on the equity spectrum by practiced, artful shadings and nuances ... not by changing THE PRESENTATION.

14

How To Present Fish And Fowl: Balanced Funds

In the last chapter, we fit three types of equity mutual funds into the Universal Five-Point Presentation simply by modulating the tone and feeling of The Presentation. The idea was to sit you behind the wheel and let you drive The Universal Five-Point Presentation around for a while, to see its responsiveness under a variety of driving conditions.

Let's take The Presentation to the next level of conceptual difficulty, and examine funds which provide two different benefits by combining stocks and bonds (or securities which are both stocks and bonds) in one portfolio (called "balanced" funds). We'll cover three groups of balanced funds in this chapter: (1) growth-and-income funds, which contain a preponderance of stocks (say 80%) and some bonds; (2) "classic" balanced funds, which usually hold close to 50% in equity and 50% in bonds or cash equivalents; and (3) convertible securities funds, in which the balanced fund concept is present within each individual security.

(Note: The labels and classification systems used to group mutual funds are mind-numbing and vary widely, depending on who's doing the classifying. I'm trying to organize funds by concept, not labels. But while we're on the subject, I'd like to say something about labels, categories, classifications and ratings — I hate 'em all. Labels, categories and ratings are very dear to the hearts of Americans and are always getting in the way of more important, albeit more ambiguous, realities. A great wine isn't always the same; it varies with the food, the friends and the conversation. Try to think of funds the same way ... not in terms of some ranking that appeared in a magazine six weeks ago. Truth is *so* much more subtle than any accumulation of facts.)

Balanced funds are more difficult to present because you need to explain more benefits, and the benefits compete to some extent. But, in this age of the dreaded disease "PRAP" (Pandemic Risk Aversion Psychosis), you may think any investment that decreases "risk" and increases "safety" is automatically easier to sell. This assumption is seriously wrong for two reasons.

First, **selling a "mixed portfolio" is inherently much more complicated than selling a single investment.** The reasons you build a portfolio may be self-evident to you, but can be very scary as they go whizzing past a prospect's head ... unless you're very careful about how you present THE CONCEPT. For instance, one of the key attractions of a balanced fund is that the debt portion will sustain only minor casualties during periods when the equity side is getting nuked. But, how do you present that notion to a 62-year-old without shorting out his pacemaker?

Second, since the debt and equity components of a "portfolio" work at cross-purposes, **lots of prospects will react favorably to one aspect and quite negatively to the other.** Human nature being what it is, the primary emotion generated will tend to be the negative one. And if you're not fast on your feet, you're going to stand there looking at a called third strike.

In this situation, if you let the primary issue become the fund — rather than the synergistic power of you and the Gronskys to find the right solution — you're done. You are emotionally dug into a position you can't defend and from which you can't advance. Game over.

But this conundrum (prospect likes half the concept and hates the other half) can be solved if you follow the advice laid down in the prospecting chapters: *When the prospect tells you why he won't buy what you want him to buy, he's told you what he will buy.* So the superstar, sensing he still doesn't have a real good "read" on the prospect, comes right down the middle. The message: **When presenting balanced funds, retain your flexibility to go either way based on the signals you get from the prospect.**

Guy's got terminal PRAP? Zig right: "Then you just want a pure play in the highest quality corporate bonds. That's fine, and the Gronsky Group also manages a superb bond portfolio." Guy's stronger than you thought (i.e. he has a better idea of what "risk" and "safety" really mean)? Zag left to a growth-and-income portfolio that's 80% stocks and 20% bonds. Or zag hard left, to Gronsky Quality Growth Fund ... your direction depends on the signals. You're not pandering to the prospect; you're getting him on board. As his trust grows — as he really becomes a client — you'll develop greater ability to vector him in the right direction.

So remember, balanced funds give prospects extra things not to like. The way you sell them is: carefully, warmly ... and nimbly. Here are the presentations you need.

PRESENTING GROWTH-AND-INCOME FUNDS

Clearly, the primary emphasis for growth and income funds is still on growth via common stocks. But, you have a significant windward anchor in the form of bonds and other short-term debt instruments. The anchor is a relatively *consistent* portfolio device and not a temporary response to market conditions. Some pure growth funds may go to 20% or 25% cash when the managers are cautious-to-mildly-negative on the equity markets. But when they're bullish again, they go back to being fully invested in stocks. But a growth-and-income fund maintains the fixed income component as the anchor to windward. The purpose is to produce enhanced income the growth segment can't deliver, while hedging against unforeseen declines in the equity market.

So you can start to see a picture of the "suitable" investor and how to present growth-and-income funds, let's isolate the benefits:

- **Growth of capital and income** — usually through a preponderant exposure (70% - 80%) to stocks of large, well-established companies that pay good cash dividends.

- **Enhanced income relative to growth funds** — partly because the equity portion is weighted toward dividend payers, and partly because income from the debt side (the other 20% - 30% of the portfolio) is higher than from stocks.

- **Deadened sensitivity to sharp market moves** — By combining debt exposure with a high-cap, high-quality bias in the equity portion of the portfolio, growth-and-income funds proved safer than any other category of equity funds throughout the Great Whipsaw of 1987-90. In an age which equates volatility with risk, this point is significant.

As always, the needs and perceived risk tolerance of your prospect match off against the fund's goals and strategies and form the first of your five presentation points, **THE CONCEPT.**

SUPERSTAR: *If you're going to accomplish the capital accumulation goals you've set for your retirement, your capital clearly has to grow substantially over the next ten years. That's pretty plain, isn't it?*

PROSPECT: *Plain as the nose on your face.*

SUPERSTAR: *Well, long-term capital accumulation, for me, is synonymous with the ownership of great common stocks. But I have a strong bias toward companies that pay generous — and growing — dividends, because compounding the dividends takes a lot of the guesswork out of retirement planning. Still making sense?*

PROSPECT: *No argument so far.*

SUPERSTAR: *I'm also a great believer in diversification, so even in a portfolio that's primarily for growth, I love to have 20% to 30% of the assets in high-quality bonds. Of course, the bonds also enhance the portfolio's current return — there's the magic of compounding again. But more than that, the bonds deaden the sensitivity of a portfolio to short-term market gyrations. And — if only psychologically — that's become real important to my clients these last few years. You feel that way too, I imagine.*

PROSPECT: *That's a big 10-4.*

SUPERSTAR: *Put it all together, I suppose it's a sophisticated approach. And it takes a smart, sophisticated money manager to put the strategy in place, and keep it in place.*

In reading through THE CONCEPT aloud, you find the prescribed length of 90 seconds. The presumption is you and the prospect have agreed retirement is the goal which requires some big-time capital accumulation — either from him or from his portfolio — to reach his destination.

Before going on, make sure you have clear, unequivocal agreement on the critical point: Equities are the only real solution to capital accumulation.

Now listen to some of the power phrases — the real attention-grabbing table setters — that came out in the last minute or so:

- *"... the ownership of great common stocks ..."*

MESSAGE: This isn't class B ball — we're playing in the major leagues.

- *"I have a strong bias ..."*
MESSAGE: I'm not just reading from a script or flogging the fund du jour. This is what I believe, and I'm prepared to be responsible for it.

- *"... companies that pay generous — and growing — dividends..."*
MESSAGE: Nobody's talking about speculating, here.

- *"... compounding the dividends takes a lot of the guesswork out ..."*
MESSAGE: You won't be looking up stock prices every day to see if you're still alive; you'll be seeing dividend checks.

- *"I'm also a great believer ..."*
MESSAGE: More of the "I'm in command of the situation" subliminal signal.

- *"... diversification ... high quality bonds ..."*
MESSAGE: It's even smarter to own different kinds of great stuff.

- *"... enhance the portfolio's current return ... the magic of compounding ..."*
MESSAGE: Reinforces the previously stated theme: Checks do not lie.

- *"... deaden the sensitivity ... to short-term market gyrations ..."*
MESSAGE: Never use the dreaded "V" word ("volatility") first. This is a corollary of Murray's Law of Riding the New York City Subways: If you don't make eye contact, you're not really there. Similarly, if you don't say "volatility," the market isn't volatile — it's just subject to those pesky little old "short-term gyrations." Get it?

- *"... that's become real important to my clients ..."*
MESSAGE: Everybody's worried about volatility, not just you. You can stop worrying now.

- *"... sophisticated approach ... takes a smart, sophisticated money manager ..."*
MESSAGE: You didn't think we were gonna do this ourselves, did you?

The washout will undoubtedly use the words "risk" and "volatility" in the first two minutes of a presentation. (No, I don't understand it, either; maybe he has to re-qualify every year or face the loss of his Washout Merit Badge.) Specifically, he'll say a growth-and-income fund lowers the risk of owning stocks and produces less volatility. Trouble is, you cannot be "less pregnant" or "less dead." And in the investor's mind today, there is no such thing as "less volatility." I say again:

You must never allow the "V" word to escape your lips. If spoken at all, the "V" word must be spoken by the investor (and we'll deal with your response in Q&A/objections handling).

Incidentally, notice we haven't said anything about a fund yet. And here we are at **Point #2: THE PEOPLE** (or, "I never did get that masked man's name, but he left *three silver bullets*..."). Once again, you use the "constant" part of Point #2, word for word, as follows:

SUPERSTAR: *My firm has a very close relationship with the Gronsky Group — a large, well-known money management firm that manages four billion dollars for institutions as well as for people like us.*

Of course, we can refer clients to a lot of money managers, but we've always been especially comfortable with the Gronsky people, because ...

Now for the variables, the "silver bullet" attributes you can load into your presentation for some of the leading growth-and-income funds. Find out the three which have the most resonance for you — that apply to the growth-and-income fund you like. (Be who you are; sell what you love.) But remember: Don't be greedy. Only three "silver bullets" to a customer:

- *They combine very good performance with excellent risk management.*

- *They emphasize mature industries such as chemicals, telephones, foods and utilities.*

- *Every stock in their portfolio pays a dividend.*

- *Management has been extremely consistent and disciplined, looking at long time horizons. After all, they've been managing the portfolio I like since 1932!*

- *The value of the portfolios they manage has increased at nearly three times the rate of inflation over the last decade.*

- *Management concentrates on blue chip stocks with above-average yields.*

Next, **Point #3: THE INVESTMENT AND WHAT IT DOES FOR YOU.**

SUPERSTAR: *The Gronsky Group manages several different kinds of portfolios, including a money market fund. And, of course, you can switch back and forth among the different portfolios whenever you want, as often as you want, at absolutely no cost. This is really beside the point, but **total liquidity** and **total flexibility** are essential to any rational retirement plan ... and, of course, Gronsky provides both.*

The portfolio I believe you want, though, is the Gronsky Fund for Growth and Income, which is actually their flagship fund, started back in 1932. Today, there's $2.2 billion in the portfolio. About 80% is spread out among 65 great common stocks — all names you'd recognize, and all great dividend payers.

*Great dividend **growers**, too. For instance, you see here that they own a million shares of General Electric. GE was paying a $.34 dividend in 1971. They raised the dividend in 19 of the next 20 years, and ended 1990 paying $1.88. That kind of dividend growth beats the pants off inflation and is going to mean a lot to you when you retire.*

The other 20% of the portfolio is in high-quality corporate bonds, Treasury securities, and cash. These bonds generate extra income, and stabilize the whole portfolio when the stock market gets the hiccups.

*This 80/20 arrangement has always been a formula for success — and it's always been successful. Why, in the last 30 years, looking at 10-year periods, the Gronsky Fund for Growth and Income has beaten the major market index in **every one** of the periods.*

*So, what the investment strategy will do for you, of course, is grow your capital in a conservative way until you retire ... and then we can switch, **entirely without cost**, to another Gronsky portfolio that produces more income. Can you see how that would work?*

(Speaking time: 2 minutes)

You've just talked for two minutes straight — which is almost a geologic age for a presentation. The justification: You've rolled together Points #3 and #4 of the presentation because it's virtually impossible to explain what a growth-and-income fund does for you without explaining how.

But look at where you stand after only three and a half minutes. The prospect has received an incredible amount of both hard and conceptual information about the fund — somewhere between 80% and 90% of all he'll ever remember. And, in a lot less than one minute — after risks/limitations and the trial close — this presentation will be all over.

Look at the tremendous wealth of information the prospect received in the last two minutes:

- The Growth and Income Fund is the Gronskys' flagship. In a business where longevity is a sure sign of strength and consistency, this fund's been around for almost 60 years.

- The fund is big and substantial: $2.2 billion is a lot of change, and you don't induce that many people to entrust that much money to you with mirrors and blue smoke.

- With $1.75 billion in 65 great common stocks, the Gronskys must build very big positions in the finest imaginable companies.

- The fund has a million share position in one of the greatest business enterprises in the world — the General Electric story. (If the prospect is interested, GE raised the dividend at about a 9% compound annual growth rate over 20 years.) Look at the implication: **Dividend growth in America's greatest companies is the ultimate inflation killer!** (This guy is starting to think, "CDs?! What could I have been *thinking* of?") And please note one more thing: *Nobody's said anything about GE's stock price!* To anyone incubating the PRAP virus, stock prices are abstract and scary — but dividends are concrete and comforting!

- About 20% of the portfolio is in high quality corporate bonds, Treasuries, and cash to "generate extra income" (I love that phrase) and stabilize the portfolio "when the stock market gets the hiccups." The superstar belittles volatility phobia … without even mentioning its name!

- Gronsky Growth and Income beat the S&P 500. Just a whiff of track-record grapeshot in the air here. But, when and if the prospect counterattacks, what a massive weapon you have. Imagine, with the millstone of 20% in bonds around its neck — even during the 1970s and early 1980s, a hellacious time for bonds — this portfolio still kicked the stuffing out of the S&P 500 stock index in every single ten-year period over the last 30 years! Impossible. But true!

See ... if you put yourself under the time constraint of five points in about five minutes, you can't get beyond the largest nuggets of all-important truth. In this respect, **the Five-Point Presentation saves us from ourselves** — from our tendency to long-windedness ... from rambling ... from bringing up a lot of secondary and tertiary points that only confuse and distress our prospects. This presentation style saves us, if nothing else, from our own nerves.

Quickly, then, move on to the final **Point #5: RISKS / LIMITATIONS.**

SUPERSTAR: *Clearly, now, a 20% exposure to bonds is an anchor to windward in a choppy stock market, but it won't keep the value of the shares from going down a little if the stock market gets hit hard enough. Just remember, portfolios of great common stocks may go down from time to time **but they never stay down.** I'm just making sure you realize that there's a limit to what the bonds can do.*

*Nor, in a wild bull market, can this fund ever triple in a year and make you the hero of the cocktail party set. Great, mature companies' stocks — not to mention bonds — won't move that much ... **in either direction.***

Considering all this, do you agree that $___ is an appropriate investment for you to start with?

From this presentation — and the running commentary — you can start to see some of the possible variations and improvisations within the Five-Point Presentation. Make the presentation a living, breathing organism, and not a dead, static, rote formula that traps you and the fund you love inside.

Again, does this presentation leave a lot out? Of course it does — the load and the yield, to name two items. But you should **never bring up the sales charge in the presentation** — it's not important enough, in the great scheme of things. Besides, when the prospect wants to know, he'll ask. And then, you'll be able to read volumes into *the way he asks.* So, let him broach the subject.

The yield is only going to be about 4%, so don't bring yield up, either. If he's human and hears a 4% current return, the prospect will think, "Well, heck, I could get more from an insured passbook savings account ..." And he'll miss the whole next minute of the work of art which is your presentation. So when and if he asks — he may not, you know — say:

> *"Well, to tell you the truth, I've forgotten to look lately, but it's usually in the neighborhood of about 4%. That's a tad more than the yield on the S&P 500, but of course it ought to be, on account of the bonds. The thing you care about, of course, is not where the dividend is, but where it's **going**. And, as an indication of what I was saying earlier about the importance of dividend growth, Gronsky Growth and Income has raised its dividend in 28 of the last 30 years ... just like the great ones always do."*

I don't want to get ahead of myself and into Q&A theory just yet. I'm just suggesting that many points the washout thinks are critical can easily wait until Q&A, where you can put your own special spin on the ball as you answer.

PRESENTING "CLASSIC" BALANCED FUNDS

"Classic" balanced funds are roughly half invested in good quality common stocks and half in good quality bonds. (We'll simply call them "balanced funds" in this section.) Balanced funds have a unique conceptual beauty shared by no other type of mutual fund. First, and without any hyperbole, **balanced funds are instantly a "rich man's portfolio."** Do you know what a really wealthy investor has in his portfolio? *Everything.* The more substantial and sophisticated an investor, the more likely he follows the three cardinal rules of investing (postulated by Republic Bank's senior portfolio strategist and developer of the concept of multifund investing, Michael Hirsch): 1. diversify; 2. diversify; 3. diversify.

Nothing beats a diversified portfolio of great common stocks for growth of capital and income. Nothing beats high quality corporate and U.S. Treasury bonds of varying maturities for safety of principal and a competitive, risk-adjusted current return. So it stands to reason, if you're the kind of investor who wears a belt and suspenders — who wants a diversified portfolio, some major part of which is "working" in any economic environment — there's a balanced fund out there with your name on it. Balanced funds are the right choice for people who can't — or won't — make a choice.

Balanced funds have been around since 1928 — which, for the

mutual fund industry, means shortly after the Dawn of Recorded Time. And some have done almost startlingly well. At least one balanced fund outperformed the S&P 500 stock index for the twenty years through the beginning of 1990 — while remaining 30% less risky since half was in bonds!! That's real performance by anybody's definition.

Perhaps **the greatest advantage to the planner/salesperson is that balanced funds give you the perfect opportunity to explore a new prospect's likes and dislikes.** You can take a middle-of-the-road approach and see which way he breaks — an extremely low-risk strategy. No one will be angry at you for offering a balanced fund. It's smart, it's classy and it's conservative. And, while not always awe-inspiring, a good balanced fund's record is usually unimpeachable, if only because so much of the return has come from reinvested dividends. And, don't forget, the largest stock holdings of balanced funds are almost always household names.

Let's round up the major attributes of balanced funds, around which we can build our Five-Point Presentation.

- **Real diversification and the stability that goes with it** — If you suddenly had to invest $100 million, chances are you'd buy some very high-quality stocks, Treasury securities, corporate debt, perhaps some world-class foreign securities, and a few good convertible bonds. Because you wouldn't want to bet the ranch, you'd spread everything out so your exposure in different markets balanced out. Well, with $10,000, you can invest the same way, efficiently and inexpensively, in a balanced mutual fund.

- **Professional management with plenty of flexibility** — You and I don't necessarily know when to lean more toward equities or debt, when to shorten or lengthen maturities, when to accentuate growth stocks, or when to go heavy into cyclicals. Great managers often do know. You can hire the expertise in a balanced fund, but then ... you have to give the manager time to work his strategy out. You're here for long-term, stable performance, not instant gratification.

- **The consistency that comes from automatic compounding of a relatively high, predictable and growing income stream** — The better balanced funds racked up total returns of 14% to 16% per year in the 1980s. But an average of 6% to 6.25% came from current income. That's a big chunk — and of course, income is more stable than the component of the return that comes from price appreciation. So total long-term returns are comfortably stabilized by the compounding of the relatively high dividend stream (half again higher than the dividends from a growth-and-income fund). Given the current volatility phobia, this point takes on extra resonance.

So, **THE CONCEPT** shapes up like this:

SUPERSTAR: *Your financial situation looks to me like you're well along the way toward the realization of your goals. You've accumulated a fair amount of capital, and I don't think you need to take a lot of risk or try to hit one out of the park to get to where you want to be. Is that an accurate reading of the situation?*

PROSPECT: (With more than a little pride) *I'd say it is.*

SUPERSTAR: *On the other hand, you sure don't want to put it on automatic pilot, and fall asleep. Maintaining an adequately diversified portfolio earning a superior return under rapidly changing market conditions ... well, that's hard work, don't you find?*

PROSPECT: *I can't complain, I guess. After all, what's the alternative?*

SUPERSTAR: *Well, unless managing your own portfolio is a lot more fun for you than I think it is, the smart alternative is first-class professional management — in a beautifully diversified but* **self-contained portfolio** *that's about evenly divided between great common stocks and very high quality bonds.*

The investment would probably enhance your total return — wouldn't be worth doing otherwise — and you would be out of the stock-picking, coupon clipping, nail-biting end of running your portfolio. Got four more minutes to learn how?

PROSPECT: *Heck, I'm a sport: take six minutes.*

SUPERSTAR: *Thanks, but I don't need 'em. All the greatest investments are the simplest to explain. And this is one of my best — and one of the simplest.*

(Speaking time (you guessed it): 90 seconds)

What did you do here? First of all, you tipped your hat to a guy who's obviously gotten on track and stayed on track. People don't want you to say their portfolio is on fire and you're the fireman. People want to hear they've done a good job. Don't blow smoke in their ear, but if you think they've done OK, don't be reticent about telling them so.

But then point out what they know: Investment success is a real chore; the markets are getting harder to figure; and a real pro can build a solidly balanced portfolio that would (a) probably do better than they're doing on their own, (b) with one heck of a lot less work and worry. Know what? Maybe nobody ever actually said to the prospect: "You don't have to carry this burden yourself anymore. You've earned a rest. Put it down. I'll get somebody else to carry it for you." (And you still think this business is about what you *know?*)

Now, push down on the accelerator and move to **Point #2: THE PEOPLE.**

SUPERSTAR: *My firm has a special relationship with a very large, well-known money management firm called The Gronsky Group. The Gronskys manage a total of about four billion dollars for institutions as well as for investors like us.*

Of course, our firm can refer clients to a lot of money managers, but we've always been particularly comfortable with the Gronsky people. I guess that's because ...

● *Their portfolios are run by a committee of senior investment professionals, which ensures continuity of sound investment policies.*

● *They really know how to buy well-established companies with positive long-term earnings prospects — when those prospects aren't reflected in a stock's price.*

● *They reward their managers with bonuses based on how well they do* **for you.**

● *They know how to attract and keep excellent people. Why, the portfolio I like for you has had the same man running it since 1967!*

● *They maintain large cash reserves, so they can always pick up a real bargain when it becomes available.*

● *They make great investments and then hang on to them. Low portfolio turnover means lower costs and higher returns for investors.*

- They haven't had a down year in fifteen years.

Since it sounds like you're talking to an older, better established prospect here, this selection of balanced fund silver bullets is very strongly relationship-oriented. Remember, the prospect for a balanced fund is virtually sure to be a "don't get killed" rather than a "make a killing" person. You tell him the portfolio is run by a 33-year-old rocket scientist with a Ph.D. in portfolio theory and a minor in Chinese poetry, and this prospect will drop you down an airshaft. Continuity, longevity, sound judgment, long-term orientation, large cash reserves and a great eye for value are the messages carried by these silver bullets.

Depress the clutch and shift smoothly into **Point #3: THE INVESTMENT AND WHAT IT DOES FOR YOU.**

SUPERSTAR: *The Gronskys' best-known portfolio — and it's been written up in financial magazines as long as I've been in the business — is the Gronsky Balanced Fund. The name tells you exactly what it is — one portfolio that is usually divided about equally between the highest quality blue-chip common stocks and a great collection of corporate bonds, US Treasury bonds, and cash. It's a very fluid, very flexible structure which lets the Gronsky Group produce superior total returns in virtually any economic or market environment. Over the last ten years, the average annual return has been about 15%, which is amazing to me, given how safe and conservative the portfolio is.*

Of course, a big attraction here is efficiency: You can compound the earnings automatically — and at absolutely no cost — so your money is never idle. If you're going crazy trying to figure out how and where to re-invest your dividends and interest, I'm sure you'll see how important this feature is. At first I thought it was just a small point, but all my clients say this feature gives them tremendous peace of mind.

And the income keeps going up, too. Gronsky Balanced Fund started in 1973, and they've increased the cash payout in 15 of the 17 years since. Of course, when you look at the portfolio, you can see why. Look, here's a million shares of Florida Progress Corp — the old Florida Power; it's the big electric utility in Florida. The Gronskys once told me that was one of the first stocks they bought when they set up shop in 1973. The company paid an $.87 dividend a share then — and when I *looked last, at the end of 1990, the dividend had grown to $2.58.*

(Speaking time: A tad less than 2 minutes)

Now here again, look at what your tone is accomplishing and how you are expanding the relationship by weaving your own personal experiences into the fabric of the presentation.

- *"Their best-known portfolio ..."*
  MESSAGE: People feel safest with things that are *well known.*

- *"... written up ... as long as I've been in the business ..."*
  MESSAGE: I've seen this portfolio admired in print for years. Haven't you?

- *"... fluid ... very flexible ...*
  MESSAGE: Doesn't it just *feel* good?

- *"... superior total returns ... any market environment ..."*
  MESSAGE: Don't even *think* of saying the "V" word to me, Mr. Prospect. The Gronskys and I do not tolerate such vulgarity, sir.

- *"... average annual return ... 15% ... amazing to me ..."*
  MESSAGE: If somebody told me it was going to do this well, I'd have probably bought more.

- *"... given how safe and conservative the portfolio is ..."*
  MESSAGE: The washout says, "This portfolio is safe and conservative." The superstar says it the other way, almost as an afterthought. Which way sounds better to you?

- *"... you can compound ... no cost ... so your money is never idle ..."*
  MESSAGE: So can every one of 3,000 other mutual funds. But, said this way, doesn't it sound like the Gronskys practically *invented* it?

- *"... I thought it was just a small point... but all my clients ... peace of mind ..."*
  MESSAGE: I just never cease to be amazed at how happy the Gronskys make my people.

- *"... income keeps going up ..."*
  MESSAGE: The income keeps going up. Is that clear?

- *"The Gronskys once told me ..."*
  MESSAGE: I know them well; we get together sometimes and talk

about the early days.

- *"... the old Florida Power ..."*
MESSAGE: I don't hold with all these fancy new names, myself. I'm just a conservative old shoe ... just like you.

- *"... $.87 (in 1973) ... $2.58 now ..."*
MESSAGE: Have you bought and held many stocks that tripled their dividend? No? See, I *know* you are going to like this fund.

Again, this presentation combines Points #3 and #4. Prospects for balanced funds aren't MBA's. They don't want a course called "Modern Portfolio Theory in Monosyllabic Words for Pre-School Children." Give 'em a break.

You're within sight of the checkered flag — just move through **Point #5: RISKS/LIMITATIONS.**

SUPERSTAR: *Now, you have to realize a fund so stable it hasn't had a down year in ten years, is too stable to explode upward in a bull market. So you may have to grit your teeth every so often when a hare goes whizzing by ... because your money is on the tortoise. OK?*

And, once in a great while, you'll see a big run-up in interest rates, which tends to put pressure on both stocks and bonds for a time. But, come to think of it, that's what caused all the trouble in 1987, and Gronsky Balanced Fund came through without a scratch ...

Well, considering all of that, is $____ a comfortable amount for you to start with?"

Incidentally, are you wondering how I know the stuff about the dividend history of GE and Florida Progress? I did the homework, that's how. When you're obviously knowledgeable about a fund's largest holdings — without being a showoff — you reinforce the prospect's awareness of your deep, long-standing relationship with the fund and the sponsor.

And since, in these dark days of PRAP, you don't want to go out on a limb talking about stock *prices*, you'd better be prepared to **take the moral high ground of dividend growth**. Income that's growing as fast or faster than inflation is what investment success is all about.

And what a sensationally powerful story. Here are examples of twenty-year dividend histories on some great companies that are widely owned by mutual funds.

	DIVIDEND GROWTH CAN WHIP INFLATION			
Company	**Cash Dividend*** **1971**	**1990**	**Number of Years Dividend Raised**	**20-Year Compound Annual Growth Rate**
Mobil Oil	$ .60	$2.55	15	7.50%
Warner-Lambert	.29	1.28	All	7.64%
IBM	.96	4.73	13	8.30%
General Electric	.34	1.88	19	8.93%
Coca-Cola	.12	.68	All	9.06%
Pfizer	.32	2.20	All	10.18%
PepsiCo	.04	.32	15	11.39%
Phillip Morris	.03	1.25	17	19.96%
Consumer Price Index				**6.40%**
*Adjusted for Stock Splits				

Not to pound this observation into the ground like a tomato stake, but these stocks have two very important common characteristics:

(1) they are among the best-managed, best-financed business enterprises on the planet; and

(2) they are the kind of stocks that individual investors *don't buy.*

The experienced, older, risk-averse client who looks at balanced funds really needs to feel a tremendous professionalism coming at him when you speak. But once he trusts you, you'll be his adviser for the rest of his life. So, do your homework ... this isn't a spectator sport. Know the portfolios of the funds you love. Know why the managers own the biggest positions, and be prepared to comment intelligently. Have the brains to really know your stuff, and the class not to be obtrusive about it.

PRESENTING CONVERTIBLE BOND FUNDS

Convertible bond funds provide benefits essentially like balanced funds. (In fact, Gordon Williamson's *100 Best Mutual Funds You Can Buy* lumps the two categories together.) The difference is a balanced fund buys two different kinds of securities (stocks and bonds), whereas each individual security in a convertible bond fund *is* both a stock and a bond.

Since they are convertible into common stock at a prescribed price, convertible bonds offer most of the advantages of stock — a theoretically limitless upside potential, the peerless ability to preserve purchasing power, and equity's record of outperforming all other classes of financial assets.

But a convertible security also offers some of the best features of a bond. First, the fixed yield is usually substantially higher than the underlying common stock's dividend. Second, the maturity date is fixed. And the price will migrate toward par as maturity approaches, regardless of interest rates or the conversion price. Finally, the debt is senior to common stock and has a higher claim on company assets. (For purposes of this discussion, I'm lumping together convertible debt and convertible preferred stock. Convertible debt is senior to convertible preferred stock, but they are both senior to common stock.)

To obtain this remarkable package of benefits, you pay a price. First, there aren't many convertible issues, and most are relatively small. A fair number of the roughly 1,200 convertible issues trade on the major exchanges, but the majority trade over the counter. The market capitalization for all convertibles combined isn't as big as many individual stocks on the New York Stock Exchange. Many convertible issues are $25 to $50 million in size, so trading markets aren't very liquid. Nor do convertibles command much research coverage.

Like most debt, convertibles have call provisions which can be complex and hard to understand. Call provisions can have profound effects on the way the bonds trade.

Finally, the price relationship between the bond and the underlying common stock isn't linear. Particularly in the early stages of market recoveries, when the common is selling way below the conversion price, the stock may have a heck of a run before the convertible reacts. Granted, that's because the bond stopped going down long before the stock did — thanks to the bond's yield. That's the great strength of convertibles. But on the way back up, you pay the price.

If you're interested in availing yourself of the benefits of convertible securities, you'd better stick with professional management — people who specialize in understanding the peculiarities of the convertible market. And when you locate a convertible fund you're happy to show your prospects, your powers of conceptualization and simplification will really pay off.

One way to simplify the concept is to use the "eagle-and-the-chicken" analogy. When common stocks are having a great, long run on the upside, a convertible acts like an eagle, soaring right along on the updraft. Convertibles would have to do that, because if the bond price lags behind conversion value, a hundred arbitrageurs' computers will ring their alarms, and the gap will quickly close.

Let the stock take a big enough dive, however, and the convertible bond suddenly starts acting like a chicken. The price falls to where it's valued fairly just based on the current coupon. From that point on, even as the stock continues tail-spinning toward the deck, the bond just sits there and says, "Don't look at me; I'm no common stock. I'm a bond. I've got a rating. I've got a coupon. I've got a fixed maturity that's getting closer every day. Most important, I'm senior to all that common stock riffraff. My issuer *owes* somebody my face amount. I'm just gonna sit here keeping my eggs warm for the duration."

The eagle-and-the-chicken analogy may be too corny. (I kind of like it, because it's apt to make a prospect smile. And, when I make him smile, he starts to become my friend.) Maybe you'd rather try a jet plane and a parachute. But give some thought to framing an analogy that feels comfortable to you. Because I promise if you start talking about call provisions, conversion premiums and non-linear price relationships, you're going to dig yourself a hole deep enough to smell the rice cooking in Beijing.

So let's **look at the key attributes of a convertible securities fund**, and think about how those features fit with the profile of a reasonable prospect.

- **Extremely competitive current yield, especially when the stock market is down** — The popular perception is convertibles are a way to cajole people into maintaining proper equity exposure even when they are afraid the stock market is vulnerable. Maybe so, but I think **convertibles are even more strategic when the market is down already, and the consensus is totally risk-averse** (at the wrong time, as always). Because, at such times, the bonds in convertible funds will be selling almost purely on yield ... which will look pretty attractive. You know how eager you are to increase clients' exposure to the equity markets at times like this ...

and how reluctant they are. This is very frustrating because all your instincts and all your experience say you'll really perform for people if you can get them into the market when it's low. Convertible funds can be the answer.

- **A style of investing the client can't, in all practicality, do for himself** — Broad diversification and dispassionate professional management are the classic attractions of mutual funds. But convertibles add a new level to the old argument. Individual investors would have great difficulty mastering convertible securities markets. An investor may cling to the conceit he can buy and hold growth stocks as well or better than a fund does, or employ relatively simple bond strategies with government debt or high grade corporates, for example. But in a thinly traded, small, under-researched area like convertible securities, the investor almost has to have a professional manager, or not invest at all.

- **The underlying security instinctively does the right thing almost all the time, relieving you of the last vestigial temptation to be a market timer.** With most securities you have to do something (i.e. sell) to stop it from taking your portfolio down. A convert will stop going down all by itself. You don't even have to pull the ripcord. When you hit the area where the yield supports the price, the parachute opens automatically. Conversely, if you're still hiding out in "mode chicken," thinking a rally can't be the real thing, the convert will listen to the tape, not to you. The convert spreads eagle wings and soars, without you having to do anything.

On to **THE CONCEPT,** then.

SUPERSTAR: *The more we go over your financial needs and your risk tolerance, the more I think we have here a classic conflict between your head and your heart. Your head says, "The only way I'm going to get where I need to go is to patch together some serious growth of capital over the next ten years, and that means stocks." And your heart keeps saying, "Safety. Income. And I support a constitutional amendment to take October 19 out of the calendar and replace it with an extra long Saturday in July." (Grinning:) Is that a fair statement of the case?*

PROSPECT: (Grinning ruefully in return — but grinning, and that's all that counts) *Yes. I suppose when you put it that way, it doesn't sound especially rational. But you have to be who you are. And that's who I am.*

SUPERSTAR: *That's terrific! And I appreciate your being so candid with me. Because my job is a lot like a doctor's, in a way:* **I can't cure you unless I know your symptoms.** *As it turns out, the "bug" you have is very common, and not at all serious. There's an instantaneous cure, and you don't even need a prescription.*

What you need is a portfolio of securities that act like common stocks when the market is rising, but suddenly start behaving like bonds — plenty of stability, lots of current income — when the stock market is hit hard. There is such a portfolio, and it's run by some of the most reliable, most experienced money managers I've ever known. Best of all, four minutes from now, you'll understand it completely. May I tell you about it?

PROSPECT: *I insist, bubba.*

SUPERSTAR: (*Launching into* **Point #2: THE PEOPLE**) *My firm has an excellent relationship with a large, very well-known money management firm called The Gronsky Group. The Gronskys manage a total of about four billion dollars for institutions as well as for investors like us. Now, my firm can refer clients to a lot of money managers, but — **when the symptoms are like yours —** only The Gronskys will do. That's because:*

● *Their risk profile is strikingly similar to yours. Which is to say:* **They hate risk.** *They want to participate in rising stock markets, but they want to be hiding out in bonds whenever the bear counterattacks.*

● *But they're not market-timers ... they believe, as I do, that nobody consistently times the markets well, and that market-timers always underperform steady, conservative investors.*

● *So one of the Gronskys' specialties is a whole class of assets that act like bonds because they are bonds; they have a credit rating, a fixed maturity date, and a very competitive interest rate. But, in rising stock markets, these bonds rise right along with their issuers' common stocks. Because they can be converted into stock ... and that's why they're called convertible bonds.*

I know you'll have a lot of questions about how this works in practice. But just stay with the concept for another minute or so. Think about it — a professionally managed portfolio of securities that sits there acting stable and throwing off a good current income whenever the stock market gets the flu, but which rises right along with the stock market when the market feels healthy again. *And the portfolio never stops throwing off all that income!*

With the scent of income still in the air, the superstar glides into **Point #3: THE INVESTMENT AND WHAT IT DOES FOR YOU.**

SUPERSTAR: *The portfolio is called — no surprise — The Gronsky Convertible Securities Fund. The total size of the portfolio is about $300 million — large enough to give you more than enough diversification. Heck, it owns almost 100 different bonds. But small enough to have a lot of flexibility and quick response.*

The fund is run very defensively — here's the issue of risk-aversion again. They only buy investment-grade convertible securities, so you always own the cream of the crop. And they usually hold a pretty high cash position — at least they have since I've been buying it, and that's almost ten years now.

The current income usually runs about 6%, but the total return over the last ten years has averaged 17%. I know that seems like an awful lot, coming from a portfolio of defensive, high-quality debt instruments. But the return just shows you what convertible bonds, managed by very smart people who specialize in them full-time, can do for you.

If you wish (it's optional) you can venture into **Point #4: HOW IT WORKS.**

SUPERSTAR: *I don't want to bore you to tears with the gearworks, here, but I would like to show you one example of how a convertible bond works in real life. Here you see the fund owns $5 million in Hippocrates Healthcare Centers 8% convertible bonds due in 2001. Those bonds, as I remember, were issued in 1986, and I think the Gronskys told me that's when they bought 'em.*

Anyway, the bonds are convertible into Hippocrates common stock at $25 a share, so a $1,000 bond can be exchanged for 40 shares. Well, Hippocrates Healthcare stock closed on the NYSE today at 30. So the bond closed around $1,200 — because that's what the bond is worth if you converted it into stock tomorrow.

If the stock goes to 50, what'll the bond be worth? (Wait for the answer. If the prospect doesn't have it on the tip of his tongue, your decision to use Point #4 is starting to look questionable, to put it mildly.) *Right. The bond will go to $2,000 ... 40 shares times 50 bucks.*

But suppose the market does one of its occasional swan dives, even while Hippocrates Healthcare continues to do well. And suppose the stock goes to 20, or even 15. What'll happen to the bond, do you think?

Well, depending on where interest rates are, the bond will probably go back to around $1,000. There, its 8% yield, and the fact that Hippocrates does have to redeem the bond at $1,000 one day, will probably keep it from falling much further. It's acting just like a bond again.

That's how it works. When the stock market is acting rational, the convertible bond rises along with the underlying common. When the market is acting depressed, the convertible turns back into a bond ... **and pays you to wait for the market to return to its senses ... which the market always does.** *As I say, that strategy has been good for an average 17% annual return over the last ten years.*

Last stop, **Point #5: RISKS/LIMITATIONS.**

SUPERSTAR: *Now, remember, you are buying a portfolio of bonds, here, and you need the folks who borrowed your money to make good on their promise to repay you. That's why having a great professional manager like Gronsky, watching credit quality like a hawk, is so critical. Considering all that, is $____ an appropriate "dosage of this medicine" to start with?*

Convertible securities funds give you a lot of advantages. But they also afford a lot of opportunities to shoot yourself in the foot if you allow your penchant for overexplaining the technicalities to muddy the pure conceptual water.

SUMMARY

- **THE CONCEPT** of this chapter is a portfolio concept: the growth potential of stocks combined with the safety and income of bonds within the same fund.

- Though anything that increases safety and decreases risk may appear easier to sell, selling a portfolio is inherently trickier than selling a single investment.

- A balanced fund is an excellent, right-down-the-middle way of taking a client's real emotional temperature.

- Forget labels, ratings and classifications. Within certain obvious tolerances the "best" fund is the one that feels right to you, and to the people who rely on you.

- They don't call them "growth-and-income" funds for nothing; the primary emphasis is still growth. The debt component is an anchor to windward that enhances income a bit and — far more important — deadens market sensitivity. Be careful how you make the last point, though. Never say the "V" word first.

- The way you sell growth to a conservative investor is by stressing dividend growth versus inflation, rather than stock prices and net asset value.

- "Classic" balanced funds (roughly half stocks and half bonds) are a comfortable concept and an instant "rich man's portfolio." They're like Sara Lee: Nobody doesn't like them. Prospects may want either more safety or more sex appeal, but nobody will ever get mad at you for presenting a classic balanced fund.

- A balanced fund's long-term record is very much a function of compounding the relatively high current income, and an excellent way to get people to give up managing their own portfolios.

- Convertible securities act like eagles in rising markets and chickens in falling markets. Moreover, convertibles are a market the individual investor would have great difficulty mastering on his own, which is one of the key arguments for owning a fund.

SUMMARY *(continued)*

• Convertible funds afford you tremendous opportunity to bury yourself by overexplaining. Beware the proclivity for unwanted nuance; try not to answer questions nobody asked you.

15

How to Present Bond Funds: Government, Corporate and Municipal

Bond funds are the hardest to present using our overwhelmingly conceptual Universal Five-Point Presentation. Why?

**DEBT BUYERS DON'T CONCEPTUALIZE —
THAT'S WHY THEY'RE DEBT BUYERS.**

A true believer in debt securities has room in his soul neither for a lot of romance nor a lot of trust. The former is the reason the debt buyer doesn't invest in stocks, and the latter is the reason he does "invest" — if that's what you call it — in bank certificates of deposit.

And yet you can't and shouldn't ignore bond funds. They are the next logical refuge for the genuinely horrifying percentage of assets investors have buried in the twin black holes of cash equivalents (money funds) and CDs. Look at the chart below from the November 1990 issue of *Money* magazine.

DISTRIBUTION OF ASSETS	
Category	**Percentage of financial assets**
Certificates of deposit	21.8%
Cash/Equivalents	21.6%
NYSE stocks	21.0%
Taxable bonds	15.4%
Small-company stocks	6.6%
Municipal bonds	4.7%
Bond funds	4.0%
Equity funds	3.5%
Real estate securities	0.8%
Gold and mining shares	0.6%

A staggering 21.8% of assets is in CDs and 21.6% is in cash equivalents. Only 4% is in bond funds, and 3.5% is in equity funds!

The last two statistics speak volumes, as well. In 1970, according to the Investment Company Institute, less than 10% of all mutual fund assets were in bond funds. Today, after two decades of exponential growth in total fund assets, bond funds account for more than half of mutual fund assets held outside money funds.

The vast preponderance of money is buried in CDs and money market funds for the wrong reasons. In the case of CDs, government insurance is the motivator. In the case of money funds, it's total liquidity and the *perception* that net asset value will always be $1.00 (although nowhere is the number guaranteed). CDs are bought out of fear and loathing; money funds reward the decision not to decide.

A lot of the cash in CDs and money funds would be better off in bond funds. Our job is to help people see why. But the not-very-attractive twin psychologies of "fear and loathing/love to not decide" are tough nuts for most of us planners/salespeople to crack. We don't think that way, and we don't instinctively care much for people who do think that way.

Let's administer a spot quiz to see if you have been internalizing the major theme of this book sufficiently to deduce the only way to break into this market.

SPOT QUIZ

There is only one way to reach the "fear and loathing/love to not decide" crowd and get them to start nibbling at bond funds. Circle the letter below corresponding to the one correct way:

(a) Show the prospect the pure intellectual truth and beauty of GNMAs.
(b) Plead.
(c) Show how corporate bonds provide a higher return.
(d) Tell the prospect all the banks are going out of business.
(e) Tell the prospect the FDIC fund is bankrupt.
(f) Show the prospect pictures of your children.
(g) Get the prospect to trust you.
(h) Show the prospect the Morningstar report that says your fund is 5-star.
(i) Show the prospect a picture of the president of the bank that holds your home mortgage.

Let's decide by process of elimination. Hyperbole is out, so (d) is disqualified. Most of the S&Ls are going out of business, but only some of the banks. Besides, you don't win the confidence of essentially frightened people by frightening them even more. So (e) is out, too. These people think everybody's out to get them, so (f) and (i) won't work. You'll get no sympathy — that also disqualifies (b).

Higher return means higher risk to this group, and besides, they're obsessed with safety, not income. So (c) is a non-starter. And (a) will send them screaming from the room.

If the prospect doesn't trust you, why would he trust a rating service he never heard of? That lets (h) out … and leaves stark, simple (g) — "get the prospect to trust you."

Of course, **with people who fear anything but a government guarantee or who can't make up their minds, THE CONCEPT is trust.** Greater returns, greater efficiency, greater diversification … those are highly desirable attributes of bond funds. But those attributes only start to register with people as they come to rely on you and trust you.

A little dissatisfaction with the yields on CDs and money market funds would go a long way toward helping our cause, as well. You know when this type of prospect was happiest? Back in 1981, when CDs were paying 15% and money funds 17%. Never mind that their *real* return was negative after taxes and inflation. The *nominal* rates were very high, and that's all folks cared about. But, many believe we're in for a period of relatively low inflation and relatively low interest rates in the early 1990s. So CD and money market savers may be in for some "reverse sticker shock."

By and large the individual investor has no real sense of the yield curve. He doesn't think in terms of yields relative to other yields. Higher nominal rates make him happy, and lower nominal rates make him sad. When he's sad — when he's dissatisfied with low rates — he may be willing to look at alternatives. That's about all you can ask.

In this product segment, you want a tailored approach for each of three broad categories of bond funds: government, corporate and municipal. Let's start with governments.

PRESENTING GOVERNMENT AND GOVERNMENT-INSURED BOND FUNDS

The single most important element to help people become

comfortable with a bond fund is to relate the investment to their own experience. Otherwise the fund investment may be just too mysterious, and therefore intimidating. Try this:

SUPERSTAR: *Did you ever invest in a bank certificate of deposit?*

PROSPECT: *Do it all the time.*

SUPERSTAR: *Do you do it for a year at a time, or do you go longer?*

PROSPECT: *Kind of depends on interest rates. They're nothing to write home about right now, so I do 'em for a year.*

SUPERSTAR: *Got it. When you go down and buy a one-year CD, what do you think the bank does with the money?*

PROSPECT: *Haven't the foggiest, old boy.*

SUPERSTAR: *They buy a one-year U.S. Treasury note.*

PROSPECT: *Fascinating. Why do I care?*

SUPERSTAR: *Because the bank is getting a higher rate on a federally guaranteed security than it's paying you. Their profit is the difference.*

PROSPECT: *Keep talking.*

SUPERSTAR: *Don't have to; I can see you've already got the message. Why not own the Treasury paper yourself? The guarantee is the same, and the rate is higher. In fact, why not own a whole portfolio of US Government-guaranteed debt and pull in more interest than CDs in the process? Did you know you could do that?*

Or, how about introducing the concept of government-insured Ginnie Maes. It's a little dicier, but might be worth the effort.

SUPERSTAR: *Got a mortgage on your house?*

PROSPECT: *Yup. (Or, if answer is no: "Congratulations. Remember when you did have a mortgage?")*

SUPERSTAR: *Every month you pay some principal and some interest to the bank, so the loan is self-liquidating, right? The ending balance of the loan is zero.*

PROSPECT: *Yup.*

SUPERSTAR: *Know who's holding your mortgage note right now?*

PROSPECT: *Sure, the bank.*

SUPERSTAR: *Probably not. See, here's where it gets interesting. Chances are the bank packaged your mortgage with a whole bunch of others and sold them. By selling your mortgage the bank got the money to make a whole new series of mortgages. The new owner of your mortgage probably bought a government guarantee, and then sold the guaranteed mortgages to other investors.*

Your bank still services the mortgage — collects the payments, sends you statements — but the people who are getting your principal and interest are probably fishing or playing golf somewhere.

It's a great deal for the guy who owns your mortgage, because he has a good loan plus a government guarantee. Last but not least, he's earning interest that just blows the doors off anything he could get — or you could get — on a bank CD.

Plus, he doesn't have to wait to maturity to get his principal back, like you have to do in a CD. Because you're paying him interest and principal in every month's mortgage payment.

PROSPECT: *What kind of interest is he getting?*

SUPERSTAR: *What kind of interest are you paying?*

PROSPECT: *About 10-1/2%, I guess.*

SUPERSTAR: *Well, then, after transaction costs, and the cost of the government guarantee, I guess he's getting 9.5%-10%, somewhere in there. Depends on where interest rates were when he bought the mortgage — just as it does in a CD.*

I can see you're really interested in this. Want to hear about a nifty way of getting on the receiving end of other people's mortgages ... with a government guarantee in the bargain?

PROSPECT: *You bet I do.*

The washout will still be only 20% through a long, abstruse, but technically correct explanation of Ginnie Mae pass-throughs while you're already signing your guy up.

The superstar is relaxed, friendly, interested, interesting, non-threatening, non-technical, and conversational. This is a dialogue, not a monologue. He's saying: **the entry-level bond fund is a government securities fund,** whether it's comprised of Treasury paper, agency paper, mortgage-backed securities, or all of the above. The reason is simple: You get a better yield without giving up the government guarantee. It's hard to dignify the approach by calling it a "CONCEPT," but that's what it is.

So **the presentation for government bond funds runs something like this.**

SUPERSTAR: *Mr. Prospect, one of the best aspects of my job is that I can go around helping people make slight improvements in the way they invest ... because, in the long run, even slight improvements can lead to big differences in results — especially when you're compounding your returns. Can you see what I mean?*

PROSPECT: *I guess so.*

SUPERSTAR: *One of my favorite targets for slightly improving portfolio performance is the bank CD.*

People don't like CDs much, and I don't blame them. The interest rate is never really competitive — and, over the last ten years, it's cratered, down from about 12% to about 7%. CDs are not really liquid — you have those killer penalties if you withdraw early. And worst of all, if you lock the money up and interest rates go higher — well, they go higher without you. And still, people hold more CDs than any other financial asset except cash. And do you know why?

PROSPECT: *Sure I know why. Because your principal is government guaranteed.*

SUPERSTAR: *(With great excitement, as if he and the prospect had just discovered a cure for a major psychological illness) Exactly!! And yet anybody can get the same guarantee directly from the government, and earn higher interest rates in the bargain, because you eliminate the middleman — the bank! Once you know how to invest this way, CDs look like a fairly bad trade. Want to see the alternative?*

PROSPECT: *Reckon I do.*

SUPERSTAR: *My firm has a very special relationship with a large, well-known money management organization called The*

Gronsky Group. The Gronskys manage a total of four billion dollars for pension plans, university endowments, and municipalities, as well as for investors like us. We can refer our clients to just about any money manager, of course. But for people who want high income and government guaranteed investments, we feel that only the Gronskys will do. That's because:

• *they manage $1.1 billion of government-guaranteed debt, so they can afford to have a team of government bond experts watching markets full time;*

• *the portfolio contains forty different bonds with varying maturity dates. So, you never have to worry that you made the wrong bet on which way interest rates are headed, because a portion of the portfolio is constantly rolling over; and*

• *the average maturity is only five years.*

The portfolio is called Gronsky U.S. Government Securities. Over the past five years, it's provided a current income stream — which you can take as monthly checks or leave to compound — of about 9.75%. You never have to make a maturity decision, roll over your CDs, or anything like that — ever again. You can add to, or withdraw from, your account at any time. You're totally liquid and totally flexible. Best of all, you'll always get the highest yield available from securities backed by the full faith and credit of the U.S. Government. In other words, the full taxing and borrowing power of the United States stands behind the bonds that provide you with each month's check.

Now there are certain limitations to this kind of investing. But I think you'll agree that they don't come close to the benefits.

First of all, you will see — if you bother to look — small variations in the price of the shares, as interest rates change. But I think that's a very small price to pay for instant, daily liquidity.

And the yield will change, very slowly over time, as interest rates rise and fall. But, here again, you'll always be getting the market yield on a billion dollar, diversified, professionally managed government bond portfolio.

Now considering all that, have you got a CD rolling over, or some excess cash in your money market fund, that could be working harder for you in Gronsky Government Securities?

I deliberately left out the headings (Point #1, Point #2, etc.), because by now you should almost hear them clicking over in your head. You should be saying, "Right; that's THE CONCEPT ... these are THE PEOPLE ... bang, bang, bang; there go the silver bullets ... here's THE INVESTMENT ... RISKS/LIMITATIONS ... trial close."

There aren't a lot of high-flying subliminal messages in the presentation, but you may have noticed a few variations and special zingers. They weren't unintentional — nothing in these presentations is unintentional. The variations amplify certain strengths of a government fund and calm some anxieties.

- *"... the Gronskys manage ... four billion dollars ... for pension plans, university endowments, and municipalities as well as investors like us ..."*
  MESSAGE: Notice the phrase expanded from "the Gronskys manage ... for institutions." We're punching up the Gronsky Group's specific institutional credentials, here, to give our prospect a warm feeling and to replicate the trust he has in his bank.

- *"... forty different bonds ... you never have to worry that you made the wrong bet on interest rates ..."*
  MESSAGE: Debt buyers, as a class of people, are relatively insecure and fear criticism. If they never have to make an investment decision again ... wow! How error free can you be? Get it?

- *"You never have to make a maturity decision, roll over your CDs, or anything like that ..."*
  MESSAGE: There is such a thing as psychic income, you know. You're relieving people of a lot of anxiety, here ... because of who you are, and because of the way you say what you say ... *not* because you're an expert on government bonds.

- *"... you'll always get the highest yield available ..."*
  MESSAGE: Shoots down the variable return argument, and makes the client, in a sense, always "right" about interest rates.

- *"... you will see — if you bother to look — small variations ..."*
  MESSAGE: Another corollary of Murray's Subway Law — if you don't look up the little squiggly price changes in the paper every day, they're *not there!*

People respect a real financial professional once you reach them emotionally, and they will respond to your signals. **Prospects will worry about what you signal them (almost entirely non-verbally) to worry about.** And they stop worrying when you signal not to worry.

Expect first-time buyers of a government securities fund to be fairly load-sensitive. In fact, all yield buyers are deeply suspicious of "hidden" costs. So, be careful to quote yields in terms of the gross price of the fund's shares, not in terms of net asset value. Or, plan to attack the load issue somewhere in the presentation — which, as you've seen, is really not my style. (We'll unload on the load issue when we get into Q&A/objections handling, because I believe the discussion belongs there. In the meantime, just realize load is a much larger issue to a buyer of current yield than to a buyer of growth or total return.)

Most people's perception of yield is much too simplistic. You can convince prospects to buy into the concept of a government securities fund, but then they'll find three others that "yield more." Well, maybe they do and maybe they don't. Anybody can juice up the current yield on a government portfolio by lengthening the average maturity, adding options, or buying higher-coupon GNMAs that are more likely to be pre-paid. So, you're right back to the threshold issue: THE CONCEPT is trust — the trust that you make people feel, for you and the Gronskys.

Remind people of what they know, instinctively: Markets are generally efficient, so higher yield almost always entails higher risk.

SUPERSTAR: *Mr. Prospect, if we do business together for another twenty years, I think I can **guarantee** you that I'll probably never — and the Gronsky Group won't — offer you the highest yielding security of its kind. There's always somebody out there willing to jazz up current return by taking risks.*

But I'd genuinely like to be your primary financial advisor for decades to come. So I have to be able to look you in the eye and say: 'I'm responsible for your owning this investment, and I'm proud of it.' Among other things, I'll never have you straining for the last eighth of a point in yield. That makes sense to you, doesn't it?"

PRESENTING CORPORATE BOND FUNDS

Corporate bond funds make the most sense in tax-deferred accounts, with their lovely ability to compound high levels of income. And that's great, because retirement accounts — IRAs, rollovers, 401(k)s, etc. — offer tax deferral and are hideously overloaded with CDs, GICs and other instruments where an investor gives up yield to protect against a risk of loss which, long-term, isn't really there.

If you're going to be a real professional, you need to know where CD rates have been over the last five, ten and twenty years. So copy this chart, and keep it handy.

A HISTORY OF CD RATES 6-Month CD Rates*			
Year	**Rate**	**Year**	**Rate**
1969	7.91%	1980	12.99%
1970	7.65%	1981	15.77%
1971	5.21%	1982	12.57%
1972	5.02%	1983	9.27%
1973	8.31%	1984	10.68%
1974	9.98%	1985	8.25%
1975	6.89%	1986	6.50%
1976	5.62%	1987	7.01%
1977	5.92%	1988	7.85%
1978	8.61%	1989	9.08%
1979	11.44%	1990	8.17%
*Annualized Average Monthly Rates Source: Federal Reserve Board			

You also ought to be able to **offer prospective clients illustrations of returns from compounding CDs versus compounding in bond portfolios** made up of the debt of America's greatest corporations —graphic proof of the terrible price they pay for risk aversion.

Also, plan to know the portfolio managers' general philosophy, as well as their current thinking, on investing in the corporate debt markets. Become familiar with the portfolio, and be able to cite some of the larger positions in high quality, household-name issues . . . just as you did with equity funds.

The phrase "corporate bonds" is an abstraction to most people, and abstractions are frightening to someone who's emotionally incapable of conceptualizing — like a bond buyer. But, the name General Electric Credit Corp. is specific, comforting, and attractive. So are AT&T, Duke Power, and General Motors. **No one thinks great companies aren't going to pay their debts, so know and use the names of the portfolio companies.** You'll make the fund come alive for people, and make yourself a knowledgeable professional. Remember: **You are seen in the light of what you sell.** Offer people quality, and you *are* quality; offer people schlock, and you are schlock.

The last point is very important because, in a corporate bond fund, you're moving the prospect away from the safety net of a government guarantee. Clearly, you're investing for the significant pickup in current return (again, a critical factor when you're compounding toward a future goal), believing the concomitant increase in risk is, particularly over the long term, well worth taking.

And there, in case it went whizzing by you too quickly, is THE CONCEPT: a professionally managed, broadly diversified portfolio of high-grade corporate bonds, affording very significant potential for incremental yield over guaranteed instruments, with little or no real incremental risk. (*Perceived* incremental risk is, as always, another factor. In the end, what you think doesn't matter; only what the prospect thinks matters.)

So **here's what the corporate bond fund presentation might sound like.**

SUPERSTAR: *Mr. Prospect, given the fact that you're only ten years from retirement, I can sympathize with your desire to keep your IRA assets (or 401(k), or whatever) in safe, sure investments. But, compounding interest is the critical issue in determining what you'll have to retire on. I think you're paying a terrible price for safety by keeping such a large percentage of your assets in bank CDs. I'd like to offer an alternative suggestion for part of that money, if I may.*

PROSPECT: *Suggest away, laddie buck.*

SUPERSTAR: *Your employer has a pension or profit-sharing plan for you and all the company's other employees, right?*

PROSPECT: *To be sure.*

SUPERSTAR: *This may surprise you, but I'll bet if you called the plan's administrator in the morning you would find that a third to a half of the plan's assets are invested in the highest quality bonds of great American corporations.* (Note: If you need a little more excitement in your life, you might consider adding, "And none of the plan's assets are invested in bank CDs." Never mind; forget I said that ... I don't know what came over me.) *Would that surprise you?*

PROSPECT: *Yes, it would.* (Or, "No, it wouldn't" ... makes no difference.)

SUPERSTAR: *Your plan's managers look on high quality corporate bonds as a core holding in a retirement portfolio. Just like you, they're compounding everything they earn, until the day they have to start paying out a retiree's benefits.*

And when you're compounding, relatively small differences in return produce very significant differences in how much money you end up with. For instance, $10,000 compounded at 8% for 20 years is around $46,000, but compounded at 9%, it grows to over $56,000 ... that's a $10,000 difference, or a difference equalling your entire original investment! High-quality corporate bonds don't have a government guarantee, of course. But when American Telephone, or General Electric, or Illinois Power & Light promises to pay ... what other guarantee do you really need? (Stop here for a reality check. If your prospect has not started to tremble and moan, proceed.)

I've found a perfect way for my clients to recreate, inside their own portfolios, what their employers' pension plans are enjoying from corporate bonds. Would you like to see it?

PROSPECT: *With pleasure.*

SUPERSTAR: *My company has an excellent relationship with a large and very well-known money management firm called The Gronsky Group. The Gronskys manage over four billion dollars for institutions, pension plans, university endowments, and for people like us. My firm can refer clients to lots of money managers, of course. But the Gronskys are our choice as the top corporate bond investor we know, and we're very comfortable with them because:*

- *they emphasize quality and consistency;*

- *they practice broad diversification … why, in the $1.5 billion bond portfolio I like for you, they own over **200 different bonds**. There's safety in numbers, don't you agree?*

PROSPECT: *Cut to the chase, kid.*

SUPERSTAR: *Right. The portfolio I have in mind is called the Gronsky High-Quality Corporate Bond Fund. As I said, it's a very large, well-diversified and extremely safety-conscious fund. You can add money whenever you want. And it pays all income monthly, which increases the effect of the compounding. Over the past five years, current income has averaged 9.8%, which is pretty impressive considering the high quality of the portfolio. On the other hand, my clients have come to expect good yield from the Gronsky Group. After all, with $1.5 billion in corporate bonds in this fund alone, they can afford to have a full-time group of bond market professionals watching the markets like a hawk. That's what superior results are made of.*

Now, of course, there are limitations to this kind of investing — as there are in every other type. The income isn't fixed, and, over time, the yield will follow the market for high-quality bonds. But you always know you're going to get the current market yield for a billion-and-a-half dollar portfolio of great quality bonds.

And the price of the fund shares isn't fixed, either. That's the price you pay for instant and total liquidity. But, the benefit goes back to the central issue of compounding. If the price of the shares comes off a little bit, your interest earnings can buy more shares. If the price rises, your interest buys fewer shares. I love that. Because it means that your average cost is always going to be relatively low.

That may not seem like such a big thing now. But I promise you, in ten years, when you're ready to retire, you'll think it was one of the fund's most important features.

Do you have a CD maturing, or some extra cash sitting in a money fund, to start your corporate bond compounding account with the Gronskys?

Keep it straightforward. You notice I didn't talk much about average maturities, for two reasons:

(1) I'm just trying to give you a generic presentation of each major fund type. Average maturity is a refinement.

(2) If you're selling an intermediate-term fund, what do you accomplish by saying so? What's the *benefit* of the feature? Of course: A shorter-maturity portfolio is less v... v... v... volatile. Oh, no! The "V" word! Now do you see why I don't mention it? (Don't worry. If the prospect wants to know, he'll ask. Besides, over ten years of compounding — i.e. dollar-cost-averaging with reinvested income — you'd actually *rather* the fund was more v _ _ _ _ _ _ e. But do you want to try explaining that to the guy?)

Once again, the overwhelming conceptual fit of a corporate bond fund to a risk-averse retirement investor is so great you don't want to clutter the presentation up and obscure the neat fit. So, **resist the temptation to pile on a lot of refinements.** There'll be plenty of time later, as the investor grows to know and love the fund from the inside, to introduce the nuances. First things first.

COMPETING FOR TAX-SENSITIVE MONEY

We've already seen one great difference between the nominal and real rate of return is inflation. The other, of course, is taxes. And taxes — specifically, the avoidance of taxes — on a fixed-income portfolio is the reason municipal bond funds exist.

Municipal bond funds compete, day in and day out, with three basic investments:

1. individual municipal bonds;
2. municipal bond unit investment trusts; and
3. CDs.

Let's size up the advantages and disadvantages of muni funds versus the competition.

● **Individual municipal bonds** — The consumer of individual municipal bonds has already figured out government and corporate bond funds basically don't work after taxes in his bracket. His net after-tax yield is higher with comparable safety from municipal bonds. However, **all but the largest, most sophisticated municipal bond investors underdiversify.**

Usually, underdiversification takes two forms. First, people tend to buy only bonds issued in their home state to beat local taxation. Sure the net return is better, but you're playing legislative Russian roulette, aren't you? Second, people tend to buy bonds of the same general maturity — either very long or very short. Go very long, and your portfolio gets very v _ _ _ _ _ _ e. Go very short, and you're probably putting your liquidity *wants* ahead of your liquidity *needs*, to the great detriment of your yield.

Moreover, in all but the largest municipal bond portfolios, efficient compounding by coupon reinvestment is difficult, if not impossible.

So, although it's a little like preaching to the choir — and although you run a certain risk in saying "my way's better than your way" — municipal bond funds offer the individual bond buyer professional management, several different kinds of diversification, and perfectly efficient compounding through reinvestment.

• **Municipal bond unit investment trusts** — Unit investment trusts (UITs) are essentially fixed, unmanaged portfolios of securities with some common theme. UITs became extremely popular in the early 1970s, after the go-go mutual fund craze of the 1960s crashed and burned in the bear market of 1969-70. Performance mania had encouraged (and richly rewarded) fund managers who took hellacious risks toward the end of the 1960s. The result was many widely owned funds performed quite a bit worse than the averages when the market broke. Amid the wreckage, the conviction arose that "professional management," far from being value-added, was value *subtracted.* Hence the rise of the UIT, whose primary attraction was offering a portfolio untouched by human (read: management) hands.

The municipal bond UIT has been far and away the most popular iteration of the format, particularly since the advent of portfolio insurance. (Indeed, for many people, an insured UIT is the only rational way to construct a single-state municipal bond portfolio.) And, for an investor who wants to establish and maintain the consistency and discipline of one investment thesis, a UIT is a pretty good bet.

Still, UITs have some significant drawbacks … or at least, some features that many investors can happily live without. Although there is no management to hurt you, there's no management to help you, either. So, in rising interest rate environments, muni bond UITs — particularly the long-term vintages — can really take a major hit. And they have.

And, if rates take a big tumble, you may sit there, watching your bonds be refunded, one by one.

There's no manager to shorten maturities if a storm's coming, or lengthen them before, or even during, a drop in rates. Trading and swapping opportunities go right by a UIT. So, a UIT's total return and its coupon are essentially the same if you hold to maturity. By contrast, a lot of better municipal bond mutual funds have captured total returns significantly (200 to 300 basis points) higher than the coupon yield, through active management.

The fact is, both mutual funds and UITs fit into a nicely diversified tax-exempt bond portfolio. You just need to understand the strengths and limitations of both.

• **CDs** — Municipal bond funds compete easily with CDs. But, most planners and salespeople attack this problem the wrong way: by showing a tired old chart of taxable equivalent yields. Accurate, but not particularly motivational.

A better bet is to take the net yield after taxes on, say, a $200,000 CD, and **show how much less you'd need to invest in a municipal bond fund to earn the same income.**

Suppose you could buy a $200,000 CD with an 8% current return. In the 28% tax bracket, you net $11,520. To have the same dollar return from a municipal bond fund that yields 6.5% (net of the sales charge), you only need to invest about $177,000. You have an extra $23,000 to invest for additional income, spend, or even put into an equity mutual fund as "mad money." Create this exercise yourself, using current CD rates and a municipal bond fund that you like. The illustration will be a real eye-opener, both for you and for your CD-addicted prospects.

PRESENTING MUNICIPAL BOND FUNDS

As in the earlier sections of this chapter, let's just concentrate on presenting the highest quality municipal bond fund. (We'll cover presenting higher yield municipal bond funds, and "junk" bond funds, in the chapter on "Niches.")

In constructing a generic presentation for high-quality municipal bond funds, let's not prime the pump by selecting one of the prospect scenarios we used so far. Let's talk to a guy who really should be paying more attention to tax-free income and buying the mutual fund format.

Here's **THE CONCEPT** and **THE PEOPLE.**

SUPERSTAR: *Mr. Prospect, you've heard the old, but true, saying that it's not what you make, it's what you keep after taxes that really counts. Some of the highest quality, most liquid fixed-income investments you can make are in tax-free municipal bonds. You're well into the 28% tax bracket, aren't you?*

PROSPECT: *Sure am.*

SUPERSTAR: *Well, no safe, liquid, taxable fixed-income investment will give you the same after-tax return as a municipal bond. But, in the long run, success isn't a function of picking one **type** of bond over another, or even picking one particular municipal bond over another.*

Long-term success is about owning a beautifully diversified portfolio of municipal bonds, and having someone smart manage the portfolio under changing market conditions. In a complex market like municipal bonds, a real pro earns you a lot more than he costs, through active management. Does that make sense to you?

PROSPECT: *I don't know yet. Get specific.*

SUPERSTAR: *Glad to. My firm has a special relationship with a large, very well-known money management firm called The Gronsky Group. The Gronskys manage over four billion dollars in assets for institutions as well as for investors like us. My company can refer clients to a lot of money managers, of course. But, when it comes to municipal bonds, we're just very comfortable with the way the Gronskys handle our clients' investments, because:*

*● they have one of the largest research departments in the investment banking business devoted exclusively to municipal bonds. That means lots of highly trained people working to spot exceptional value for **you**;*

● they invest exclusively in top quality bonds, the ones rated single-A through triple-A. They could certainly get higher yields by coming down in quality, but that's not their style — or mine;

● with $2 billion of bonds in the portfolio, you have diversification usually only available to the largest, wealthiest investors or institutions.

Next, **THE INVESTMENT.**

SUPERSTAR: *The portfolio they run for individual investors is called The Gronsky Tax-Free Income Fund. It's a big portfolio containing about 300 different bonds — a great cross-section of debt from the higher credit states, cities, and public agencies. Over the past five years, the portfolio has produced an average cash return of about 7.25%, entirely free of federal taxes. That's very impressive, considering the portfolio's high quality. On the other hand, it's what my clients have come to expect from the Gronsky Group.*

*Now, the things you need to focus on are that you can add to your account whenever you like, in any amount you like ... and take out whatever you want, whenever you want. You can take your income in monthly distributions, or leave it in to compound automatically. In addition to buying the best bond managers I know, you're getting **total flexibility** and **total liquidity** ... all in what I believe is one of the classiest municipal bond portfolios in America.*

There are limits, of course, to any investment. And that's true in Gronsky Tax-Free Income. The yield isn't fixed, and, over time, it will migrate toward the level of current interest rates. But you'll always get the competitive rate on comparable quality municipal bonds.

Nor is the value of your fund shares fixed, not that they'll move around that much. But they'll always accurately reflect the value of the bond portfolio — and again, there's no finer portfolio I know of.

Considering all that, would $____ be an appropriate amount for you to start with comfortably?

* * *

The essential elements in this chapter are always the same: **stress the quality of the people and the portfolio, accept personal responsibility, and don't trim on the risks and limitations.** Though the three kinds of bond funds are very different, the principles involved in selling them are perfectly consistent.

Too much money in this country, with the goals of safety and income, is poorly invested. You have the power to do something about that. But first, you have to begin to forge a bond of trust ... with a class of people who don't trust easily.

Where there's no trust, it doesn't matter how pressing the need or how suitable your solution — you're shooting blanks. Where you can establish trust, there's no limit to what you can accomplish.

SUMMARY

- Far too much capital is buried in the twin black holes of cash equivalents and CDs. It's waiting for you to "establish trust" and propose a better solution.

- Bond funds now account for more than half of all mutual fund assets. They're the logical place for CD and money fund assets to go first.

- THE CONCEPT in government funds is this: With the help of professional management, you can capture higher yields while still holding federally guaranteed debt obligations.

- Relate government bond funds to things an investor can see and touch: what his bank buys with his CD money, or who now holds his home mortgage. That's the easy way to explain Treasury paper and Ginnie Maes.

- Treat the potential for small price fluctuations with dismissiveness. Variability is not fatal, despite what some investors think — the difference between hitting an ice cube and hitting an iceberg is considerable. A long-term perspective helps calm morbid sensitivity to small price movements.

- Make sure somebody is always selling a higher yielding instrument than you are. That's how you keep people safe. Reaching for yield always increases risk. Reaching for the outer limits of yield increases risk dramatically.

- The compounding effect of the incremental yield from corporate bonds in a tax-deferred retirement account just blows the doors off CDs. Most people are not afraid to be creditors of the great American companies. Remember: To the prospect, you are what you're selling.

> ## SUMMARY *(continued)*
>
> - High quality tax-exempt bond funds are an elegant way to introduce people to the joys of tax-free income ... or to save them from the classic mistakes they make buying tax-free bonds on their own.
>
> - This chapter covers the highest quality funds in each of three categories. No options, no high-yield debt, no funny stuff. Keep your presentation as straightforward as are the funds themselves.

16

How To Present Niches — Part I: Global Funds And High-Yield Bond Funds

With our broad survey of the major fund types now complete, let's turn to an examination of some other popular funds. In this chapter, we'll work on crafting presentations for two categories of niche funds:

- **Global funds** — both equity and debt;
- **High-yield bond funds** — both corporate and tax-exempt.

In Chapter 17, we'll cover other niche funds:

- **Gold Funds**
- **Sector Funds** — and other investments specializing in energy, health care, the environment, and real estate.

But before we start work on presenting these products, we would be wise to step back and put niche funds in perspective — particularly with respect to when and to whom you should present them.

First of all, inclusion of any special fund in a portfolio is, for most people, a *want* and not a *need*. Yes, partisans of energy, real estate and gold will argue that no portfolio is adequately diversified without a representative of one or all. Advocates of international investing will point out that owning only U.S. securities is like only buying stocks whose names start with the letters A through E. In fact, a sophisticated iteration of the argument holds that the greatest negative correlation —i.e. the most reliable inverse price relationship — in the universe is between international stock funds and U.S. government bond funds.

Finally, many students of the debt markets believe that high-yield "junk" debt reached extreme undervaluation in 1989-90. And they think the combined forces of economic recovery, de-leveraging of the debtor companies, and a general decline in interest rates will create a great bull market in "junk" as the decade progresses.

Any of these arguments may be true — but all are completely beside the point.

This book isn't about portfolio theory or asset allocation — it's about marketing. We salespeople and planners must take people as we find them, and hope they'll allow us to make small, incremental improvements in their portfolio mix — when and as they learn to trust us.

I think all **niche funds are investments** *clients* **may listen to but** *prospects* **won't** ... if you see the not-too-subtle distinction. Niche funds require one or more layers of additional explanation. In presenting niche funds, you ask the client to have a higher tolerance for ambiguity than is reasonable to expect from folks who don't know you well. In areas where the consensus is highly negative ("junk" and real estate, to name two at this writing), the medium — a scary asset that most people fear — will completely cancel out the message. Which is, of course: "Learn to trust me."

So, niche funds have three very important common characteristics:

(1) they are a *refinement* of a portfolio, not an essential component. They are not matters of life and death, the way common stocks are to real growth of capital;

(2) the client has to give you a significant benefit of the doubt, while you explain why you want him to own one;

(3) niche funds require careful and sometimes complicated explanation.

And because niche funds have these common elements, I call them "low concept" funds. This phrase is used in movie and television production. Simply stated, the easier it is to explain the plot, the "higher" the concept and the wider the potential audience. Here's an example:

Young man falls in love with strange, beautiful girl — doesn't know she's a mermaid who can only stay on land for a week.

This "high" concept movie is the big hit, *Splash*. You get an immediate, complete understanding of the dynamics of the plot, and you're ready for everything that happens (in restaurant, mermaid eats lobster, shell and all; mermaid is captured by evil scientists who want to dissect her; boy swims away with mermaid).

Here are some other "high concepts." Sixteen-year-old-boy-genius-surgeon, the thesis of a television series called "Doogie Howser, M.D.," is extremely "high concept." In ten minutes, without ever having seen the show, you and I could probably dope out most of the plots in the series' first thirteen weeks (cantankerous old millionaire refuses to let Doogie operate on him; thirtyish lady doctor gets major crush on Doogie ... etc., right?). How about this: divorced father and estranged teen-age son switch brains? (They actually made this movie twice one year. I liked the version with Judge Reinhold and Fred Savage, *Vice Versa*. Very "high concept.")

Now check this one out:

*A burnt-out British spy is persuaded by his superiors to stage a fake defection, so he can plant false evidence that will make the East Germans think their own intelligence chief is a British spy. Too late, the Englishman realizes that his "target" really is a British spy, and that this is all a plot to destroy the number **two** guy in East German Intelligence, a very decent man who figured out his boss was really working for London.*

That's the concept of John Le Carre's classic, *The Spy Who Came In From The Cold*. It's a great story, which revolutionized the spy novel when it was published in 1963. But it's about as "low concept" as you can get. It's long, complex, and hard to understand. Even when you read the concept a second time, you may not be sure you get it. ("Wait a minute ... run that by me again, slowly ... international stock funds go *up* whenever U.S. government bond funds go *down* ... or is it the other way around ... oh, it's *both*? Uh ... *why*, again?)

When you're talking to an existing client, most or all of the major issues in your relationship are already resolved. The client knows who you are and what firm you're with. He knows you understand his financial goals and constraints. And he knows your investment philosophy and what kinds of investments you favor. Most important, he's comfortable with you and your philosophy; otherwise he wouldn't be your client.

Because those issues are out of the way, the existing client can focus all his attention on the particular investment you're discussing. You have the opportunity to tell a relatively "low concept" story — one he may have to work on a little to understand.

But suppose your current favorite investment is an equity mutual fund whose objective is aggressive growth. The fund invests mostly in small foreign stocks and can use leverage, sell short, trade futures, and employ complex option strategies.

Talk about "low concept!" This mutual fund makes *The Spy Who Came In From The Cold* seem as simple as a Nancy Drew mystery. Nevertheless, you may decide to take it on, because you believe the fund will be the megawinner of the 1990s.

Fair enough. Just realize you'll have to work very hard, sustain very high levels of rejection, and experience a miniscule closing ratio. That's because the fund you're selling is highly specialized, narrowly focused, and inherently volatile with respect to potential returns. So it makes much more sense to show this fund to friends, not strangers.

Even the plain vanilla funds in the previous chapters can be ranked "high" to "low" in terms of concept. (See accompanying box.) Remember, though, that all these previously discussed fund types are a lot "higher concept" than anything in this or the next chapter.

RANKING MUTUAL FUND TYPES BY "CONCEPT"		
High Concept	**Medium Concept**	**Low Concept**
U.S. Government Bonds	Balanced	Growth & Income
High-Grade Corporates	Equity Income	Convertible
High-Grade Muni's	Aggressive Small Cap	
Growth		

The addition of a seemingly small refinement in a fund can dramatically lower the "concept." A fund that's 60% Treasuries/40% GNMAs is on the same "high concept" plane as a fund that's 60/40 the other way. (It would take a fourth-level black belt washout to disagree with this. Or an MBA. But I repeat myself.) However, if you suddenly add call options and leverage to the fund, the "concept" drops like a free-falling safe. Ditto the addition to corporate or muni funds of even the smallest representation in high-yield bonds.

Generally speaking, then, **the newer and more tenuous your relationship with your prospect or client, the more you should move toward "higher concept" funds.** So the funds in this chapter and the next should probably be discussed only when you and your client are strolling back and forth on a solidly built bridge of trust.

PRESENTING GLOBAL EQUITY FUNDS

Guy jumps out of bed in the morning, flicks on his Panasonic TV, and starts his Braun coffeemaker. He watches the news while shaving with his Norelco electric shaver. A quick shower, and then he puts on his Daks slacks, Turnbull & Asser tie, Harris tweed sport jacket, and Ferragamo loafers. He's in a hurry, so he mixes himself some Carnation instant breakfast, then jumps into his Volvo (in which he just installed a Blaupunkt sound system). Gets to the office, answers a message from his travel agent about his upcoming vacation to Italy on an Alitalia package tour. She also confirms his reservations at a Holiday Inn (owned by Bass plc.) on his business trip to Chicago tomorrow; asks if he wants to grab a quick lunch later at Burger King (owned by Grand Met). He declines politely, redials his Toshiba cordless phone, calls you, and asks what you like today. You say the Gronsky Global Equity Fund. He says: *"I just don't get the concept of global investing!"* (To which you reply, with your debonair savoir-faire, "Au contraire.")

If global investing was any closer to this guy's life, THE CONCEPT

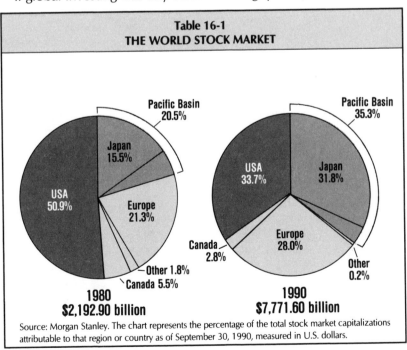

Table 16-1
THE WORLD STOCK MARKET

Pacific Basin 20.5%
Japan 15.5%
USA 50.9%
Europe 21.3%
Other 1.8%
Canada 5.5%

1980
$2,192.90 billion

Pacific Basin 35.3%
USA 33.7%
Japan 31.8%
Europe 28.0%
Canada 2.8%
Other 0.2%

1990
$7,771.60 billion

Source: Morgan Stanley. The chart represents the percentage of the total stock market capitalizations attributable to that region or country as of September 30, 1990, measured in U.S. dollars.

would bite him on the, uh, ankle. (Maybe he'll finally understand when he arrives at his hotel in Rome, turns on the TV ... and watches CNN.) And, if a picture's worth a thousand words, the two on the previous page are worth about a million. Notice the U.S. securities markets are only 34% of the total value of the stock markets of the world.

And the pie chart only tells half the story. **In only one year during the 1980s did the U.S. stock market finish among the five best performing markets in the world!** (See Table 16-2)

And if *that* doesn't make your brown eyes blue, check Table 16-3.

Table 16-2 RANKING OF WORLD'S BEST PERFORMING STOCK MARKETS 1980 - 1989				
YEAR		**RANKING**		
	1ST	**2ND**	**3RD**	**4TH**	**5TH**
1980	ITALY +80%	HONG KONG +73%	SING/MAL +63%	AUSTRALIA +55%	U.K. +42%
1981	SWEDEN +39%	DENMARK +25%	SING/MAL +18%	JAPAN +16%	SPAIN +13%
1982	SWEDEN +24%	U.S.A. +22%	HOLLAND +17%	GERMANY +10%	BELGIUM +10%
1983	NORWAY +82%	DENMARK +69%	AUSTRALIA +56%	SWEDEN +50%	HOLLAND +38%
1984	HONG KONG +47%	SPAIN +42%	JAPAN +17%	BELGIUM +13%	HOLLAND +12%
1985	AUSTRIA +177%	GERMANY +136%	ITALY +134%	SWITZ. +107%	FRANCE +83%
1986	SPAIN +123%	ITALY +109%	JAPAN +100%	BELGIUM +81%	FRANCE +79%
1987	JAPAN +43%	SPAIN +38%	U.K. +35%	CANADA +15%	DENMARK +14%
1988	BELGIUM +55%	DENMARK +54%	SWEDEN +49%	NORWAY +43%	FRANCE +39%
1989	AUSTRIA +105%	GERMANY +47%	NORWAY +46%	DENMARK +45%	SINGAPORE +42%

Source: Morgan Stanley Capital International.
Note: Return in U.S. dollars (with gross dividends).

Table 16-3 AVERAGE ANNUAL STOCK MARKET RETURNS*	
FIVE YEARS ENDING 9/30/90	
Spain	30.57%
France	27.65%
UK	19.85%
Japan	19.59%
Hong Kong	19.25%
Germany	15.37%
USA	**14.41%**
*In U.S. dollars (with gross dividends). Source: Morgan Stanley	

Thank goodness it's not quite as simple or bleak. Why? Look at the asterisk at the bottom of the last chart for a minute, and the reason may hit you — average annual return *"In U.S. dollars."* The issue is currency translation, as in the phrase "something gets lost in the translation."

Taking nothing away from the importance of global diversification, you have to realize that a very large portion (Republic Bank's Michael Hirsch estimates as much as half) of the shoot-the-lights-out performance numbers for global funds from 1985 through 1990 came from currency translation. In other words, if you parked your money in foreign currencies and stuck them in a vault, you made money because of relative devaluation of the dollar.

The currency translation factor does not vitiate the performance in any way. Had you the perspicacity to invest in foreign stock markets you would have really earned fabulous returns. But, you shouldn't be selling global funds by extrapolating performance numbers. (Yes, that's right, you shouldn't be selling *any* fund by extrapolating the performance numbers ... *especially* global funds.)

You see, in September 1985 the U.S. and its major trading partners agreed in the "Plaza Accord" on a program of dollar devaluation. The dollar plunged more or less straight down for three years, rallied a bit from November 1988 through September 1989, but then resumed its downward course. By the time of this writing, the dollar had made new lows against the mark, though not yet against the yen. (I don't mean to bore you with a course in international currency. I just want you to understand that *part* of the recent performance of international funds has been caused by the hand of man, not by intrinsic stock market performance.)

However, I don't want you to walk away thinking global funds are an indispensable part of a balanced portfolio only if somebody turns the clock back to 1985, or foreign ministers give you a big assist. Properly understood, global funds are potentially even more likely to be excellent investments in the future, now that the Cold War has ended and the whole world is groping toward capitalism.

For global funds (and for each fund we discuss in this chapter) we'll suggest THE CONCEPT. By now, you should be able to clone the whole Five-Point Presentation from THE CONCEPT, more or less as follows:

- **Point #1: THE CONCEPT** will state the investment/portfolio thesis.

- **Point #2: THE PEOPLE** will say that, for this specialized investment niche, only the Gronskys are to be relied upon. This assertion will be treated as a given, and need not be amplified with three "silver bullets" unless there's one that's an absolute knockout.

- **Point #3: The INVESTMENT** will talk about the fund and its strategy, ritually stressing how the investor could never dream of implementing the strategy himself.

- **Point #4: HOW IT WORKS** — Fageddaboudit!

- **Point #5: RISKS/LIMITATIONS** becomes very important in "low concept" funds, now doesn't it?

Let's **look at a complete presentation on global equity funds:**

SUPERSTAR: *Mr. Client, everything I've learned about you in the time we've been investing together says you are always interested in strategic diversification — in other words, exploring new ways to get greater returns without taking substantially more risk. Do you think that's a fair description of your approach?*

CLIENT: (Looking quite pleased) *I sure hope so.*

SUPERSTAR: *No, there's no doubt about it. You are one of a number of my clients — and it's a distinct minority, I assure you — to whom I'd like to talk seriously about the opportunity to diversify by global investing. Have you ever looked seriously at this concept?*

CLIENT: *Always wanted to; never have.*

SUPERSTAR: *Same here. So recently, I've been spending some serious time with a money management firm that my company recommended to me as our favorite global investor. And I learned some very eye-opening things. Got a few minutes to hear about 'em?*

CLIENT: *I'm all ears.*

SUPERSTAR: *Well, with the whole world now going capitalist, and with Europe set to become one huge economic nation in '92, I'm convinced global investing isn't a vogue or a fad. It's here to stay, and there are some phenomenal opportunities. At the same time, it was obvious to me that I couldn't do the necessary research, or pick individual foreign securities. For global investing, you must use a very smart international money manager, or you'd better not do it at all. Check?*

CLIENT: *Check.*

SUPERSTAR: *So I met with some of the senior guys in my firm, to get some guidance on how to go up the learning curve. Their advice was: Don't even bother. If you want to put serious money to work overseas, you hire a large, very well-known global manager called The Gronsky Group. Our people feel that the Gronskys are head and shoulders above everybody in the field. Not just because they make great returns — although they certainly have — but because they realize that **American investors like you and me have very little risk tolerance for overseas adventures.** That really got my attention. Want to hear some specifics?*

CLIENT: *Desperately.*

SUPERSTAR: *Well, they offer American investors a $250-million portfolio called Gronsky Global Equity Fund. Their concept is pretty simple: (1) find a great, growing business; (2) find the country which is better at that business than anybody in the world; and then (3) find the best local companies. For instance, The Gronskys own stock in great Japanese electronics companies, German heavy machinery companies, Southeast Asian manufactured goods companies — and a couple of superb biotechnology stocks from right here in America! One* *hundred stocks in all — dominant companies in the countries I've mentioned, and also in places like Canada, the U.K. and Australia.*

An investment of $10,000 in Gronsky Global Equity ten years ago has compounded to over $60,000 now. And the manager, Jean-Claude Gronsky, told a meeting I attended that, given the end of the Cold War and European economic unification in '92, he thinks the last ten years were the pre-game warmup.

Now, there are some important risks to this kind of investing. First of all, the falling value of the U.S. dollar has been a big factor in the return — but currencies can move around. And overseas stock markets aren't as liquid as ours. I guess I sound like a broken record, but ... you do this kind of investing either with super professionals or not at all.

I'm suggesting that my more knowledgeable clients start by putting ten percent of their growth capital into Gronsky Global Equity. In your case that would be about $25,000. Does it feel right to you?

(Speaking time: 4 minutes, 30 seconds)

Let's stop and review the subliminal information transmitted here (though you've probably already picked up much more than you would have a few chapters ago).

- *"... everything I've learned about you in the time we've been investing together ..."*
  MESSAGE: I'm not a salesman, and you're not a customer. *We are partners.*

- *"... you are one of a number of my clients ... it's a distinct minority ..."*
  MESSAGE: I know you're smart enough to understand this, *even though most people aren't.*

- *"... I've been spending some serious time with a money management firm ... our favorite global investor ..."*
  MESSAGE: I've done my homework, and these are the right guys. (Remember: It's never the wrong time to hire the right guys.)

- *"... global investing ... not a vogue or fad ... here to stay ..."*
  MESSAGE: This is serious, and you should be a player.

- *"... I couldn't ever learn to do the ... research, or pick ... foreign securities ..."*
  MESSAGE: The superstar never, ever says, *"You* can't do it." Though true, it's vaguely insulting. *So he takes the incapacity and puts it on himself.* And the client instinctively takes an emotional step toward the superstar out of sympathy and understanding. We're not acculturated to confess our limitations to other people; so when we do, people find it immensely attractive.

- *"... something you have to do with a very smart international money manger, or you'd better not do it at all."*
  MESSAGE: In all "low concept" funds, access to difficult markets is THE MEGA-CONCEPT. You hire the best professional guide you can find or you *stay out of the jungle!*

- *"... not just because they make great returns — although they certainly have ..."*
  MESSAGE: My God! The superstar is *belittling* the superb track record! He's saying it's a secondary concern!! *Bravissimo, maestro!*

- *"... they realize ... investors like you and me have very little risk tolerance ... "*
  MESSAGE: All riiiiight!

- *"Their concept is pretty simple ..."*
  MESSAGE: Hey, maybe this global investing isn't so complex after all ...

- *"... the manager ... thinks the last ten years (when the fund took $10,000 to $60,000) were just the pre-game warmup ..."*
  MESSAGE: Friends, this is your author speaking. Whenever I write phrases like that, I realize once again that there's a big part of me which has no shame. I hope you don't mind my sharing this very private, very personal observation with y'all ...

- *"... important risks ... the dollar ... overseas stock markets aren't liquid ...*
  MESSAGE: In "low concept" funds, the risks/limitations point lets you restate THE MEGA-CONCEPT: no pro, no go.

- *"... my more knowledgeable clients ... (put) ten percent ..."*
  MESSAGE: Just a reminder that the superstar thinks this client is smart enough to do this.

- *"Does it feel right to you?*
  MESSAGE: Disengage brain. All ahead full on heart power. Get it?

PRESENTING GLOBAL BOND FUNDS

The Universal Presentation, as always, will take you through 40% of everything you have to do before you need to vary a word. So you'd get all the way to, "Well, they offer American investors ..." before anything changed between debt and equity presentations. From that point on, you say:

SUPERSTAR: *Well, they offer American investors a $150-million portfolio called the Gronsky International Income Fund. (Grinning) GIIF is kind of like a shark that swims through all the oceans of the world, swallowing only those bonds with the* **highest real yield.** *So, for instance, say a one-year Australian government bond pays a 15% coupon. And say the Gronskys think inflation in Australia is a dead duck and that the Aussie dollar will actually rise a little versus the American greenback. A double play. CHOMP! GIIF bites off about $5 million in Aussie government bonds ... and swims away. See?*

PROSPECT: *Got it.*

SUPERSTAR: *Well, over the last five years, the strategy has been good for an average return of 18% per year. Granted, they had help from a declining dollar ... but when you win the Super Bowl, you earn a Super Bowl ring to wear for the rest of your life, even if the other team blew the game. No questions asked. Comprende?*

PROSPECT: *Si, muy bien.*

SUPERSTAR: *Now, there are some important caveats to this kind of investing. First of all, as I suggested, the dollar is a big factor in the return. If you bought the 15% Aussie bond, but the Aussie currency declines 20% against the U.S. dollar ... well, throw another shrimp on the barbie, 'cause your total return is a negative 5%. And overseas bond markets aren't usually as liquid as ours. So, forgive me if I sound like a broken record, but ... you do this kind of investing with super professionals or not at all.*

I'm recommending that my more knowledgeable clients start by putting 5% of their bond portfolio in GIIF. In your case, that's about $20,000. How does that **feel** *to you?*

Of course, global investing has a lot of subsets. Funds aimed at particular regions or countries are the obvious examples. Still, you need not change one syllable of the basic presentation until it's 40% over, and you're on to the specific opportunity.

A WORLD OF CONCEPTS

Here's THE CONCEPT for each of several international approaches, from which you can clone an entire presentation (like the alien in the movie *Starman* who became Jeff Bridges by entering one cell in a lock of his hair).

- **CANADA** — Now a free-trade zone with the U.S.; soon may become part of a hemispheric free-trade zone that includes Mexico. *$200 billion stock market.* Huge reserves of land, zinc, nickel, silver (Canada is already the world's largest mineral exporter). The most stupendous wild card: natural gas — the U.S. needs Canada's huge reserves to kick its addiction to imported oil.

- **EUROPE** — The trade walls are scheduled to come a-tumblin' down in 1992 — leaving you with a unified economic nation of 320 million people with $4 trillion in purchasing power — *the wealthiest single market in the world.*

- **EASTERN EUROPE** — The Rip Van Winkle of regions, awakening from the long, painful slumber of Communism. The paradigm is East and West Germany. West Germany is the most advanced economy after the U.S. and Japan. In East Germany, when the Wall came down, we learned: (1) most manufacturing plants date from the early 1950s; (2) the country had only 40 (count 'em, 40) international phone lines; and (3) only 16% of East German households had phones. Elsewhere: Levi Strauss put up a jeans plant in Hungary, offered twice the going wage, and recouped its capital inside a year!

- **JAPAN** — As one wag said: "The Cold War is over … the Japanese won." Electronics, cars, film and TV production, Rockefeller Center … ignore it at your peril.

According to Morgan Stanley, Japan has:

- 5 out of the world's 10 largest electronics companies;
- 8 out of the world's 10 largest apparel companies;
- 7 out of the world's 10 largest appliance manufacturing companies;
- 8 out of the world's 10 largest utility companies;

- 8 out of the world's 10 largest machinery and engineering firms;
- 9 out of the world's 10 largest financial service firms; and
- 14 out of the world's 15 largest banks.

- **PACIFIC BASIN** — Question: Why did God create the Pacific Basin? Answer: Out of pity for the people who neglected to invest in Japan in 1950. God *always* gives you one more chance ...

Look at the chart of wage rates; suddenly, all will be clear to you.

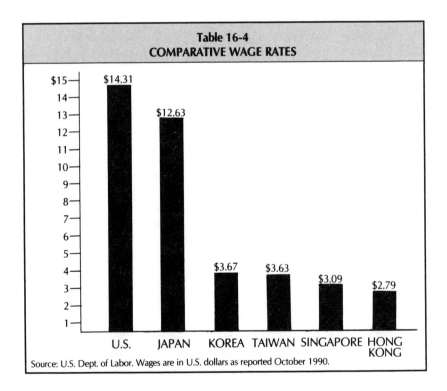

Table 16-4
COMPARATIVE WAGE RATES

Source: U.S. Dept. of Labor. Wages are in U.S. dollars as reported October 1990.

So — and this has nothing at all to do with the U.S. dollar — you shouldn't be surprised at the average annual total return from the respective stock markets from 1985 to 1989. (See Table 16-5 on the next page.) If I can manufacture in the lowest wage-rate countries in the world, it stands to reason that I'm going to beat my competitors' brains out, and my company's stock is going to soar.

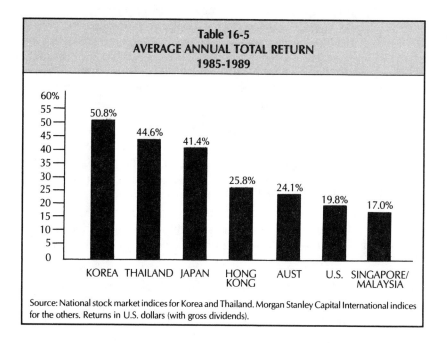

Table 16-5
AVERAGE ANNUAL TOTAL RETURN
1985-1989

Source: National stock market indices for Korea and Thailand. Morgan Stanley Capital International indices for the others. Returns in U.S. dollars (with gross dividends).

CHECK YOUR PULSE

If you aren't excited about trends abroad, your heart is telling you to forget the whole idea of global investing. Somehow this concept is literally alien to you. "Why" isn't really important. Just know that *you cannot sell, because you yourself are not sold.* Live with it. Don't fight yourself. There's so much natural good in you, and so many ways for you to help people achieve their financial goals, that it makes no sense to obsess about refinements you can't get your arms around.

PRESENTING HIGH-YIELD CORPORATE BOND FUNDS

High-yield debt was once the province of a select, highly expert few. Then came a huge, unprecedented boom, and a great wave of popularity. Then, Armageddon.

Investors wanted someone to tell them, despite the extraordinarily high coupon, that somehow high-yield debt was safe. And, for a while in the 1980s, this mutual hypnosis worked ... until the trance snapped. As far as the individual investor is concerned, high-yield debt became the ultimate expression of the awful conundrum:

PEOPLE SAY THEY WANT SAFETY AND INCOME, BUT WHAT THEY REALLY WANT IS INCOME AND THE ILLUSION OF SAFETY.

Let's go to the video tape and replay some history. Understanding some investment history can help you relate to your prospect's mindset and avoid opening some old scars.

Years ago, the debt of companies rated below investment grade offered huge premium yields. The reason: The universe of debt investors — trusts, insurance companies, pension plans — weren't permitted to buy debt rated below investment grade. So the yield differential related to lack of demand rather than to credit quality. In the late 1970s, a new generation of potential junk investors concluded yields were far too high in relation to the real risk. On this high intellectual plane, the modern junk bond phenomenon was born.

In the 1970s, the preponderance of high-yield bonds were once investment grade but the issuers' financials had deteriorated — the so-called "fallen angel" phenomenon. The new junk generation said, "Why can't we develop a new-issue market for high-yield debt of smaller companies which have *not yet become* investment grade?" That's when the market really took off. From $1.5 billion in high-yield bonds issued in 1978, the market grew to $7.4 billion issued in 1983.

Look what happened next. The world discovered the leveraged buyout, and from there it was only a short step to takeover mania. And how was all the activity financed? With high-yield debt (and, it must be said, commercial bank borrowings). New high-yield issues mushroomed to $48 billion in 1986 ... and the deals got bigger and bigger.

Then cracks began to show. A large and prominent issuer of high-yield debt, LTV Corporation, suddenly and unexpectedly filed for bankruptcy in June 1986, defaulting on $2.1 billion in bonds. In November of the same year came the Boesky indictment and the insider trading scandal. A sharp run-up in interest rates in the first half of 1987 led ultimately to the crash (which was triggered by a proposal in Congress to end the deductibility of interest on takeover debt).

The high-yield market staggered through all this, but stayed on its feet. Then came the fateful Friday in October 1989 when the financing for the UAL buyout collapsed. And the voice of a little child was heard, simply stating what everybody knew: The emperor had no clothes. The game was over. Junk went into a huge bear market, compounded by the invasion/recession massacre of 1990, which brought a new wave of defaults.

Suddenly, folks who'd bought into the illusion of safety in high-yield bond funds were unpleasantly surprised. (Not as badly as people who bought *individual* junk bonds, of course.) The press discovered a study done at Harvard suggesting junk defaults were really much higher than anybody suspected. The Great Extrapolator, the media, trumpeted this "news" to the sky, completely ignoring the issue of portfolio yield net of defaults. (Ah, but that's a nuance, and the business of journalism has no time or tolerance for nuance.)

As the smoke clears and the emotions start to subside, I suspect we'll end up where we were at the beginning of the story. Namely, we'll see a growing conviction that high-yield bonds provide a significant long-term incremental return, even after loss through default. In fact, a study by First Boston found junk bond yields averaged 437 basis points over Treasury bonds from 1977 through 1988, while annual losses due to defaults averaged less than 200 basis points. And, that's THE CONCEPT for high yield corporate bond funds. In a diversified portfolio of lower grade bonds …

**THE HIGHER YIELDS
MORE THAN COMPENSATE YOU FOR
THE HIGHER RISK OF LOSS …
ESPECIALLY IF YOU'RE COMPOUNDING THE HIGHER YIELDS.**

In the 1990s, you'll probably see de-leveraging, a return to gradual but sustainable economic growth, and perhaps a period of lower interest rates. So, most likely, **people who eschew high-yield bond funds are doing what the crowd always does: looking through a rear-view mirror and avoiding a brilliant investment opportunity.**

Again, I'm not trying to sell you high-yield bond funds. I'm just trying to clarify the record (which you may have found clouded by emotion or journalism) and state the issues in a useful way. You can consult your own heart, and find out whether you believe this way of looking at high-yield bond funds will, over the long run, prove correct. If you find you *do* believe … then you'll *be* believed.

Typically, you'll want to **take the idea of high-yield bond funds to a client who already has a reasonably well-diversified bond portfolio.** Here's what you might sound like:

SUPERSTAR: *Mr. Client, I recently spent some time talking with the senior guys in our firm who oversee the money managers to whom we refer our clients. Right now, they're pretty excited about a strategy for capturing historically high yields in a bond portfolio, without having to take unacceptably higher levels of risk. Would you like to hear their thinking?*

CLIENT: *You bet.*

SUPERSTAR: *Well, my firm has a special relationship with a large, very well known money management company called the Gronsky Group. They manage four billion dollars in assets for institutions as well as for people like us. We refer clients to a lot of different money managers, of course, but the Gronskys have an extraordinary level of expertise in the high-yield bond area — and that's where our firm thinks there's a great opportunity right now. If you have a couple of minutes, I'll explain the concept to you. OK?*

CLIENT: *Sure.*

SUPERSTAR: *Well, the Gronskys have been doing a lot of research, and they feel that high-yield bonds right now are about where common stocks were early in 1982 — beaten down out of all relationship to reality, with all the major risks behind them, and right on the edge of a long period of superior performance.*

The Gronskys offer individual investors a $1 billion portfolio of about 200 very carefully selected, carefully managed high-yield bonds. The portfolio is called the Gronsky High Yield Fund. And — I found this a little hard to believe myself, at first — they've provided investors with an average return of 13% per year over the last ten years.

And, to hear them tell it, the 1980s were a nightmare. A few of us had a conference call with Dr. Hezekiah Gronsky, who runs GHYF, and he called the '80s "amateur night." He said something else that really struck me, too. He said he's perfectly comfortable when high-yield bonds pay four percentage points over investment-grade debt — but that, right now, the spread is more than eight percentage points! Dr. Gronsky said he thinks that in just a few years, we'll look back at today's market in high-yield debt the way we look back at stocks in 1982.

Both our firm and the Gronskys feel that, in the past, people tried to ignore the incremental risks of high-yield bonds — and believe me, those risks are real. But if you've got a broadly diversified, brilliantly managed portfolio of high-yield bonds, like GHYF, the premium return more than compensates you for the extra risk.

Our firm is recommending that clients with fine bond portfolios like yours take some profits in their investment-grade bonds and create a 10% portfolio weighting in GHYF. Does that sound about right to you?

This presentation says several very powerful things. First, the investment thesis is agreed upon by the highest levels of your firm's management and by your firm's favorite junk bond manager. You make the analogy to another cyclical financial asset — common stocks — at a time when they, too, were the focus of a too-bearish consensus. You state the extraordinary performance of your chosen portfolio, without carrying on about it. You suggest — out of the mouth of the portfolio manager, with whom you've personally spoken — that current yields are extraordinarily high and will come down. And you couch the recommended fund purchase (if this is how your firm really feels) in terms of a firm-wide asset allocation recommendation. The presentation is very powerful — but it will only work if you really *feel* it.

PRESENTING HIGH YIELD TAX-EXEMPT FUNDS

High yield tax-exempt bonds are particularly intriguing, and you can expect to see a growing interest in this investment.

THE CONCEPT: A municipality or public authority may simply decide not to obtain a rating because the costs are so burdensome in relation to the small size of the bond issue. So, the bond may be perfectly safe, but not rated. (Bonds having a relatively low rating also fit here.)

So you sell a high-yield municipal bond fund essentially the same way you sell a fund of investment grade municipals. You just **sell management and its research disciplines a bit harder, and stress the significant yield pickup.** Risks are higher, but broad diversification and really smart management make the risk acceptable for a portion of an investor's tax-exempt fund holdings.

SUMMARY

- Niche funds are "low concept" stories and are harder to explain. They're refinements of a portfolio, requiring the client to give you the benefit of the doubt. For these reasons, they are better suited for clients than prospects.

- THE CONCEPT becomes doubly important when you present "low concept" funds. But from THE CONCEPT, you can easily clone the whole presentation. Cut back on the silver bullets — the client will stipulate to a manager's particular "low concept" expertise, just by virtue of the fact that your firm has chosen that manager above all others.

- Respect a client's "affiliation" needs. When presenting a "low concept" fund, stress the involvement of the senior people in your firm.

- The client can't do "low concept" investing on his own, but don't you dare say so. Take the limitations and put them on yourself. People will find your approach surprising and attractive. Besides, it's true.

- In all "low concept" funds, access to difficult markets is THE MEGA-CONCEPT. Continue to soft-pedal the track record.

- Whenever you find a "low concept" fund that your head likes but your heart doesn't, your heart is right. You have to be who you are, and — especially in "low concept" funds — you have to sell what you love.

- Global funds are great portfolio diversifiers and balancers. They're not a panacea. The track record of the last half of the 1980s is due in part to a swan-diving dollar. Still, the potential for managers who know their stuff is tremendous.

- High-yield corporate debt had a richly deserved comeuppance in the shakeout of 1989-90. But, all the evidence suggests high-yield debt does provide a premium return much larger than the incremental incidence of default.

- In the tax-exempt area, non-rated paper has interesting potential, provided the manager can hack the additional research work.

17

How To Present Niches — Part II: Gold And Other Sector Funds

Let's continue our presentations of "low concept" funds with gold funds and other sector funds (health care, energy, real estate, etc.)

Gold is the ultimate international currency. Gold tells you the sum of the world's expectations for the dollar, more efficiently and dispassionately than any other single asset. When the preponderance of market participants around the globe thinks that U.S. inflation is accelerating, the price of gold in dollar terms will rise. (Or, conversely, the value of the dollar will fall in relation to gold.) And, though it was certainly undervalued by being pegged to the dollar at $35 for so long, gold has turned in a stellar performance since its price was permitted to float back in 1971. (See Table 17-1 on the next page.)

When U.S. inflation is moderate to low, stocks and bonds do well and the price of gold does poorly. Let inflation heat up, and stocks and bonds get hurt, but gold goes up. So, gold is not merely a near-perfect inflation hedge but also a very practical hedge for a stock and bond portfolio. People who know much more about asset allocation than I do say that a 5% to 7% portfolio weighting in gold is an essential insurance policy in a stock-and-bond dominated portfolio.

The insurance analogy is the one to use with clients regarding gold.

GOLD IS LIFE INSURANCE FOR YOUR PORTFOLIO.

You pay the premiums and hope you never collect on the policy. In a sense, you hope your gold holding never "works" ... because if it doesn't your stocks and bonds are performing beautifully.

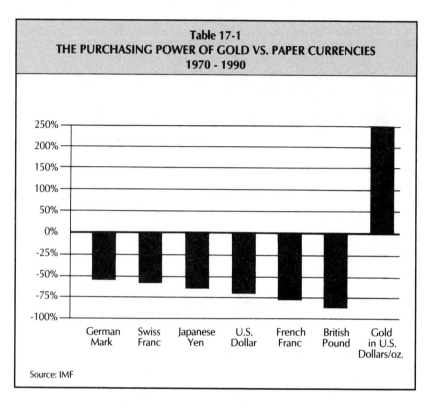

Table 17-1
THE PURCHASING POWER OF GOLD VS. PAPER CURRENCIES
1970 - 1990

Source: IMF

So the presentation goes this way:

SUPERSTAR: *Mr. Client, after the Summer and Fall of 1990, when both stocks and bonds took a major hit, the professionals I exchange ideas with started talking about using gold as a portfolio hedge.*

None of us are gold bugs — and we'll certainly never be part of the doom and gloom crowd — but the 1990 experience was very dramatic. In June 1990, when the Dow Jones Industrials were struggling to close at 3000, gold was lying around at $345 an ounce. In the Kuwait invasion/recession massacre of August through October 1990, the Dow went to 2350 without leaving a skid mark — and suddenly, gold was shining — up 20% at $415 an ounce!

When you do the homework, as my colleagues and I have, you find this relationship has been exceptionally reliable over the twenty years since the dollar was taken off the gold standard. Gold never lies, and always goes in the opposite direction from stocks and bonds. So, adding gold to a stock and bond portfolio keeps performance tacking along on a more steady keel.

But who knows how to play gold? Do you buy bullion? And who knows anything about gold mining stocks? So we had a conference call with the senior guys in our firm who oversee our relationships with money managers. And they came up with one of the best ideas I've heard in a long time. If you have a couple of minutes, I'd like to share it with you.

CLIENT: *I thought you'd never ask.*

SUPERSTAR: *Sorry, I guess I'm really wound up about this idea. You see, our firm has a close relationship with a large, well known money management company called The Gronsky Group. They manage about four billion dollars for institutions as well as for people like us. We refer clients to a lot of money managers, of course, but our top people said that, for expertise in gold and precious metals, the Gronskys wrote the book. They're the people we trust. That's what I really care about, don't you?*

CLIENT: *Absolutely.*

SUPERSTAR: *Well, the Gronskys offer individual investors a $200-million portfolio of about 40 gold-mining stocks from the major gold-producing regions of the world. It's called Gronsky Gold Shares Fund. They also hold gold bullion from time to time, when they think the outlook for gold is particularly good — which, of course, means when they think the outlook for stocks and bonds is particularly spooky.*

Even during the '80s, which was a golden age for stocks and bonds and a time of relatively low inflation, GGSF performed superbly. It had an average annual return of 14% during the decade — as surprising as that may seem, since this was an insurance policy you hope you'll never collect on.

There are some definite limits to this kind of investing, of course. Gold and other precious metals really move around a lot, so you don't want to drive yourself crazy looking up quotes in *the papers every day. And remember, it's a hedge. In a very real sense, you're hoping it won't be a big winner, because the implications for the rest of your portfolio wouldn't be good. So we're recommending that you just put about 5% of your portfolio in GGSF. In your case, that's about $15,000. How does that sound to you?*

Selling people something that both you and they hope won't work out is a relatively difficult exercise. The only defense: It's the right thing to do.

OTHER SECTOR FUNDS

You put part of a client's portfolio in a specific industry or sector for two reasons, each of which requires a somewhat different presentation approach:

- **The "play"** — You may want to "play" the sector because the industry has short or long-term prospects to outperform the overall market. So, you want clients to take a portion of their assets and participate in a professionally run cross section of companies in a particular industry.

- **The hedge** — You believe a particular sector's performance will run counter to the rest of the portfolio in some significant way (like owning gold). Real estate and energy prices, for example, correlate positively with inflation (go up), while financial assets like stocks and bonds correlate negatively with inflation (go down).

A sector recommendation is a fairly sophisticated, "low concept" strategy — often taking a good deal of extra explaining. "Playing" health care, the environment, etc., is easier to explain, and easier for a client to accept, than "hedging" — but "easier" doesn't always mean "better."

LEVEL 1: PRESENTING A SECTOR "PLAY"

Let's see how a particular sector fund play, say health care, might fit into the Universal Five-Point Presentation. As always, THE MEGA-CONCEPT is access to difficult markets. The specific twist in health care is that the industry is too hard to stay ahead of. But you know clients should be participating, because health care is one of the megatrends of the 1990s. So you'd probably say something like this:

SUPERSTAR: Mr. Client, I've been thinking for some time about how to get clients' equity portfolios positioned for the phenomenal growth of health care. You know, health care expenditures in this country hit $750 billion in 1990 — about 12.5% of the gross national product. And health care expenditures are projected to grow at 12% to 15% a year — three times inflation — at least through the mid-'90s. This is one of the great growth industries of our whole investing lifetimes. You can see that, can't you?

CLIENT: Sure, but what do I do about it?

SUPERSTAR: That's exactly the problem. Who knows where the next big breakthroughs are coming? Biotechnology, drugs and pharmaceuticals, diagnostic imaging — I knew I'd never stay ahead of the curve.

So I talked to some of the senior people in my company who oversee our relationships with money management firms. And they gave me what I now realize is the only right answer. If you have a couple of minutes, I can tell you about it very simply.

CLIENT: Shoot.

SUPERSTAR: Well, it turns out that our firm has a special relationship with a large, very well-known money management company called the Gronsky Group. They manage about four billion dollars for institutions as well as for individual investors like us. Our firm refers clients to a lot of different managers, of course. But in the health care area, our guys think the Gronskys are light years ahead of their competition in understanding what American health care will look like five and ten years from now. That really got my attention. Want to hear the specifics?

CLIENT: Very much.

SUPERSTAR: The Gronsky Group offers individual investors a $250-million portfolio called Gronsky Health Care Fund. Gronsky Health Care holds about 50 very carefully researched stocks in all the major disciplines of health care: pharmaceuticals, medical/dental/optical products, biotechnology, medical diagnostic, biochemical research, and the operation of facilities like hospitals and nursing homes.

GHCF has provided investors with about an 18.5% average annual return over the last five years. But what really amazed me *was that GHCF was up almost 20% in 1990 — a year when the stock market really took a beating.*

It shows you that, whatever other issues exist in health care, the industry is completely recession-proof — another reason to include health care in the growth segment of your portfolio.

Make no mistake about it, health care does have serious issues — government regulation and reimbursement policies, rapid technological change, and a chronic need for capital. That's why our guys rely on the Gronsky Group to stay out in front of those issues for us.

We're recommending that 5% of your growth capital be invested in health care, through GHCF. In your case, that's about $12,000. Sound about right to you?

Let's re-cap the sector "play" presentation:

- this industry is one you have to be in;

- the industry is moving way too fast for the individual investor to be able to stay on top of it;

- my guys say hire the Gronskys;

- it's not without risks and limitations, so: **no pro, no go;**

- this amount seems right to me — how does it seem to you?

Combine this approach with the industry-specific CONCEPT, and you can efficiently roll out any sector play that feels right to you. Here's THE CONCEPT for some of the leading sector plays for the 1990s:

- **The Environment** — Our country bore the burden of explosive economic growth for two hundred years. Now, as our economy matures, the environment is presenting the bill. Landfills, acid rain, hazardous waste, air pollution and plain old garbage will demand the expenditure of hundreds of billions of dollars in the next two decades. Companies with products, services and processes in pollution control and waste management will grow at very rapid rates. (Which ones? Trust the Gronsky Group to know.)

- **Computers** — "Transparent computing," the next wave of change, will make computers almost as easy to use as telephones. Huge demand exists in the industrializing areas of Eastern Europe and the Third World.

- **Broadcast and Media** — People everywhere have an insatiable appetite for inexpensive entertainment. Disney World is in Paris and Tokyo. Sony acquires Columbia Pictures; Matsushita buys MCA. Tune in CNN on your hotel TV in Vienna and "I Love Lucy" re-runs in Rio. The whole world says, "I want my MTV." Cable, fiberoptics ... what next?

- **Consumer Products** — Trade barriers going, going, gone. Global media means global advertising. Pizza Huts in Moscow, Pepsi in Pakistan. Who will own the great global consumer franchises?

In summary, sector "plays" give you an opportunity, for a relatively small investment, to have a managed portfolio in a specific industry you think investors should be exposed to over a five to ten year horizon.

You know the trend has many more years to run. But, investors always look at the great stocks — Intel, Disney, Waste Management or Pfizer in their respective sectors — and say, "I missed it." You need an effective way to **overcome the fear that the trend has left without the client.** The answer: Turn a sum of money over to the manager of a sector fund, and let him go fight the battle for you.

LEVEL #2: PRESENTING SECTOR "HEDGES"

If the number-one enemy of a stock and bond portfolio is inflation — and it is — then that's an enemy you have to fight every day for the rest of your life. Sometimes the battle is easier than at other times (i.e. when inflation is more moderate). But you don't ever win the fight, because the enemy never quits the field.

And, if you can't or won't use gold, you have two income-producing operating businesses available in sector funds (and in other forms, as well) that may effectively serve the same purpose.

But, as opposed to gold, THE CONCEPT for these businesses is not primarily hedging. THE CONCEPT is: *a great cyclical business near its low ebb.* In fact, THE CONCEPT in the two sector "hedges" I'm going to describe — energy and real estate — is a long-term cycle so broad and gradual that it utterly defeats any short-term investment approach. (That's why the perspective of journalism — The Great Extrapolator —is the permanent, implacable arch-enemy of the truth about these two businesses.)

And yet both businesses very effectively hedge a portfolio principally composed of stocks and bonds. Energy is an engine of inflation. (You could argue that energy was *the* engine of inflation in the 1970s and early 1980s.) Energy is the ultimate commodity; its price ripples through every good and service produced on the planet. When energy prices are rising, corporate profits are under pressure, as companies struggle to pass on increased energy costs to the consumer. That's bad for stocks.

Energy price-induced inflation also puts upward pressure on interest rates. And, the danger of inflation increases as energy-importing nations are tempted to monetize the increase in their balance of payments deficit caused by rising oil prices. So stocks — and, more painfully, bonds — are under pressure when energy prices rise. Meanwhile, of course, investments in energy do well.

Real estate is another operating business which correlates positively with inflation. Simply stated: Inflation increases the cost of new construction, so new construction ceases ... until, with supply constrained, rents rise to levels justifying new construction again. Higher rents, higher cash flows ... higher values.

The peaks and troughs of these two businesses have been wildly exaggerated over the past couple of decades. And extreme booms and busts (further exaggerated in the case of real estate by the lending policies of S&Ls and banks) make people very emotional, in both directions.

At this writing, in fact, both real estate and oil and gas are psychic free-fire zones as far as most investors are concerned. But where you find great emotion (especially where great consensus surrounds the emotion), you usually have lifestyle-changing profit opportunities ... if you're willing to invest counter to the consensus. Remember: While "contrarianism" is the purest imaginable common sense to professionals, to the folks we counsel it's very "low concept" and always will be. (I say again: Woe betide you, when everybody likes what you're selling.)

But if you can help people take a long-term cyclical approach to these businesses (as opposed to a *USA Today*/six o'clock news/where-did-it-close-today perspective), you may make them some serious money while, at the same time, effectively hedging financial assets.

In crafting an effective presentation straight from your heart, you can't be sure of the answers until you're sure you have the questions framed right ... remember? So, let's just spend a little time pulling some historical perspective together to lay the groundwork for presenting each business.

● **ENERGY** — Energy is something the world had so much of for so long we forgot to keep investing in it. But by the early 1970s, energy demand and supply — and, therefore, energy prices — were on a collision course. (You'll find the best discussion of how America went to sleep about energy — and Japan didn't — in David Halberstam's wonderful book, *The Reckoning*.)

The October 1973 war in the Middle East was the catalyst. Energy prices tripled overnight, and OPEC became the dominant force in energy pricing. Prices began a long upward march — culminating in another sudden doubling in 1979, after the revolution in Iran. (Lee Iacocca described this second energy shock as "the day the Shah left town.") Prices continued upward for another three years, peaking in 1981-82. Then the consensus said prices would keep going up faster than double-digit inflation, forever.

But, conservation had finally become a reality. Businesses and people cut back on energy use. New supply came on line — through exploration and development spurred by higher prices — and a glut suddenly appeared.

Prices crashed, from near $40 a barrel in 1981 to, briefly, $8 in 1986. The independent oil and gas exploration business in this country was liquidated. The city of Houston looked like a saloon emptying out after last call (on the six o'clock news, anyway).

Investment cratered, particularly after the 1986 tax law curtailed the intangible drilling cost deduction and the depletion allowance. The North Slope quietly started a long, downhill slide in production ... with nothing coming along behind. And, after *Exxon Valdez*, opening up new frontiers for exploration looked out of the question. America had gone back to sleep.

But, the cycle was about to re-assert itself, as cycles always do. In 1990, days after OPEC set a benchmark price of $21 — a price that looked like it would stick — Iraq took over Kuwait. And, the price shot to $40 a barrel.

Yes, the price fell right back again (most precipitously, of course, the day the consensus predicted an upward spike — the day the Allies attacked Iraq). But many professionals believe the panicky price action is a warning, pointing a prudent path to investors looking into the 1990s and beyond.

A huge part of the world's reserves are in the Middle East, which may prove to be less stable now than ever. And no new North Slopes are being found, by us or anyone else. Meanwhile, Eastern Europe is resurgent, and the Third World is continuing to industrialize, portending continuing growth in the demand for energy.

Cyclically, investment in energy will surge in the 1990s. And energy investment will produce far-above-average returns for the investor who can be induced to get his head out of today ... and look at the long-term cycle.

With this perspective, by now you ought to be about able to prepare a **presentation for energy funds** in your sleep:

SUPERSTAR: *Mr. Client, I'm part of a professional group — all of us involved in counseling more substantial individual investors — and we meet by telephone once a week to plan our strategies.*

One of the issues we've been researching is the role of energy in the portfolio of the '90s. Energy had a perverse impact on people's portfolios in the '70s and '80s. In the '70s, energy investments performed well, but energy was underweighted in people's portfolios. And then energy really hurt people in the '80s — when everybody owned too much of it and the cycle cratered. Now, by and large, nobody owns energy again. Why? The consensus is you're going to be hurt by sagging prices again — much like what happened in the early 1980s.

But, we see a familiar industry pattern. After a decade of weak pricing, the energy industry is underinvesting, which leads to undersupply, and then to better pricing, and better investment returns. Does this sound completely farfetched to you?

CLIENT: (If the client starts screaming, frothing at the mouth, and telling you how his mother lost her inheritance in the Petro-Lewis programs, you are excused from making the rest of the presentation. If, on the other hand, he says anything like, "No, not too farfetched," you can continue.)

SUPERSTAR: *Well, my group talked to some of the senior people in our Research Department, who had some specific recommendations along the lines of individual stocks like Unocal and Schlumberger. But frankly, individual stocks are **tactics**, and we weren't even sure we knew what our **strategy** should be yet ...*

even though our people agreed that our basic investment thesis is right. So we decided to look for an investment manager who was expert at investing in energy. We talked to the head of our department that selects money managers, and she gave us a terrific idea. If you have two more minutes, I'll tell it to you.

CLIENT: *Please do.*

SUPERSTAR: *It turns out our firm has a special relationship with a large, well-known money management company called The Gronsky Group. They manage over four billion dollars for institutions as well as for individual investors like us. Our firm refers clients to a lot of money managers, of course. But our people feel that, with regard to energy, the Gronskys are in a class by themselves.*

They offer individual investors a complete portfolio, with about $200 million diversified among 50 stocks of companies in every important phase of the energy business. Not just oil and gas producers, but drilling companies — onshore as well as offshore — manufacturers of drill bits and other equipment, and even companies that solve the environmental problems of drilling. The portfolio is called Gronsky Energy Fund.

I want to make it very clear that the Gronskys are not just speculating on the price of oil, here. There are lots of high-risk, high-potential ways to do that, all of which are too rich for my blood.

The Gronskys are investing for a cyclical upturn in exploration and production activity, so the portfolio gives you several different ways to profit from the world trying to replace the reserves we burn up every day. And in this complete energy portfolio, you own four dozen of the best managed, best financed energy companies in the world.

Moreover, investing in the energy business gives your whole portfolio a terrific hedge. If you think back to any period when energy prices surged (1973, 1979, 1990), you'll note that, in general, stocks and bonds were hit pretty hard — but energy issues made people serious money.

There are real limitations to energy investing, of course. Energy prices do tend to gyrate a lot in the short term, and the

> *headlines are always screaming — usually the wrong thing at the wrong time — about energy. So GEF isn't like owning a utility fund. In part, that's why you go with world-class professionals like the Gronskys. And, too, if you wait for the headlines to tell you you're right — then you're virtually guaranteed to be wrong.*
>
> *We're recommending people with fine, diversified portfolios move about 5% into energy via GEF. Does that feel comfortable to you?*

This presentation stresses some fairly interesting points. You and a group of like-minded professionals have been thinking seriously about the issue of energy — in other words, you're not just shooting from the hip. Then, in two sentences, you put the 1970s and 1980s in a proper cyclical perspective — thereby suggesting strongly what the 1990s may be like. You looked at individual stocks, and decided you'd never be able to pick them right ("they're tactics ... we weren't even sure we knew our strategy") — putting the limitation onto yourself, not the client. Remember the words of "Dirty" Harry Callahan: "A good man always knows his limitations." But state them as *your* limitations, not the client's.

So, you went to the head of your asset management group, and she gave you the Gronskys — money managers in a class by themselves. The fund: four dozen of the "best managed, best financed" energy outfits in a "complete portfolio." Next, with nearly surgical precision, you destroyed the price objection that may have been forming in the client's mind. ("This investment won't work because oil prices aren't going to go up." Get sucked into that argument, and you're history.) You said speculating on price is "too rich for my blood," with becoming modesty and conservatism. You repeated the theme of under-investment: We have to replace the reserves we burn up every day. Just common sense, right?

Then you fired off your "hedge" point, which is a honey. In stating risks/limitations, you managed to take a particularly vicious swipe at journalism, bless your heart. Then you did your trial close. Nothing is coincidental (only small children and dead spies believe in coincidence). Nothing is left to chance.

● **REAL ESTATE** — The other great sector "hedge" is real estate, a cyclical business with an unprecedented boom and bust over the last twenty years. For those of you who didn't live through the entire cycle (or who did, but still can't figure out what happened), a quick review is in order.

The beginning of the end was the Tax Reform Act of 1976. In a massive swipe at abusive tax shelter (this phrase was not yet perceived as a redundancy), TRA '76 said if you weren't personally liable for a partnership's debt, you couldn't write off any more than your cash investment. Only one economic activity on the face of the planet was spared from this draconian dictum. Of course: real estate. So, real estate became the only big write-off tax shelter in town. That's when gigantic amounts of capital — doubling and doubling again every year — began flowing into real estate ... *for completely non-real estate reasons.*

This tax shelter frenzy went on for five years. (During the early years of the boom, hyperinflation was obligingly making everyone who owned real estate look like a hero.)

Then, in 1981, the new tulip mania of bricks and sticks went into high gear. Congress was drafting a new tax law, called the Economic Recovery Tax Act ("ERTA"). The prime rate, meanwhile, was in the upper teens, as Fed Chairman Paul Volcker was single-handedly breaking the back of inflation by sucking the money supply out of the economy. The real estate lobby came to Washington and said, "If you really want to get this economy going again, you have to incentivize real estate construction. Because with the prime at 16%, there isn't a nail going in a board anywhere in the U.S. of A."

So, Congress threw into ERTA a radically shortened schedule for depreciation of real estate (the Accelerated Cost Recovery System, for you students of the genre). And just then, Paul Volcker won, and interest rates cratered.

(You may not remember Volcker. He's not on the six o'clock news or in *USA Today* anymore, so, in a sense, he doesn't really exist. He's sort of the Cyndi Lauper of our economic life. But I'll bet you remember your money market fund going from 18% to 6%, fast.)

Real estate thrives mightily on low interest rates and didn't need the added stimulus of the Tax Code at all. But ACRS was pouring gasoline on the fire.

And then, the situation *really* got worse. How do you halve interest rates in a hurry? Why, of course, Watson: the Fed liquefies the banks and S&Ls. And what did the stuffy bankers do with all the money? Right — they threw embarrassing amounts on the real estate conflagration. More fuel for the Overbuilding Firestorm.

The boom ended as suddenly as it started. Congress came out on the front porch at 3:00 AM one night in 1986, and whispered, "No more tax shelter ... period," and then went back to bed. Every developer who could do so rushed to start a new project before TRA '86 went into effect ... and the overbuilding firestorm went thermonuclear.

It would be a mistake to think of the 1986 Tax Act as the straw that broke the camel's back — more like the giant sequoia that fell on the camel, rendering him into a large but very flat camel pancake. Five years later, real estate development had completely stopped; two thirds of the country's S&Ls were gone or going; real estate loans were taking banks under, left and right; and real estate — a business that has always been financed preponderantly with borrowed money — was literally unfinanceable, on any terms, anywhere. The firestorm had blown out. The great boom had been incinerated ... wait now ... did you just see something moving in the ashes? Looks like a phoenix?

Several real estate mutual funds are available which own real estate investment trust ("REIT") shares and the stock of entities which own, operate and develop real estate. The REIT format, itself, has proven to be a good way to hold real estate if you want a liquid security. For this reason (and because I'd like to demonstrate that the Universal Presentation easily encompasses any form of managed money) **here's a REIT presentation:**

SUPERSTAR: *Mr. Client, as I think I've mentioned to you before, I'm part of a professional group within my firm — a group of senior professionals who deal primarily with more substantial individual investors.*

We get together by conference call to talk about the markets and try to synthesize intelligent strategies. For the last couple of weeks, we've been working on kind of a novel idea, and I'd like to share it with you if you have a couple of minutes.

CLIENT: *Please do.*

SUPERSTAR: *Well, after watching the markets get whipped around for the last several years, it's become clear to us that big, noisy consensus is nearly always wrong. You're much better off keeping part of your serious capital on the lookout for great businesses when they are really out of favor. Does that make sense to you?*

CLIENT: *Conceptually, it does, I guess.*

SUPERSTAR: *Well, good. Anyway, three weeks ago, this group I belong to — there are seven of us — decided that we'd each come to the next meeting with an idea of the most downtrodden major business we could think of. But it had to be a business where you could make a case for a very large potential cyclical recovery. Otherwise there'd be no justification for taking the risk.*

CLIENT: *Don't tell me ... you picked banking.*

SUPERSTAR: (Gleefully) *No, it's even worse than that! Actually, we talked about banking, but concluded that none of us understood it. And that, even when a bank's run right — if one ever is run right — banking is a boring, low-growth, low-margin business.*

We went upstream, to the business popularly credited with having brought down the banking system (even though the system could only have been brought down by the low quality of its management). Can you guess what we named?

CLIENT: *Yes, I can: real estate. You're not trying to get me to buy real estate, are you?*

SUPERSTAR: *I have too much respect for you to try to "get you to buy" anything. But if you ask me real nice, I'll tell you what the seven of us collectively agreed was the greatest real estate story we'd heard in ten years, and which we're now all buying for ourselves and our best clients. But first, let me ask you a question. When was the last time somebody tried to sell you a real estate investment?*

CLIENT: *I don't even remember. Certainly not since the spaghetti hit the fan about real estate, in all the newspapers and everywhere. Two years? No, it's probably more like three.*

SUPERSTAR: *BINGO!* (Superstar now just sits there, saying nothing, grinning at his client ... waiting for the beautiful truth to dawn on him.)

CLIENT: (Finally) *Oh, OK. So what you're saying is when everybody was pitching me a real estate deal, that's when real estate was about to eviscerate everybody. But now that no one would dare* say the words "real estate" in polite company, maybe you can make some money in it.

SUPERSTAR: I was going to say that... but I was afraid I'd sound like I was trying to sell you something.

CLIENT: All right, wise guy. Knock it off, and tell me the story.

SUPERSTAR: Well, OK... but only because you asked so nicely. You see, real estate is somewhere in the trough of its greatest depression in your and my lifetime. Banks, S&Ls and insurance companies have foreclosed and are now selling assets at panic prices. No one is building anymore, because all the existing stuff is for sale below replacement cost. And besides, it's unfinanceable. Picture walking into a bank today, trying to get a mortgage on a new construction project. They'd treat you like Dracula trying to negotiate a loan from a blood bank. Does this scenario remind you of anything?

CLIENT: It reminds me that I've been meaning to ask you: Are you on drugs?

SUPERSTAR: Au contraire. Sorry, but the correct answer is: It's hauntingly reminiscent of the stock market in the week after October 19, 1987.

CLIENT: Ouch. That hurts.

SUPERSTAR: It's supposed to. No pain, no gain.

CLIENT: I'm sure this is a very bad sign, but this is suddenly starting to make a whole lot of sense. Could I induce you to cut to the chase, here?

SUPERSTAR: Gladly. My firm has a terrific relationship with a large, well-known real estate advisory and management outfit called The Gronsky Group. The Gronskys apparently missed out on the whole real estate boom and bust. Because, as the smoke starts to clear, there they are, doing their old conservative thing. Which is: buying small to medium sized neighborhood shopping centers **at prices substantially below replacement cost,** fixing them up, putting some serious professional management in, and making them really hum. The Gronskys have been doing this, pretty much the same way, for 20 years now. And today, they own 50 shopping centers, totaling about 7 million square feet of space. I *don't know how you're going to take this, but — the centers are 95% occupied.*

CLIENT: *So you want me to buy a shopping center?*

SUPERSTAR: *Heck, no. I want you to do what one of the largest British trade unions just did for its pension plan:* **buy a slice of all 50 of 'em.**

You see, the vehicle through which the Gronskys conduct their real estate activities is a New York Stock Exchange-listed real estate investment trust called Gronsky Realty Trust. It closed last night at $18 a share, and it pays a $1.30 dividend — up from $.45 ten years ago. (Yes, the dividend tripled, and in fact they've raised the dividend every ninety days, through the worst real estate depression since World War II. But I digress.)

They're headquartered in Philadelphia, where the Gronsky family is from, and they own property in 15 states. As I said, a large British pension plan recently bought $100 million of GRT shares directly from the Trust. So the Gronskys have a $100-million war chest to go out and buy foreclosed shopping centers at bargain-basement prices from banks that are bleeding to death. My associates and I are going along for the ride; you come, too.

Now, there are major limitations to real estate investing. It's illiquid — which is why you may want to own it in a REIT vehicle you can sell whenever you like. And, in a sense, real estate is risky. Not as risky at today's prices as it was three, five, seven or ten years ago. But not an electric utility, either. So you want the steadiest, most reliable people — namely the Gronskys — managing your real estate for you.

Would you feel comfortable owning 1,000 shares, and would you want the dividends in cash or reinvested in additional shares?

Clearly, this conversation was between a professional and a client who have a very good relationship. Unless you're totally insensitive to rejection or independently wealthy, you probably don't want to jump out of the bushes at total strangers, asking them to buy arch-contrarian stuff. But, if you've got the courage to begin trying the idea on people who respect you and the way you think, you may start a referral machine that will carry you into the next century.

SUMMARY

- Gold is the ultimate international currency and as efficient an inflation hedge as you're likely to find. Gold belongs in all portfolios that are preponderantly in stocks and — especially — bonds. If all else fails, think of gold as the portfolio's life insurance.

- Two basic kinds of sector funds are "plays" and "hedges." "Plays" are an entré into a sophisticated area the client is excited about but fears he's missed. "Hedges," like gold, are real businesses that tend to head in the opposite direction from stocks and bonds.

- Health care, the environment, computers, consumer brands, and broadcast/media are some sector "plays" with lots of appeal in the 1990s.

- Energy and real estate are two great — and, at the moment, under-appreciated and under-owned — sector "hedges."

- Note that the Universal Presentation is a perfect vehicle for presenting a REIT ... and, by extension, any other managed money vehicle you can think of.

18

Q&A/Objections Handling 1: General Theory

Q&A is where the rubber meets the road.

After your presentation monologue, Q&A re-establishes a genuine exchange of information and feelings. Q&A lets the prospect open up and show you his deepest fears and concerns. You'll get clear access to the wealth of misinformation he may have picked up over the years —about investing, about funds, and even about how life works. You can show how calm and imperturbable you are, and how much you genuinely believe in your product. Finally, Q&A is the critical, indispensable final step in your interview. After Q&A, nothing stands between you and a favorable decision to invest.

But, if Q&A has all these wonderful attributes, why do salespeople and planners hate and fear it so? The answer is: Because we misunderstand Q&A completely and therefore handle it badly. The real problem with Q&A isn't what the prospect says — the real problem is what *we think*.

Recognize these symptoms of chronic Q&A anxiety — all of which begin in your own head — and you'll be on the road to recovery.

• **A morbid fear of the question you can't answer** — In part, our somewhat fragile egos equate a question we can't answer with looking foolish. But this equation is only for washouts. The superstar knows — and never lets the prospect forget — that he is selling himself, not the accumulation of facts and technical detail he knows. (By the end of this section on Q&A, you'll never fear the question you can't answer again. So, put the fear completely out of your mind.)

• **Combat stress** — In the deep recesses of your mind you know that Q&A, no matter how polite and professional, is an intrinsically adversarial process. The longer Q&A goes on, the more potential to get out of control and turn ugly, as the prospect's mind starts leaping from one imaginary fear to another.

We all know this. Indeed, we have all had it happen to us too many times. We've prospected, qualified, and gone to see Dr. Jekyll, made our presentation … and suddenly, during Q&A, this guy Hyde is trying to tear out our lungs. Or we've had several conversations with Mr. Straight Arrow, just-give-me-the-bottom-line-I'm-a-busy-businessman-I-make-decisions-all-day-long. But during Q&A, we suddenly find ourselves talking to Casper Milquetoast, who can't make a decision to go to the bathroom.

• **Sisyphus strain** — This anxiety says, "Please don't let me have come all this way — through prospecting, qualifying, getting the appointment, fact-finding, feeling-finding, and the presentation — only to lose the sale. I just don't know if I'm strong enough to go back down to the bottom of the hill and start rolling the rock back up again."

Trouble is, these symptoms reflect what is going on in our own heads and have nothing whatever to do with what is going on in the prospect's head. And, the more our attention is diverted by anxiety, the less spontaneous, flexible and focused we become. We lose the calm, centered concentration the prospect initially found so attractive. Because, after all, *maybe it's not just the prospect who has a mood swing during Q&A.* Don't you think he started picking up our own anxious vibes on his non-verbal-communication radar screen?

So, to re-state a central theme of this book: *You are responsible* for what happens during Q&A. If you thought you established genuine communication earlier in the relationship, but communication broke down during Q&A … either the guy was operating from a hidden agenda all along, or

YOU LOST IT.

Let's get the hidden agenda issue out of the way. Just because you managed to talk your way into the prospect's office, and prevailed on him to sit still while you made a presentation, you may never have *communicated.*

This fact is particularly hard for aggressive,. transaction-oriented salespeople to accept. They've been taught to fight for yardage — on the first call, get the appointment. Take the sales process to the next successive step — get ten yards within four downs. They don't really listen to what a prospect is saying, because listening isn't in the playbook the coach gave them. So they fight to within the ten yard line, and what happens?' The prospect says, "I only buy no-load funds."

While preparing this book, I asked mutual fund wholesalers for the most common/most vexing objections salespeople run into. On one list — in quotation marks, so I knew it was very real — appeared this unutterably sad objection: "You don't care about me; you hardly know me, and yet you're making a specific recommendation!"

The transaction-oriented salesperson hears this reaction every day… if he's lucky. If he's not lucky, the prospect never bursts out so honestly. He hides behind the load, volatility, or some similarly vapid non-issue.

Boys and girls, you just don't sell relationship-oriented products (e.g. *managed money*) in a transaction-oriented way. That's trying to put a square peg in a round hole. Selling managed money isn't football — a titanic struggle of strength and will so painful and intense you can only play ten or twelve times in a season. It's more like baseball — warm, pastoral, subtle (a lot happens beneath the surface, visible only to the real fan). And, like baseball …

YOU PLAY THIS GAME EVERY DAY.

So if you're constantly being "stopped inside the ten" of Q&A, the problem isn't necessarily your ability to handle the issues — it's that you're *not listening*. Q&A isn't at the back of this book by accident. Creating the relationship, making the prospect know you care, and letting him feel you really listen to his hopes and fears are the groundwork you need to establish, even before you present something. Then Q&A becomes a mopping-up operation — a way of gently clearing up any remaining misconceptions.

In selling managed money, a prospect or client tells you where he needs to go, and you tell him how to get there. Picture a guy coming up to me outside my office at 47th Street and Park Avenue in New York. He says, "Are you a New Yorker?" I say, "Yup. Lived here all my life." He says, "Well, I'm from out of town, and I'm trying to get to the Museum of Modern Art." "Piece of cake," says I. "Walk two blocks west on this street — 47th — and you'll come to Fifth Avenue. Turn right, and walk uptown six blocks to 53rd Street. Hang a left into 53rd and two-thirds of the way down the block, you're there." Can you see the guy arguing,

"That's not how you get there"? Neither can I.

Anxiety about Q&A puts your energy in the wrong place. You can do so much psychic conditioning of the prospect first, so that Q&A is simply the peaceful conclusion to the interview. Q&A is the place the investor's last few lingering fears are gently put to rest, before he accepts — as you know he will — the perfect fit of the investment to his needs.

DO YOU BELIEVE?

If it's becoming clear during Q&A that you're not being believed, ask yourself if you believe. In other words, do you think some aspect of this money management product could surprise or hurt the investor in a way you haven't prepared him for? Do you think something intrinsic renders the product inferior? (For instance, do you really fear that no-load funds outperform?)

If so, you've probably slanted the presentation because of your view of the product — a slant your prospect can consciously or unconsciously tune into.

IF YOU DO NOT BELIEVE,
YOU CAN'T EXPECT TO BE BELIEVED.

You can't shuck and jive your way to the Super Bowl. So if you don't really believe, and you come up empty on fourth and goal from the one yard line (during Q&A), well ... you ain't got nobody to blame but your own self, bubba.

You must know that your recommendation has no hidden fatal flaw.

THERE IS NO SMOKING GUN.

If a superior managed investment really fits the client's needs and is presented fairly and honestly, the client has nothing to object to which invalidates the investment. (If, on the other hand, you were somehow too busy to mention the currency translation issue in the global fund, and you got blown out ... well, who's to blame? You planted a smoking gun on yourself and then called the cops.)

A client may tell you why your recommended investment isn't right *for him*. But nobody can tell the superstar his recommendation is objectively bad. If the prospect (or the prospect's advisor) says, "I've found the one aspect that makes this a bad investment," the superstar, without a flicker of fear, can say (though not in so many words), "Like hell you have."

It's your responsibility to do whatever it takes to get yourself to that supreme level of confidence. Because without that iron conviction, you will never achieve money management superstardom. So, the first principle in my philosophy of Q&A is:

KNOW AND BELIEVE THAT YOUR RECOMMENDATION IS AN INTRINSICALLY SUPERIOR SOLUTION TO THE PROSPECT'S NEEDS.

That's the moral high ground. Make any attack on that position a difficult, uphill battle.

STATED VERSUS REAL OBJECTIONS

The second principle of my Q&A philosophy is:

THE PROSPECT'S STATED OBJECTION IS NOT HIS REAL OBJECTION.

Take as much time as you need, and roll that one around in your head very slowly. To the cynical observer, the statement appears to say the prospect is always trying to head-fake you and is deliberately raising "red herrings" to hide his real objections. But if you're *sincerely* prospecting people who are *sincerely* trying to understand your recommendations, you won't end up talking with prospects playing mind games.

No, the issue is more complex ... and more human. You see, people are bombarded with all kinds of contradictory misinformation about markets, the economy, and particularly about managed investments. Most misinformation comes from journalism (and is therefore one-issue-at-a-time and focused on today) or from competing, and sometimes less scrupulous, salespeople/planners ("my fund is safer ... has a higher yield ... isn't as volatile"). This leaves prospects battered and confused, not to mention suspicious. So often, your prospect is just trying to remember the question he thinks he's supposed to ask. ("I read something ... didn't *Money* magazine say ... uh ...")

You just can't ask investors to have the same depth of understanding or appreciation of investment nuances you have. In fact, assume just the opposite: The prospect has not thought out the point he's raising.

This observation puts an entirely new light on handling questions and objections in a managed money sales situation. Instead of bearing the terrible weight of the obligation to answer, crisply and correctly, every question your prospect can conjure out of thin air, shift your attitude to this perception:

"I don't think he understands what he just asked me."

For instance, suppose you were trying to convince somebody who is planning to retire in 15 years to dollar-cost-average into an equity mutual fund, but the prospect says he won't invest in the stock market.

PROSPECT: *I don't want that much volatility.*

SUPERSTAR: (With the utmost serenity) *Neither do I.*

(Then, the superstar just sits silently, for as long as it takes, until the prospect says something else.)

The washout will try to show, with charts, graphs, circles and arrows, that when you're dollar-cost-averaging around a rising trendline, volatility is actually your friend. (And the sad fact is, the assertion is true. See Appendix I: "Presenting Dollar-Cost-Averaging in Volatile Markets.") But the washout ends up digging himself a very large hole. Why? Two reasons. First, he's ceded to the prospect the admission that the equity market is "volatile." Second, and far more damning, he has no idea *how the prospect defines "volatility,"* or what he infers from his definition.

Remember the second major principle of our philosophy of Q&A: You simply have no reason to suppose that a question or objection, *as stated,* is an accurate reflection of what's really troubling your prospect.

So the only possible correct response to the objection, "I don't want that much volatility," is the serenely truthful statement, "Neither do I." (What's that? You don't see why that's the right answer? Please stay tuned. "All," as Agatha Christie's Hercule Poirot always says when assembling the suspects in the drawing room, "will be revealed.")

THE PATRIOT MISSILES OF Q&A

To become a managed money superstar, you have to have a complete, built-from-the-ground-up philosophy of handling questions and objections. That philosophy, like everything else in this book, must be rooted in an appreciation of the real emotions and feelings of your prospects.

Let's review the bidding to key into the prospect's feelings. First, we've agreed the prospect may not have a clear understanding of how markets and managed investments really work. Second, your Universal Five-Point Presentation focused completely on the big picture, to the exclusion of a great wealth of detail. And, finally, you tried to close by asking the prospect for an appropriate dollar commitment … which probably made him snap out any half-baked question or objection that popped into his mind. Now, when a question comes tumbling out of his mouth, why on earth would you take it seriously?

Right: You wouldn't. Instead, start from the premise that, when it first hits the table, neither you nor the prospect knows what his question/objection really means. So, any direct answer you give is almost certainly (a) wrong, or (b) beside the point.

If you try to answer the question as stated, not only will you be firing back at a mirage, but you may end up wrangling like a high-school debater over every question or objection — not a very smart way to show you're reasonable. Think of the Kennedy-Nixon debates in 1960. Kennedy spoke always to the television audience, and always to the larger issues that he thought people really cared about. Nixon, following the narrow definition of the format, "debated" each of Kennedy's points, trying to refute them. Those debates probably changed the outcome of the election.

The correct response to the incoming objection — a verbal Patriot missile — startles the prospect slightly, buys you some time to figure out what's really on his mind, reinforces the impression that questions don't disturb your confidence, and forces the prospect to rethink his own question.

So, when you hear the sirens for an incoming objection, sit back, relax and never speak directly to the stated objection. Assume, instead, the stated objection is not a clear statement of the client's real concern. Then, in a sincere attempt to make your prospect examine what his objection means, launch one of these Patriot missiles:

- **THE NON-ANSWER ANSWER.**
- **ANSWERING WITH A QUESTION.**

Let's test fire our Patriots against two of the most common objections you hear to equity mutual fund investing: "volatility" and "risk."

Non-Answer Answer:

Q: *Stocks are too volatile.*
A: *I'm inclined to agree.*

Answering With A Question:

Q: *Don't you think the stock market is too risky?*
A: *How do you define "risk?"*

The first response is a non-answer answer. The second is answering with a question. After responding in either one of these two ways, **always wait five full seconds before you say anything else.** This pause lets the clear understanding sink into the prospect's consciousness that his challenge has not disturbed you, and that you have unshakeable confidence in the product you're offering. Far from being required to dispense answers on cue like a trained monkey, you see your real mission as helping the prospect reason out the answers for himself. (If your instinct is to shy away from this approach — to feel instead that your prospects will never rise to the challenge — then you are prospecting people you don't like. That's *your* fault, not theirs.)

INCOMING VOLATILITY OBJECTION: "FIRE ONE"

At the end of the five-second silence, when you know you have the prospect's full attention, you can mop up after the Patriot's impact.

PROSPECT: *Stocks are too volatile.*

SUPERSTAR: *I'm inclined to agree.*

(5-second pause)

The market's short-term moves, both up and down, have certainly become more jagged over the last few years. A lot of people find that disturbing. I know I do, having to work with it every day.

But, of course, the long-term trend of the market can never be different from the long-term trend of the economy, which is up. That's the way it's been all our lives, and that's how it will always be.

Since you're investing for the long term, that's all you really care about — not where the market will be today, tomorrow, next month or next year ... but where a brilliantly managed portfolio of America's greatest companies will be fifteen years from now, when you're ready to retire. You can see the wisdom of that, can't you?

Have you seen the PBS Civil War series? If you haven't — even if you have — buy the tapes, and watch the way the historian, Shelby Foote, speaks. He has the ultimate calm, and a gentleness — even when he's speaking about the horrors of war — that takes you over. He never raises his voice or gets excited. Foote radiates great charm, and his fine attitude and quiet humor shine through everything he says. The net effect is that *you would never dream of doubting him.* You take every word he says as if it were God's truth. Because of what he says? No, of course not: because of *the way* he says the things he says. Keep that in mind while I suggest a couple of other variations, after the five second pause, to the "Stocks are too volatile/I'm inclined to agree" colloquy.

SUPERSTAR: *It's basically the sharp up and down movements of stock prices that convinced me over the last few years that my clients* **who needed the growth only common stocks provide** *should have money managed by superb professionals, rather than by me.*

We remind ourselves always that the stocks of great companies can **go** *down, but they never* **stay** *down. As long as the basic trend of the economy is up, the basic trend of the value of great common stocks has to be up, as well — because the economy is the sum of all the businesses in it.*

But when the market goes up or down several hundred points in a short time, it's hard to keep your emotions out of it. That's where the value of dispassionate management — such as the Gronsky Group provides — is a great comfort. You can see the value of that, can't you?

-OR-

SUPERSTAR: *The market's short-term moves, both up and down, have certainly gotten more jagged over the last few years. But, as long as the basic trend is up — and it always is — short-term swings can't hurt you — unless you let them make you do something irrational.*

It's like a housefly buzzing around your head. The fly is awfully annoying, but doesn't have the capacity to hurt you …

unless you try to smack it with a tire iron while it's sitting on top of your head.

(Note: The washout, because he's wound up tighter than a cheap watch, comes off rigid and humorless. The idea of the fly and the tire iron would never occur to him in a hundred million years. The superstar is supremely relaxed and confident, and sees that his clients are worried about volatility. Because he really cares and doesn't want them to be worried, he uses a little gentle humor to lighten their burden. This is just one more reason that the superstar's clients really like him. *Do your clients like you?*)

Now, look at the clip of subliminal tracer bullets you fired off in the response, and how they light up the night sky of the prospect's unconscious:

- *"... the market's short term moves, both up and down, have ... become more jagged ..."*
  MESSAGE: Volatility goes both ways. Journalism's use of "volatility" is a code word for "down a lot in a hurry." But the week the Allies attacked Iraq was also very volatile — the biggest *up* week the market ever had. So if you're using "volatility" as a euphemism for "risk," Mr. Prospect, you'll have to try harder than that.

- *"... long-term trend of the market can never be ... different from ... the economy ..."*
  MESSAGE: More and more, thanks to journalism, the stock market becomes an abstraction, a casino where the results are somehow known every night by six o'clock. People no longer realize that the prices of stocks are ultimately governed by the value of companies. And the value of companies and the trend of the economy must, over time, head in the same direction.

- *"... not where the market will be ... tomorrow ... but where a brilliantly managed portfolio of America's greatest companies will be fifteen years from now ..."*
  MESSAGE: When you buy an equity mutual fund, you're not buying a stock or even a basket of stocks. And you're certainly not buying "the stock market," whatever that is. You're buying a *brilliantly managed portfolio of America's greatest companies.* And you're buying it for the long term.

- *"... my clients who needed the growth only common stocks provide ..."*

MESSAGE: I'm sorry if the volatility of stocks offends your sensibilities. But unless you plan to retire on food stamps, dare I ask what you think the alternative is?

- *"... clients ... should have their money managed by superb professionals, rather than by me."*
  MESSAGE: What am I going to tell you, that the market is *not* volatile? Of course it's volatile. That's why I've given up my sinful life as a stock jockey and now go from town to town preaching the good news of the Gronskys. Listen up.

- *"... the value of dispassionate management ... is a great comfort ..."*
  MESSAGE: Self-explanatory.

Now, what set you up to offer all these great answers? Was it what you *knew* — about volatility, the market or about anything else? Of course not. You simply refused to be cast as a character in your prospect's own particular psychodrama — by the startling effect of beginning with your non-answer answer.

You could not possibly have known what the prospect meant by "volatility." The word is so commonly used by so many people to describe such a frightening abstraction ... that, in the end, you can't imagine what it means to one individual. Hence, your non-answer answer.

INCOMING RISK OBJECTION: "FIRE TWO"

Let's look now at how to use the second Patriot missile, "answering with a question," to shoot down the risk objection.

PROSPECT: *Don't you think the stock market is too risky?*

SUPERSTAR: (Smiling, but clearly somewhat puzzled) *How do you define "risk?"*

If the prospect doesn't say anything for the next ten minutes, you shouldn't either. "Risk," in the public mind, is even more misunderstood than "volatility." So you can sit there and pander to — or, even worse, argue with — this prospect's as-yet-unknowable notion of risk. Or you can try to *draw him out,* to the accompaniment of a fair amount of non-verbal communication from you that says "Stocks? Risky? What a peculiar notion."

PROSPECT: (Starting to stammer) *Well, you could lose ... I mean, it goes down a lot sometimes ... what if you lose? ..."*

SUPERSTAR: *Sorry, I just didn't understand at first. Yes, indeed, over relatively short periods of time stocks can go down, sometimes a lot.*

> *But, of course, over any major time frame — and certainly a 15-year period such as your time until retirement — I don't personally think it can be done ... losing money, I mean.*

> *People who jump in and out of stocks on a short-term basis can lose, of course. Personally, I think they usually do. But lose on a long-term basis? No, I just don't think it can be done. Certainly the Gronskys have never done it — or anything remotely like it. And they've been managing people's retirement money since before the Second World War.*

> *No, looking at Gronsky Quality Growth Fund over the last 40 or 50 years, I'd have to say the major risk was **not** owning it. You do see that, don't you?*

Let's try it another way:

PROSPECT: *The stock market is too risky.*

SUPERSTAR: *How do you define "risk?"*

PROSPECT: *The chance my investment may go down!*

SUPERSTAR: *Let me understand: Are you worried about your investments going down and then going up? Or are you worried about them going down and **staying** down?*

PROSPECT: *I don't know what you're talking about!*

SUPERSTAR: (With becoming modesty) *I'm sure that's my fault; I'm not explaining myself very well.*

> *Here's what I mean to say: The common stocks of America's greatest companies — IBM, Pfizer, Coca-Cola, General Electric, Procter & Gamble — will go down from time to time. I can't insulate you from that; it's the natural ebb and flow of the market.*

> *But, of course, those stocks never stay down. In fact, year after year, they go higher, and then higher ... because they're good companies, and keep getting better.*

I wish we could own these great companies without the annoyance of short-term fluctuations. But we can't. So I figured out the next best thing. You buy a little Gronsky Quality Growth Fund once a month. And then you don't look it up in the paper every day.

Can you imagine the spectacular things that America's greatest companies are going to accomplish in the next fifteen years? No, neither can I. But the Gronskys can. They've been anticipating change — and making superb returns for their investors — for nearly half a century. I'm ready to put them to work for you. Are you?

The major message of the second version is one you've heard often in this book: People have a hideous misperception of risk. Older people, in particular, equate risk with the variability of the price of investments, rather than with the inexorable erosion of purchasing power due to inflation.

The specific message here is that there's an enormous difference between *quotation* risk and *capital* risk. If I buy the specific stocks mentioned in this presentation — or a fund that holds them — I certainly may see prices lower in a day, a month, or even a year — that's "quotation risk." But if I hold the stocks or the fund for the long term (and particularly if I add systematically to my holdings) my capital risk is, historically, non-existent. In fact, you can honestly say — about great common stocks and the great equity funds that own them — that **the major long-term risk in this century has been not owning quality stocks.**

Incidentally, the phrase "stock market" (like "risk" and "volatility") is another hopeless abstraction, the meaning of which to any one investor is impossible to hypothesize. Used in a question or objection, "stock market" is always pejorative. The phrase may carry any or all of the following emotional baggage:

- The market is unitary, as in "a falling tide lowers all boats." All stocks are the same; none is higher quality than another.

- The market is a casino. Or it's manipulated; the "little guy" hasn't got a chance.

- The market is irrational, and not rooted in any objective or knowable reality.

Never try to challenge this kind of pernicious abstraction head-on. These objections are smoke; if you stumble into them, trying to find where the prospect is, you'll never be seen or heard of again. Stand where you are, and call the prospect out by changing the terms of the discussion. In the foregoing example, the prospect says "stock market." The superstar starts talking about America's great companies (note: "*companies*," not "*stocks*") — IBM, Pfizer, Coca-Cola, GE, Procter & Gamble. The superstar completely re-defines and re-sets the agenda —his agenda, not the prospect's — in a very useful, but totally non-argumentative, way.

This is a skill the washout somehow never acquires. He not only repeats (thereby accepting the prospect's definition of) "stock market," but he usually blunders into an overstated answer. "No, the 'stock market' isn't really risky," or, even worse, "This fund never really goes down." He's doomed himself by confirming the prospect's worst suspicions: that the washout is just another hyperbolizing lightweight who'll say anything to make a sale.

"THAT'S RIGHT"

Here's a refinement of the non-answer answer.

PROSPECT: *The stock market can go down 500 points in one day!*

SUPERSTAR: *That's right.* (Silence)

The washout will jump in and give the prospect seventeen reasons why the "stock market" will never crash again. And he'll come off sounding like every other salesman who tells people, "Buy this investment, because all the possible good things will happen, and all the possible bad things won't." Then, the washout wonders why nobody believes him. (Isn't that an awful way to go through life?)

The superstar sits back and says to himself, "That's right, Jack. This style of investing has some risk, like every other. And you've identified it. Now, what are you going to do with it?" The superstar knows the prospect is trying to draw him into a false position (without consciously meaning to), and with the greatest courtesy he refuses to be drawn. Saying, "That's right," and then not saying anything else, forces the prospect to amplify the question, narrow its focus, or do *something* to clarify the issue for both of you.

PROSPECT: *Well, don't you think I should be worried about that?*

SUPERSTAR: *I don't think you should be* **worried** *about anything. That's what I get paid to do in this relationship. I do think you should be properly concerned, in the sense that you know such a sharp one-day move is theoretically possible. You have to go into any investment with your eyes open, so you don't panic out at the bottom.*

But short-term jagged moves in stock prices, both up and down, are largely emotional. Emotions don't last; the value of the great companies in America, like (superstar fires off a clip of blue chips) does last ... and, over time, that value always increases — as has the value of Gronsky Quality Growth Fund.

So, a year or so after that 500-point down day you mentioned, all those great companies, and Gronsky Quality Growth Fund, were making new highs every day. That's the way it always works.

Panic and euphoria are both short-term phenomena. The values of great American companies are the ultimate long-term phenomena. You can see that, can't you?

If you read through the superstar's response again, you'll notice several interesting things:

- The prospect wasn't really saying the market will go down 500 points in one day again, even though that's what the washout would assume he meant. The prospect just wanted the superstar to tell him not to worry about it — a fact the superstar uncovered by giving the non-answer answer, "That's right."

- The little, soft "Pfft" sound you may have heard was from a silencer, as another large caliber bullet was fired into the "load" objection. The superstar said, almost as an aside, that he is paid to do the worrying in this relationship. This was so fast, so deadly and so unobtrusive, the "load" objection is standing there with a neat, round hole at the bridge of its nose, not even realizing that it's dead. *No word is coincidental;* this just looks effortless.

- After the real objection was answered, and long after it ceased to matter, the superstar did note the fact, just in passing, that one year later, as always, good funds were making new highs.

THE "WHY" WEAPON

The third great Patriot missile of Q&A responses is the wonderful, all-encompassing, "Why?"

PROSPECT: *I don't think that common stocks are a good investment right now.*

SUPERSTAR: *Why?*

Here's a classic example of an objection that's so amorphous, so non-specific — so *smoky* — that even the washout must realize he doesn't have the foggiest notion what the prospect means.

The superstar, marveling at the smokiness of the objection, just sits back, vaguely *but perceptibly* mystified, and asks "Why?" You are clearly saying you feel no obligation to respond to this objection. Indeed, you are placing all the incumbency to clarify the statement squarely upon the prospect. Here again, if the prospect doesn't say anything for ten minutes, neither should you.

Let's look at a couple of the ways this conversation could go from here.

PROSPECT: *I read several articles that said we're in a recession.*

SUPERSTAR: *I see. (Pause) What do you infer from that?*

PROSPECT: *Well, stocks go down in a recession, don't they?*

SUPERSTAR: (Gently shaking off this non-issue) *No, actually. Stocks go down **before** a recession, because the market anticipates the economy by about six months. Generally, right around the time the government officially confirms a recession — stocks go up, because the next economic upsurge is within sight, about six months away.*

That's why it's so maddening to try to invest based on what you read in newspapers and magazines ... but never mind all that.

We've agreed that you need to achieve substantial growth of capital in the 10 to 15 years until you retire. We've agreed that only high-quality common stocks can get you where you need to go. Finally, we've agreed that Gronsky Quality Growth Fund is a brilliant long-term managed portfolio of the highest quality equities. Right?

PROSPECT: *Well ... yes ...*

SUPERSTAR: *It would be a mistake — a very human mistake, but a mistake — to let the long-term decision to hire a great money manager be blurred into a short term market-timing decision. We always face short-term uncertainties — and always will. But investing for retirement is a marathon, not a 100-yard dash. And it's simply never the wrong time to hire the right people. You can see that, can't you?*

Now, suppose the colloquy had gone like this:

PROSPECT: *I don't think common stocks are a good investment right now.*

SUPERSTAR: *Why?*

PROSPECT: *I, uh ... read an article in Forbes ...*

SUPERSTAR: (Genuinely interested) *Yes? What did it say?*

PROSPECT: *I, uh ... I don't remember.*

The superstar will let this hang in the air for a few beats, and then do his famous soliloquy from the previous example that started with, "We've agreed ... and we've agreed ... and finally we've agreed." The soliloquy ends, of course, with "It's simply never the wrong time to hire the right people."

The superstar knows that "not right now" doesn't usually mean "no," but rather means "I don't know how to make up my mind." And, since he knows the managed money decision is always about time (the long-term result of investing with talented managers), and never about timing, he gently returns the focus to its proper place.

Here again, **you profit to the extent you previously established conceptual points of agreement during your five-minute presentation.** The washout doesn't see this. In his nervousness about Q&A, he allows any question to become the whole focus of the discussion. The superstar, on the other hand, in effect says, "Wait a minute ... This is certainly an interesting little question, but it's only part of a much larger conceptual framework — most of which, Mr. Prospect, *you've already agreed to.*"

You have to develop a sense of the relative weight of questions to do this really well. Your ability to turn a question around gently on the prospect will be enhanced by an appreciation of how important — or how peripheral — each particular question really is. Judging the importance of questions *only* comes from the act of practicing your presentation skills, as opposed to learning more facts. They don't pay Pavarotti for how well he reads music; they pay him for how he makes the music sound when he sings.

You also have to temper your competitive sales instincts — the visceral urge to drop-kick the objection through the goal post of life — with a little human warmth and understanding. Look, the prospect knows he's coming closer and closer to having to buy or pass on the opportunity. So, he unconsciously rebels against having to make the decision, and he is liable to come up with any objection, or try to hang the conversation up on any small debating point. That's why you never speak directly to the stated objection.

Have a little sympathy for your conflict-ridden prospect. Smile. See if you can learn to **stay mentally tough, but in a soothing kind of way.** Remind him that picking the right managed investment is a cooperative process. You're both working through a shared perception of his investment goals, and you've both agreed on a particular form of investing which fulfills the goals. If you hadn't, the conversation never would have gotten this far.

You'll notice that all the hypothetical answers in this chapter accomplish the same thing:

TAKE THE PROSPECT BACK TO
THE LAST ESTABLISHED LEVEL
OF COMMON UNDERSTANDING.

When you say, "We've agreed that ...," you are re-focusing the conversation back to the larger, agreed-upon principles. Fall into the stated objection, and the sales interview will degenerate into an endless ping pong game, played without a ball.

ADDING BACKSPIN

Just as you can refine the non-answer answer with "That's right," you can also refine the tactic of answering with a question by adding "backspin." Here, you (quite literally) turn the prospect's question around simply by rephrasing it, either with or without the preface, "I'm not sure I understand your question."

PROSPECT: *If these are such great money managers, what do they need me for?*

SUPERSTAR: *I'm not sure I understood your question. Are you asking why a money manager wants new clients?*

When you get good at this, you'll be able to backspin the question so it's already half-answered by the way you rephrase it.

As with all of the tactics recommended in this chapter, be careful to express your responses in a sincere and genuinely thought-provoking way. Avoid being smart-alecky, like this:

PROSPECT: *If these are such great money managers, what do they need me for?*

WASHOUT: *If IBM is such a great company, why do they want to sell stock to the public?*

This answer-with-a-question correctly suggests that all great business enterprises seek to leverage, directly or indirectly, off other people's money. But the response comes out with an argumentative undertone. Adversarial flavoring usually poisons a sales interview. In fact, **all great salespeople know that arguments in a sales context are unwinnable**, much like arguments about religion or politics.

Being argumentative is a fairly easy trap to fall into. You worked hard to learn all you can about a fund; you invested in it yourself; and you're sure it's right for the prospect. If the prospect asks "smoking gun" questions (which seem to communicate a feeling that something must be fundamentally wrong with your fund), you can be angry and tempted to respond in kind.

Don't do it! Maybe people distrust your prospect all day long and make him prove everything he says. Or maybe he's just made this way. Maybe he wants you to really work to get his capital. Relax. It's business — not personal.

Don't let anybody set your agenda. Q&A is the hardest time to keep this principle in mind. But it's also the most critical time.

MAKE THE EMOTIONAL CONNECTION

The poor washout who constantly tries to overcome objections with fact and reason misses more than a lot of sales. He misses the opportunity to let his prospect *ventilate* his feelings. And thus he misses the chance to *validate* those feelings by demonstrating that he, and lots of other people, feel the same way.

Making a real emotional connection with the prospect leads to the best selling. One sure way to insure that you're never in any danger of connecting is to answer the stated objection. (Right — because the prospect's stated objection never accurately reflects what he feels.)

Listen to what the superstar sounds like:

- *Why?*
- *What do you mean?*
- *I'm not sure I understand. Are you asking ...?*
- *That's a very valid concern.*
- *Why does that bother you?*
- *We all feel like that.*
- *Do you see what I mean?*
- *That's interesting; I'd never looked at it that way.*
- *Don't you feel that's true?*
- *Don't you agree ...?*

All these responses say: I'm open; I'm interested; I care about the way you feel; I'm thinking about what you said; I want to understand you ... and (last but certainly not least) I'm confident we will reach agreement.

It's very hard (though not impossible) for a prospect to stay rigid, cold and challenging when you deal with him this way. When he does continue to be stiff and adversarial, he's telling you he doesn't care what you say — he's made up his mind not to do business with you. And, he's probably never going to tell you why.

"C'est la vie," thinks the superstar. "You're just another hashmark on my daily baseline prospecting calendar. I have to let you disqualify yourself, if that's what you've made up your mind to do."

CLIMBING THE MOUNT EVEREST OF OBJECTIONS

Now, please try to maintain that sense of perfect calm and serenity as we set out to climb the Mount Everest of objections:

"The load is too high."

Let's pause for a moment, and take another spot quiz to see whether you're getting the *real* Q&A message:

SPOT QUIZ

The correct answer to the objection, "The load is too high," is:

(a) *That's a very handsome tie you're wearing.*
(b) *No, it's not.*
(c) *I have to let you disqualify yourself, if that's what you've made up your mind to do.*
(d) *In relation to what?*
(e) *Actually, this fund has the lowest load of any Morningstar 5-star-rated aggressive/small cap growth fund.*
(f) *Have a nice day.*

Once again, let's do this by process of elimination. It isn't (a) or (f). Those are non-answer answers, all right, but not in the thought-provoking way we recommend for this technique. It isn't (c), either ... at least not yet. Don't be a quitter.

The answer can't be (b) — that's argumentative; (e) is definitely out, because it commits two cardinal sins: speaking directly to the stated objection, and using pure jargon.

Which leaves you with (d). Relaxed, gently challenging, answering-a-question-with-a-question (d):

"In relation to what?"

What does the prospect mean? What is he comparing the fund to? Another load fund? A no-load fund? All no-load funds? Buying his own stocks or bonds? The superstar has no idea. Since the superstar doesn't even understand the question yet — or simply wants to appear as if he doesn't understand — he won't say anything. He asks, "In relation to what?" (Here we discuss the philosophy of the load objection. In the next chapter we'll offer several specific dialogues.)

This prospect drives around in a Mercedes. If he ever found out what the car cost when it rolled off the assembly line in Stuttgart versus what he paid for it in the dealer's showroom in Phoenix, Arizona, all his hair would turn white and fall out. He's wearing a suit that he bought from the fanciest haberdasher in town for $325. If he ever finds out it cost $29.68 to make in Singapore, he'll have apoplexy. Now, is this person really worried about "markup?" No, there's something else going on here. Could it be the mighty pen of journalism?

Look at the supreme irony: The load/no-load debate today has intensified just when the differences between the two classes of funds have begun to disappear. Back when the load was 8.5% (versus 0% for no loads) the prospect had an argument. But with sales charges dropping into the 3.5% to 5.5% range, with the outbreak of vanishing back-end loads, and especially with the popularity of 12(b)1 "trails," the force of the load argument should be considerably blunted, if rationality prevails.

But, of course, rationality isn't prevailing — journalism is. Several financial magazines seem to have a mission in life to stamp out the evil of funds with sales charges. But their way of manufacturing the debate is seriously flawed, in several important respects. Understanding the flaws will help you respond more effectively to the objections you hear.

• **The load objection suggests that money management is a commodity** ... and that the governing variable in fund performance is the presence or absence of a sales charge. But load is not the governing variable. The best-performing equity mutual fund of the 1980s, bar none, had a 3% sales charge; still does, in fact. And as Standard & Poor's *Outlook* stated not long ago, "... the longer you hold a fund, the less significant the (front-end charges) become. If you expect to stay in the same fund for five years or more, load is a factor, but not a major one." The only thing I'd add is that the statement remains true even if you only intend to stay in the same fund family — where there's no charge to switch funds — for five years or more.

• **The load objection values the investment advice of people compensated through the sales charge at zero.** This conclusion would merely be bizarre, if it weren't so frightening. Look at the implication. Somehow, a financial planner who charges his clients a fee of 3% of assets under management is "right" to sell a no-load fund. Yet a planner who takes no fee and sells his client a fund with a 3% load is "wrong."

The most frightening part of the no-load argument is this: It presumes investors will make good decisions and *stick to them* in the most frightening times without professional guidance. Perhaps our great-grandchildren may someday live in a world where it's true!

In the meantime, I have two questions: (a) Did you ever meet anyone who became, and remained, a good investor because of what he read in a newspaper or magazine? and (b) How many people do you think went to the phone between October 19 and 23, 1987, intending to liquidate their no-load equity funds, but stopped and decided to wait a couple of weeks to see what *Money* magazine said?

I mentioned earlier that Oscar Wilde defined a cynic as someone who knows the price of everything and the value of nothing. So it is with journalists. They know what the investor *pays,* but they ignore what he *receives.* And journalists have been extraordinarily successful at getting investors to think the same way. The washout will break his lance on this conundrum. The superstar vaults over it almost effortlessly (as we'll see in the next chapter).

• **The load objection suggests investors in a no-load fund are somehow not paying the prodigious costs of a marketing/sales effort.** Of course, they are.

Yes, I know — the sales charge *does* become important when you're comparing two funds whose returns can't differ very much (two short-term government bond funds, for example). Similarly, if the investor's time horizon is particularly short (two to three years, say), the sales charge is a legitimate concern. But, in considering an equity fund over a ten, fifteen or twenty year horizon, the sales charge issue is a non-starter.

On every page of this book, you are reminded again and again that a successful money management sales practice must be intensely personal and relationship-oriented. The sales charge issue is just another important reason why this is true. Because …

**WHEN INVESTORS BELIEVE
YOUR COUNSEL IS CRITICAL TO THEIR SUCCESS,
THEY BECOME ALMOST TOTALLY INSENSITIVE TO PRICE.**

And when they don't believe you care, no matter how low the price is … it's too much.

SUMMARY

• **The Q&A anxiety that cripples many salespeople is self-induced. Besides, what you know can never be as important as demonstrating you care.**

• **The real problem isn't what the prospect says. The real problem is what we salespeople think.**

• **If communication is lost during Q&A, either it was never there or you lost it. If the context is "Tell me where you need to go and I'll tell you how to get there," the conversation is unlikely to end in an argument.**

SUMMARY (continued)

- The prospect's stated question or objection is not a particularly accurate reflection of what is really bothering him. So, the worst thing you can do is answer it.

- Put the burden of amplifying and clarifying the objection squarely on the prospect. The three Patriot Missiles of Q&A accomplish this:

  - The non-answer answer
  - Answering with a question
  - Asking "Why?"

- "Volatility," "risk" and "the stock market" are concepts about which investors have varying, and essentially journalism-induced, notions. Never address them head-on. Use the Three Patriots to draw the investor out, so you can begin to understand his views.

- The superstar uses gentle humor to help prospects over their fears. The washout never knew you were even allowed to do that.

- The equity market is very risky short-term. Long term, the greatest risk is not being in it. Great stocks, and the funds which own them, often go down — but they never stay down. That's the difference between "quotation" risk and capital risk.

- Money management is about time, not timing. Don't let the all important long-term money management decisions get hung up on today's uncertainties. Take your prospect back to the last established level of common understanding, and start in again.

- For most investors looking at most funds over longer time horizons, the sales charge is simply a non-issue.

- People who believe your counsel is critical to their success are almost completely insensitive to price.

19

Q&A/Objections Handling 2: Powdering Today's Most Popular Objections

When I started researching this book, somebody told me that no matter how many wholesalers' lists of the most common, vexing objections I solicited, in the end they would all come down to three issues: load, risk, and volatility. He wasn't far wrong. The list actually comes down to four: load, risk, volatility, and ... your relationship with the prospect.

We'll examine these and other objections, but the main purpose of this chapter is to expand your firing range using the three Patriot Missiles of Q&A (the non-answer answer, answering with a question, and "Why?") by showing the various *forms* these four objections come in.

Before we refine your targeting, let's formulate "General Principles of Response" to each of the major perceived objections to money management.

GENERAL PRINCIPLES OF RESPONSE	
OBJECTION	PRINCIPLE
The Load	I'm much more than worth it, because I'm going to bring you safely home.
Risk	The ultimate risk is purchasing power. An investment's variability isn't its risk. Variability is the key to real return. "Quotation risk" is not "capital risk." Great stocks/funds go down, but never stay down.

Volatility	Volatility cuts both ways. It has no power to affect you unless you panic, because it never lasts. Volatility exists only in the short run; value is forever.
Relationship	This is the "real," overriding issue at the core of the "stated" issues above. So, turn the focus directly on you and the prospect's trust in you.

These cornerstone principles apply to all the variations of questions and objections you'll hear in each of the main categories. Keep the principles in mind, and you will be able to launch instantly a Patriot response to any variation of the standard objections.

The goal is not to have you memorize canned responses; that makes you more rigid, not more flexible. But if you know the core — the deep, inner truth — of the General Principle, then the particular answer to the particular variation becomes a refinement.

Let's look at some variations of the "Big Three" objections.

REVISITING THE LOAD OBJECTION

Let's go back to handling the load objection. (I faithfully promise, however, not to subject you to the cliched response "you-don't-mind-leaving-a-waiter-in-a-restaurant-15%-so-why-do-you-object-etc., etc." If I hear that one again, I think the top of my head will blow off. What has a restaurant tip got to do with anything? Yes, bozo, I leave ten bucks on a fifty dollar restaurant tab. I sure don't see any analogy between the tip and forking over $1,000 of the $20,000 I'm investing for retirement.)

The load objection, first and foremost, signals that you may not have established a relationship to the extent you hoped. (Or maybe *Money* or *Forbes* told the guy not to buy a fund with a sales charge, and he's simply looking for you to reassure him that it's OK.) The prospect is saying:

"I don't trust you yet."

So, you need to craft answers to the load objection that are intensely relationship-oriented and which stress your commitment to the prospect and his goals as being your value added. That builds the exchange of confidence and trust — the pre-condition for everything. But do you ask people in so many words to trust you? Do you say your services really add value? Most of us, I believe, are not as sure of ourselves in these areas as we would like to be. And that's too bad. Because only through the media of trust and value-added service —and not by analogizing ourselves to waiters — can we consistently overcome the load objection.

Where it's not journalistically induced blue smoke, the load objection is invariably a conscious or unconscious statement by the prospect that he doesn't trust you, doesn't believe you, or doesn't perceive the value of your service to him. You must therefore:

FOCUS THE ENTIRE LOAD DISCUSSION COMPLETELY ON YOU.

You are the bridge. And the issue is not even remotely the presence or absence of a sales charge. The overriding issue to focus on is the presence or absence of sound, consistent professional advice for as long as it takes to get the prospect where he wants to go. And, after the terrible shocks of Black Monday, Friday the 13th and the Kuwait invasion/recession massacre, your advice is more critical than ever. And the sales charge doesn't *begin* to compensate for it. The one-issue-at-a-time press ignores the cost of the emotional mistakes no-load fund holders may make because they don't have anybody to keep them on track.

Let's look at some ways to use our Patriot Missiles to re-direct the focus of a load objection back to you:

PROSPECT: *I don't buy load funds.*

SUPERSTAR: *Why?*

Please note, incidentally, the prospect did not say he buys no-load funds. (We'll look at that variation in a minute.) He said, for reasons the superstar cannot even imagine, that he doesn't buy load funds. And he said it *after* he allowed the superstar to sit down with him, agreed on his goals and how to fund them, listened to a wonderful presentation of a great group of people and their terrific fund, and was properly cautioned about the risks/limitations. Suddenly the critical issue is the sales charge. Why?

PROSPECT: *Because no-load funds do better.*

SUPERSTAR: *Mr. Prospect, if that were even remotely accurate, I would know it, and I would never offer my clients a fund that had a sales charge.* (Silence)

Please observe the enormity of what the superstar accomplishes in these few words. First, he makes *himself* the issue. He doesn't contradict the prospect directly ("No, they don't," or "There's no evidence of that"). He says, in effect, you must know funds with a sales charge can't be inferior *because I'd never offer clients a second-rate investment.*

PROSPECT: *But what about all this stuff I read in Money and Forbes?*

SUPERSTAR: *I can't speak directly to that, because I didn't see the articles. But I suspect they say — although I can't imagine how they derive this conclusion — that no-load funds outperform load funds, purely based on the presence or absence of a sales charge. Is that about right, or am I oversimplifying?*

PROSPECT: *No, no; that's exactly it.*

SUPERSTAR: (Shaking his head in sadness) *Hard to believe ... well, never mind.* (Looking up at the prospect, real hard) *Mr. Prospect, only two factors determine how successful you'll be reaching your retirement goals over the next 15 years in an equity fund. And, God knows, what you paid or didn't pay to acquire the fund shares can't possibly be one of them.*

*The first is management. Why, if the Gronskys did even half a percentage point a year better than another fund ... and you compounded that, year in and year out ... well, they could have practically **given** you the other fund, and you'd still be better off with Gronsky Quality Growth.*

And, of course, the other thing is discipline. When you buy a no-load fund, your only investment counselor is the mailman ... or some $18,000-a-year telemarketing trainee at the fund. Who keeps you from panicking out on October 19? Or gets you to add to your account in the fall of 1990? Or talks you out of being afraid to keep buying after the market runs up? At times, that's all I do all day — keep people on track in times of stress. That's when I really earn my share of the sales charge ... a couple of times over. You can see the benefit of that, can't you?

Now let's look at how to respond to the prospect who says he "only" buys no-loads:

PROSPECT: *I only buy no-load funds.*

SUPERSTAR: *That's interesting. Which ones do you buy?*

If you hear a lot of coughing and throat-clearing at this juncture, you know the response was a stall. The guy read somewhere you ought to buy no-loads if you do buy mutual funds. So this seemed to him like a good way to bow you out.

Or, let's say he has an answer:

PROSPECT: *I buy the Midas Fund.*

SUPERSTAR: *Really? What got you interested in it?*

PROSPECT: *It was Money magazine's top-performing fund in 1988.*

SUPERSTAR: *I see. How's it doing for you?*

PROSPECT: *Well, actually we ... uh ... sold it.*

SUPERSTAR: *Oh. When?*

PROSPECT: *In October of 1990. The damned thing was down 25%.*

SUPERSTAR: (Quietly, with empathy) *Yes, that's the fatal flaw in the no-load approach. You haven't paid anybody to tell you what to do with them **after** you buy them.. So nobody does.*

Now, we've agreed ... and we've agreed ... and, finally, we've agreed ... (Here, the superstar re-sets the agenda, and goes back to the last established level of agreement about how the prospect will reach his retirement goal.)

Alternatively, the prospect may say, "I'm holding on," or "It's not doing very well," or simply "I don't know how it's doing." The reply would be:

SUPERSTAR: *Well, then, I guess it turned out to have a plus and a minus. The plus, as far as it goes, is that you didn't pay a sales charge. The minus — and, if I'm reading you right, this is far more important — is that it's not getting you any closer to your retirement goals. Is that a fair summation?*

PROSPECT: (Ruefully) *Yes, I guess it is.*

SUPERSTAR: *Well, we've agreed ... and we've agreed ... and, finally, we've agreed ...*

Let's try it another way:

PROSPECT: **Why should I pay a sales charge?**

SUPERSTAR: (Smiling but clearly serious) *Only one reason: The sales charge buys me.* (Silence)

The washout doesn't have the guts to say this, because, deep in his heart, he thinks paying the sales charge to get him is a bad trade. (I dare not stumble into the dank swamp of self-image psychology, so I'll just let that statement stand. But you'll find no more important sentence in the book, so you might just want to camp out here and observe it for a while.)

The superstar sits in silence, looking levelly at the prospect. Sometimes the prospect understands, right then and there, what a superb professional he's dealing with. Why? Because the superstar said, in so many words, "I make the difference." No guts, no glory.

So the prospect either sits there stunned, or asks why he should believe that's a good trade. In either case, the superstar continues:

SUPERSTAR: *I've been doing this for ____ years. To me, it's as important a profession as medicine. I treat my clients' capital, and their financial goals, as if they were my own. I'm here for you, in good times and bad, for the duration. And the sales charge is how I am paid.*

You don't really want to be burdened with this, but just let me get it off my chest — it's a really dumb and completely inadequate way for me to be compensated. I'd much prefer to be paid by the hour — because this investment buys you 15 years or more of my service — even though, if you never invest again, I never get compensated again.

And ideally, of course, I'd love to be paid a percentage of your assets. Someday, when my profession wakes up, that's how it will be. Because, look: if you put your $25,000 in Gronsky Quality Growth Fund in 1980, I'd have been paid a percentage of that initial amount. Today, with that account standing at about $150,000, I'd be getting a lot of satisfaction, but nothing else. Between you, the Gronskys and me, who made by far the worst trade?

Sorry, I didn't mean to unload on you like that ... and I try never to over-explain things. But that's my philosophy of the sales charge. Is that OK with you?

You see the way this works? Here's another variation that leads into the speech you just read.

PROSPECT: *I don't want to pay a sales charge.*

SUPERSTAR: *Can you afford not to?* (Silence)

PROSPECT: *What are you talking about?*

PROSPECT: *The sales charge is what keeps me working with you on your retirement goals for the next fifteen years. I've been doing this for ____ years. To me, it's as important ...*

Here's another way into "the speech":

PROSPECT: *I don't think the sales charge is fair.*

SUPERSTAR: (Explodes) *Thank you! Neither do I!* (After stunned silence) *You don't really want to be burdened with this, but ...*

Or, how about this:

PROSPECT: **The sales charge is just a waste of money.**

SUPERSTAR: (Quietly and slowly) *If the time you spend talking with me over the next fifteen years is a waste of time ... then you're right — the sales charge is a waste of money.* (Silence)

PROSPECT: (If he's a real prospect, he doesn't say anything. He's too ashamed — as, indeed, he should be.)

SUPERSTAR: *You see, I've been doing this for ____ years. To me, it's as important as ...*

REVISITING RISK

Let's launch a few Patriots at the risk objection and follow up using the appropriate General Principle of Response.

PROSPECT: *I refuse to get involved in anything that fluctuates.*

SUPERSTAR: *Then how are you dealing with the prices of food, fuel, and medicine?* (Silence)

-OR-

And yet you're still involved with the Consumer Price Index. (Silence)

Clearly, the superstar perceives the prospect's objection as an attempt to re-set the agenda in terms that are not useful. So he simply refuses to play and instead returns the agenda, gently but firmly, to where it belongs.

After the responses above, the prospect may sit there, nonplused, moving his mouth soundlessly, or stammering, "What do you mean ... what's that got to do with it ... huh?" But, boy, does the superstar have his full attention!

Now, on to the General Principle:

SUPERSTAR: *You see, we invest to produce an income, either now or in the future. And, if our expenses were fixed, it would make all the sense in the world to invest entirely for a fixed income.*

The trouble is that our expenses are not fixed. They go up every single day, and will go on doing so for the rest of our lives.

Sometimes our expenses go up gently, manageably. And sometimes — as with fuel in the '70s, or medical costs these days — they go up ... I can't think of another word for it ... horrifyingly. But they always, always go up. So that, if you live long enough and are on a fixed income, you get to watch your lifestyle destroyed.

But people who've invested so that their incomes rise — at the same or a greater rate than living costs rise — maintain or even improve their lifestyles.

That's the central logic of owning Gronsky Equity Income Fund. You see, the great companies in America raise the dividends they pay fairly often. And the Gronskys are therefore able to raise Equity Income Fund's dividends nearly every year— 23 of the last 24 years, as I recall ... and the dividend has quadrupled in that time.

You can see the value of investing this way, can't you?

Once again, note the superstar's magisterial calm, and his refusal to be a wise guy. With the washout, who is quicker to anger, the colloquy might have gone like this:

PROSPECT: *I refuse to get involved in anything that fluctuates.*

WASHOUT: *Even if it's only fluctuated up for fifty #!*x* years?!?*

The washout, whose anxiety keeps him on the emotional ragged edge, may respond argumentatively. He just patiently showed his prospect a fund which has never done anything but make fortunes for its shareholders — larger fortunes for people who've owned it longer, smaller fortunes for people who've owned it for shorter periods … but fortunes, for anyone who ever bought and stayed with it. Now his prospect starts moaning about "fluctuation," or some such thing — and the washout blows his stack.

Who's the washout really mad at? Himself, I think. The washout tends to carry the weight of the world on his shoulders and to think that everything bad that happens to him is his own fault. (Somehow, he never learned to distinguish between *responsibility* and *fault*.) So, the washout is angry that he deluded himself into thinking this yutz was a prospect in the first place. He's angry at himself for making the same tired old facts-and-numbers approach. And he's angry at himself for being unable to break the pattern of failure.

This is a real emotional downward spiral. Anger is the single most destructive force in the life of a planner/salesperson. No matter who or what the apparent object of the anger is, the anger is always directed *inward*. (Who are *you* mad at, right now? Are you sure?)

MORE "RISK" VARIATIONS

In raising objections (or asking questions in an apparently challenging way), a good prospect is often merely seeking reassurance. Listen to *the way* the prospect says what he says, not to *what* he says. Behind that serious, confrontational exterior, hides a very decent fellow (if you've qualified your prospect right) who is struggling to get out and shake your hand. *Listen*, and select your response in a way that really reaches him.

Here's an example of a good guy trying to shake off his fears:

PROSPECT: *I'm nearly 65; I can't afford to take risks.*

SUPERSTAR: *What's the single greatest risk you face?* (Silence)

PROSPECT: *Well, obviously, it's the risk that I'll lose my money!*

SUPERSTAR: (Shaking his head very firmly) *It really isn't. If you're going to be dealing with someone like me — someone who really knows about investing and cares for his clients' capital as if it were his own — that's not much of a risk at all.*

No, the greatest, most implacable risk you face — and you

have to go on facing it for the rest of your life — is the loss of your purchasing power.

People don't seem to have a clear understanding of that, perhaps because they're still looking at their life expectancies in terms of their parents' ... I'm just not sure.

But a sixty-five-year-old man today is an even money bet to see eighty-four. If his wife is 65, she'll likely live to be 88. That's an average of more than 20 years. Do you remember what prices were twenty years ago — six cent postage stamps, 35 cent gasoline? Compare them to prices today and you see that the greatest risk you face is the risk that you'll outlive your income.

That's why fixed-income, so-called "riskless" investments — CDs and government bonds, for example — can never be the whole answer. Some significant part of your portfolio has to be in something whose income stream can grow as your cost of living goes up.

That's the central logic of owning Gronsky Equity Income Fund ... (Superstar repeats the "great American companies and Gronsky Fund raise dividends" paragraph).

You can see the value of investing in that way, can't you?

PROSPECT: Yes, but what about the value of the investment?

SUPERSTAR: What about it? (Silence)

PROSPECT: Well, it changes every day!

SUPERSTAR: Yes. Up, mostly ... if history and common sense are any guides. And they are.

PROSPECT: What are you saying?

SUPERSTAR: Simply that when you own a beautiful portfolio of great American companies who raise their dividends year after year, the value of that portfolio must be going in the same direction as the dividends. That's the common sense part.

The history part (brushing a hand over the chart in the fund's prospectus/brochure) bears out the common sense part. Simply stated, the value of an investment in Gronsky Equity Income Fund has been steadily growing since ... well, since before I was born.

Once again, depending on who you're dealing with, you may want to move quickly from the general (which is abstract, and therefore frightening) to the specific (which is familiar and solid, and therefore comforting) by naming some of the largest blue chip holdings of the fund. In these days of PRAP (Pandemic Risk Aversion Psychosis), nearly everyone is afraid of "the stock market." But I have never met anyone — nor have you — who was afraid of AT&T.

In the long dialogue you've just read, the superstar answered with a question twice ("What's the single greatest risk you face?" and "What about it?" He also gave a kind of semi-non-answer-answer ("Yes. Up, mostly ..."), although a real purist might maintain that was an answer. The superstar used these techniques to set and maintain his own agenda, and refused to discuss the issue of the fund's share price and what can happen to it day to day. He knows "quotation risk" is the wrong issue and can only take the prospect's focus off the long-term reality of dividend growth versus inflation.

In short, the superstar kept the discussion focused always on THE CONCEPT (inflation is your dragon; dividend growth via GEIF is your St. George).

Try the hospital analogy to re-focus the risk objection:

PROSPECT: *I'm very afraid of the stock market.*

SUPERSTAR: *Yes, I feel the same way. I'm also afraid of hospitals. (Silence)*

PROSPECT: *What? ... What on earth are you talking about?*

SUPERSTAR: *Well, I think for most people these days, owning common stocks and going to the hospital are very similar — you wish you never had to do either, but sometimes you do.*

We've agreed that you have to have an income stream that can grow over the years to keep pace with inflation. And we've agreed that among all financial assets only owning great common stocks can do that for you. And now we've agreed that we're scared, and we wish we didn't have to.

(Grinning) That just makes us human. And I do mean us, by the way. I don't like short-term market gyrations any more than you do, and probably a lot less.

That's why I promised myself that whenever a client's

financial situation necessitated equity investing — as yours and mine both do — I'd hire the very best professional managers I could find: The Gronsky Group.

That makes it a little less frightening, doesn't it?

Similarly:

PROSPECT: **I don't want to own stocks.**

SUPERSTAR: Neither do I. (Silence)

When the prospect stops spluttering, you can pick up from "We've agreed ..." above. Or craft a new response that says "When your head knows you need the growth only stocks provide, but your heart still doesn't want to own stocks, say yes to both your head and your heart. Don't buy common stocks (so your heart is happy) but do hire a superb money manager to run a portfolio of some of America's greatest companies for you (so your head is happy)."

Or, use the CPI shuffle:

PROSPECT: **The stock market is too risky.**

SUPERSTAR: I'm afraid the Consumer Price Index is even riskier. (Silence)

Again, when the spluttering stops, use the colloquy you had a few pages back with the 65-year-old.

The process points up the critical nature of establishing THE CONCEPT. Nobody likes stocks. Everybody is afraid of the market. But once you've established THE CONCEPT (inflation's the dragon; growth is St. George; only stocks grow), what's the alternative?

Prospect says he hates the stock market: (a) washout tries to prove he "should" love the stock market; (b) superstar says, "Of course you hate the stock market; everybody, including me, hates it; but what's the alternative?" (Then, and only then — after you've made common cause with the prospect's emotions — should you go back and show the prospect that for half a century, equities via the Gronskys have been the only place to be. Or, as the superstar puts it, "The major risk, over the last half a century or so, has been not owning it.")

REVISITING VOLATILITY

Use the same approach of making common cause with the

prospect's emotions when you deal with volatility:

PROSPECT: *I can't deal with the market's volatility.*

SUPERSTAR: *Neither can I ... nobody can.* (Silence)

-OR-

PROSPECT: *The market could be down 500 points tomorrow.*

SUPERSTAR: *Or, what's even worse, the market could be up 500 points tomorrow!* (Silence)

-OR-

PROSPECT: *I could buy this fund at $11 today, and see it at $9 in a week.*

SUPERSTAR: *Or at $8 ... or $13!* (Silence)

-OR-

PROSPECT: *The market has become far too volatile for the individual investor.*

SUPERSTAR: *Exactly!* (Silence)

Several common themes run through these four non-answer answers:

- **You couldn't agree more** that the market is too volatile, or that its short-term course is impossible to predict.

- Beyond agreeing intellectually with the prospect's hatred and loathing of volatility, you want the prospect to know that **you have the same feeling.**

- For reasons the prospect can't imagine, **you are serenely unperturbed** by all this ... implying the objection doesn't matter!

When the prospect is finally able to lift his jaw off the table, here's how you can amplify the non-answers:

- *"Neither can I ... nobody can."*
  AMPLIFICATION: What's the alternative? Re-state your agreement that growth is critical to the prospect's goals. Only stocks grow. Nobody can deal with volatility; you have to have the best manager you can find. Hence: Gronsky.

- *"Or, what's even worse, the market could be up 500 points tomorrow."*

AMPLIFICATION: Volatility cuts both ways, and can only hurt you if you react to it. Even worse than panicking out after a big drop is to stop buying after a big run because the market suddenly is "too high," or taking a quick profit and then seeing the market keep going up for years. That's why you need the dispassionate management of the Gronskys.

- *"Or at $8 ... or $13!"*
  AMPLIFICATION: Again: What's your alternative? Volatility cuts both ways. Nothing that happens short term means anything, because it doesn't last. Did the prospect expect you to deny the market's volatility, or tell him it's benign?

- *"Exactly!"*
  AMPLIFICATION: But the individual investor has no alternative to growth. So he better hire a dispassionate, brilliant pro ... quickly.

Notice this approach always comes down to the spot where you want the discussion to focus. For the washout, the debate over whatever silly objection pops up becomes the life-or-death struggle. For the superstar, the only reality is THE CONCEPT. Yes, the equity market is risky and volatile in the short term. But in the long run, it's the greatest creator of real wealth that's ever been designed. Which do you want to focus on?

Imagine your car breaks down in the middle of Death Valley. If somebody doesn't come along soon, you'll die. Then, as the sun beats down and your tongue begins to swell ... just when you're at wits' end ... there on the horizon is an oncoming car. It's getting closer ... closer ... and ... oh, no! It's green. *You hate green cars!* So ... you wave the guy on.

Put this book down right now. Find somebody in the office who's good at calligraphy and have that person make you a sign. Get the sign framed, and hang it prominently in your office — where it should remain until I personally tell you to take it down. The sign says:

"VOLATILITY" IS THE GREEN CAR.

MARKET TIMING OBJECTIONS

A kissing cousin of the volatility objection is the market timing hangup. Indeed, it's hard to say where one leaves off and the other begins. For instance, the objection "I could buy this fund at $11 and see it at $9 tomorrow" could just as easily be a market timing concern as a volatility objection.

The fact that the two issues are so closely linked should tell you the responses, too, are very similar. All responses to timing objections will center around the General Principles.

GENERAL PRINCIPLE OF RESPONSE	
OBJECTION	**PRINCIPLE**
This is the wrong time to buy.	What's your alternative? All successful investing is about time, not about timing. Short-term market swings are only important if you're investing short term. If you're investing for the long term, short-term zigzags don't matter at all. It's never the wrong time to hire the right guys.

Let's try on a few responses.

PROSPECT: **The market is too high.**

SUPERSTAR: *Too high for what?*

PROSPECT: *To buy now.*

SUPERSTAR: *Why?* (Silence)

The prospect really expected you to say "No, it's not." Then, he would have drawn you into an argument you could never win, because you can't predict the future, any more than he can. By getting you to stake out an untenable position (i.e. "now is the right time to buy"), the prospect, albeit unconsciously, is trying to bring this interview to an end without having to act. Instead, after your ubiquitous "Why?," the prospect finds himself having to defend *his* statement. His response will be very revealing.

PROSPECT: *Because we're in a recession ... the S&P 500 is at 16x earnings ... my neighbor says so ... it went down yesterday ... a guy on "Wall Street Week" said so ... my tummy hurts and I don't want to talk about this anymore ...*

The superstar wants to know how deep the prospect's conviction is, and whether the attitude comes from study of the markets, some snippet of journalism, the guy's gut, or whatever. Regardless, the response is always the same.

SUPERSTAR: *Yes, I see. Well, you may be right, or you may not be. In either case, just let me ask you:* **What has any of that got to do with your retirement date, fifteen years from now?**

PROSPECT: *Well ... not much, I guess.*

-OR-

PROSPECT: *Well, it underlines how little I can afford to make a mistake.*

SUPERSTAR: *Right. And the record of the equity market in general, and of Gronsky Quality Growth Fund in particular, suggests that, long term, the only real mistake anybody could make was* **not buying it.**

But lots of people didn't. Why? Because of a fear of short-term market considerations.

Let me ask you: Have you been good at timing the market in the past? ... knowing when to get in and get out — and actually getting in and getting out?

PROSPECT: *No, of course not.*

SUPERSTAR: *(Beaming) Welcome to the club! You're in great company: Neither have the Gronskys!! I've been in six meetings with their senior people over the last two years, and they always say the same thing: "We are not market timers. We do not predict short-term market swings well, and we do not know anyone who consistently does. We are long-term, value-oriented investors, and we buy shares in very high-quality companies whenever those shares are reasonably priced."*

But you know, Mr. Prospect, ten years ago this very day, someone didn't invest $25,000 in Gronsky Quality Growth precisely because (superstar repeats prospect's timing objection word for word). And that person's $25,000 didn't become the $150,000 it would have been today. I can't let that happen to you.

If history teaches us anything, it's that **successful investing is**

always about time, never about timing ... *and that, when you have to invest for the single most serious financial goal of your life,* ***it's never the wrong time to hire the right guys.*** *You can see the wisdom of that, can't you?*

Here's a variation on the same theme:

PROSPECT: ***The market is too high.***

SUPERSTAR: *I suppose that would be an important concern, if I were trying to induce you to play the market.* (Silence)

PROSPECT: *Huh? ... What?*

SUPERSTAR: (More magisterial silence, together with heavy, unblinking eye contact)

PROSPECT: *I don't understand.*

SUPERSTAR: *I'm sure that's my fault. I somehow must have given you the impression that an intelligent decision to begin investing in Gronsky Quality Growth Fund is a function of where stock prices will be tomorrow, or next month, or even next year. That's a complete misconception, and, to the extent that I gave it to you, I sincerely apologize.*

This decision is about hiring one of the most prominent, most accomplished money management teams in the history of American finance ... and putting that team to work for you over the next fifteen years.

I don't know what those 15 years will bring (although, with the end of the Cold War, I have some strong suspicions). Just as, 15 years ago when the Dow Jones Industrials were in the 700 to 800 range — and a President had recently been driven from office, and America had just lost its first war in history — I didn't know we'd have hit 3000 today.

I only really know two things. Luckily, they're the only two things you ever really need to know: (1) successful investing is always about time, and never about timing; and (2) when you have to invest for the single most serious financial goal of your life, it's never the wrong time to hire the right guys.

Here's how to handle a market timing objection to a bond fund:

PROSPECT: ***Interest rates are too low.***

SUPERSTAR: *That would probably be a worthwhile concern, if I were trying to induce you to buy a bond.*

PROSPECT: *Huh? … What? … I don't … well, what are you trying to do?*

SUPERSTAR: (Mildly but visibly distressed) *I'm sorry. You see, I love the Gronsky High Quality Corporate Bond Fund. And I've told the story so many times over the years, maybe I'm up too close, and I'm not explaining it well anymore.*

You've asked a fair question: What am I trying to do? Two things, really. First, create within the framework of your IRA account a mirror image of your firm's pension account — in other words, a 30% to 40% weighting in a superb portfolio of America's highest quality corporate bonds.

And second, hire the most accomplished, most trusted corporate bond fund managers I've ever known, or ever hope to know, to manage your portfolio — all day, every day until you retire.

I can't predict the cycle of interest rates, and I've never known any individual who consistently could. Frankly, I only know two things — but, luckily, they're the only two things I've ever really needed to know.

First … and second … (superstar repeats "time/timing" and "wrong time/right guys" points). You see the wisdom of that, don't you?

DEFUSING EVENT SHOCK

Another major species of the market timing delusion is connecting the decision to invest with current events. Specifically, "I can't invest now, because the market is about to get clobbered by _____."
The alleged "logic" motivating this view is twofold:

(1) The movement of the market is governed by current events (i.e. the market is what economists would call a "coincident indicator").

(2) When current events resolve themselves, all will be clear, and then the investor will be able to — and will — make a decision.

This "logic" is complete fiction — and horror fiction, at that. The market is a leading indicator, of course, and is usually about six months ahead of all but the most shocking events.

The market has always been a leading indicator of the economy — it's on the way down months before a recession starts, and on the way back up months before a slowdown ends. The conundrum is that the stock market usually goes up — and often, up a lot — just when journalism is bombarding investors with the "facts" of a recession. (Recession itself is invariably reported in the press as "The End of Economic Life in America As We Have Known It." In fact, the average recession since 1954 has taken GNP down about 1% — equivalent in percentage terms to slowing down your car from 50 mph to 49.5 mph. BULLETIN ... traffic on the beltway slowed down one-half mile per hour today!)

And, "shocking" events tend not to have any lasting effect on markets or on the economy. The single most shocking event in my lifetime was the death of President Kennedy. The Dow Jones Industrials closed that day at 711. The Dow was 25% higher a year later and 33% higher two years later.

In a much larger sense, perhaps the most horrifying event in our national life since World War II was Watergate. But if you started systematically buying stocks the day Vice President Agnew resigned in October 1973 and continued until President Nixon left office ten months later, you were up about 60% by the end of 1976.

The lesson may be that you "buy crisis" and "sell resolution." But setting a trading strategy misses the point, which is: Buy, and keep buying. Period. From any long-term perspective, **the time to buy great American common stocks is when you have the money.**

The investor can always find a short-term unresolved issue to justify not buying. And he's always wrong. Yet, when you show him the realities of economic and market history, he shakes them off. How can this be?

Pandemic Risk Aversion Psychosis is one explanation — after all, it's a psychosis, the ultimate divorce from reality. But PRAP is probably a cop-out whereby you give up, and don't face the fact that when a prospect hides behind an intellectually indefensible short-term issue, he's really saying, "I don't trust you."

The failure isn't in the prospect ... nor in the lists of crises, recessions and disasters the wholesalers give you to show how the markets always shake 'em off. These lists and charts are nice, and perfectly true, as far as they go ... which isn't very far. The trouble is, pieces of paper don't sell people things. People sell people things. Not even a ream of paper will induce a man and his wife to trust you with their life's savings. Only you can.

So, go into Q&A remembering that the stated issue (recession/war/tax bill/budget deficit/Presidential election) is rarely the real issue. The real issue is "Can I trust you?"

People don't buy for four reasons. In descending order of importance, they are: no trust, no need, no help, no hurry. In voicing a current events objection, the investor appears to be saying, "There's no hurry." In fact, he's saying, "There's no trust." (Remember, people have trouble verbalizing what disturbs them most. So a guy may say, "I don't trust Wall Street," but he means "I don't trust you.") The prospect doesn't necessarily think the market is going to go against him from here. More ominously, he fears you'd sell him this fund even if you thought the market was going in the tank.

Thus, answering the stated "current event" objection is certain death. You need to shake the prospect up, and get the focus on you, as fast and as hard as you can.

Let's see how it's done.

PROSPECT: *I want to wait until after the recession ... war ... election ... etc.*

SUPERSTAR: *What will you know then about your son's college education (your retirement) that you don't know now?*

PROSPECT: *Huh? ... What? ... No, no, I mean I want to see what the market does.*

SUPERSTAR: *Why?*

-OR-

Let me save you the trouble. After the recession (war ... election ... etc.), the market will be a little higher ... or a little lower. (Silence)

PROSPECT: *What? What's that supposed to mean?*

SUPERSTAR: *It means a whole lot of things; I'll just focus for a moment on two of them.*

First, and most important, neither of us has any idea what "the market" will do in the next ninety days. And in the context of your son's education (your retirement), the next market zig or zag is immaterial. Believe me, if I thought you had a prayer of changing the outcome of your Gronsky Quality Growth investment over the next twelve years by waiting... you wouldn't have to put me off, I'd be putting you off.

*But nothing that you do in the next 90 days will affect the 10-year outcome one iota. If you'd put $12,000 a year in Gronsky Quality Growth in only the **lowest** month in each of the last ten years... and I'd put in $1,000 **every** month for the same ten years... our returns wouldn't differ by more than about 1.5% a year! And who can pick the year's lows every time?*

I only know three things, but those are the only three that matter: (1) the Gronsky Group and I are your partners in this thing. You bring the need and the discipline, we'll bring the expertise and the character... and together, we'll get you where you need to be; (2) successful investing is always about time, never about timing; and (3) it's never the wrong time to hire the right guys. So you have to believe the Gronskys and I are the right guys.

Do you believe that?

Here is a variation:

PROSPECT: *I want to watch it for a while.*

SUPERSTAR: *What exactly do you want to watch it do?* (Silence)

PROSPECT: (Spluttering, choking sounds)

SUPERSTAR: *Seriously, in the next sixty days, this fund will either go up or down, probably less than 5%. If it's up, that won't make me right; and if it's down, that won't make me wrong.*

The only thing we can say conclusively is that, over the next 60 days, two of the 144 months until your boy goes to college (you retire) will have slipped away.

And for what? Over the last ten years, GQGF turned $25,000 into about $150,000. But if you look at it in two month clips, you'd probably say: "Nothing happened."

Also, two months from now, you won't know any more about

the Gronskys' expertise — or about my professional and personal commitment to helping you reach your goals — than you do right now.

It's never the wrong time to hire the right guys. **Do you believe that we're the right guys?**

Always end the response with the question, "Do you trust me?" That's where the focus has to be. Otherwise, you'll sit there prattling about the Berlin Blockade/Korean War/Ike's heart attacks/Nov. 22/Tonkin Gulf/Cambodia/Kent State/Watergate/Challenger/Black Monday/Saddam... and the prospect will say, as he always does, *"This time it's different."*

You are the bridge. That's your right, your responsibility, your challenge and your privilege. Stand by your guns; hold the bridge.

THE COMPUTER BOOGEYMAN

Another recent variation on the market-timing/volatility/current-events theme is the notion of the computer as boogeyman. This objection focuses on "program trading," or "computerized trading," as an evil force waiting to destroy the investor as soon as you trick him into stepping into "the stock market."

A time-honored tradition, going back to the Luddites, is seeing the machine itself as the repository of evil. (For those of you whose 19th century British history is a little rusty, the Luddites were factory workers who, during the Industrial Revolution, smashed the new machines they feared would take their jobs.) After the stock market crash of 1929, a serious movement arose aimed at banning the entry of buy and sell orders for stocks over the telephone — as if the telephone, and not the people who used it, caused all the trouble.

So, the program trading phobia is in this great tradition. The "logic" of the phobia appears to be as follows:

(1) Computers/programs have the power to drive the market down (*never up, only down,* like "volatility") suddenly and hellaciously.

(2) When the real long-term values of the great American companies come up against the evil PC, the PC will win.

This is technological McCarthyism (a couple of hundred communist conspirators, tunneling inside the State Department, can bring down America, regardless of the strength and resilience of the American system and regardless of the commitment of the American people to their traditional values). It's another symptom of the widespread fear that the market is a casino at best — a huge conspiracy against the small investor at worst. And it's another signal that people today can only focus on the *price of stocks,* rather than on the *value of companies.*

In fact, program trading is, long term, the ultimate non-event … unless, like PRAP itself, program trading phobia turns out to be a long-term positive. How? The phobia may be keeping large amounts of capital out of the market — capital that will come pouring in like Niagara Falls the next time the Great Shunt of public psychology switches from fear to greed … *after* you, your clients, the Gronskys and I are in there with both feet.

While we're waiting to find out, let's craft a response to the program trading objection:

PROSPECT: ***I'm not going to make an equity investment; program trading will kill me.***

SUPERSTAR: *How?*

PROSPECT: (Sputtering, with or without random, unfocused vituperation)

SUPERSTAR: *Program trading not only can't kill you, it can't touch your long-term investment results at all.* (Silence)

PROSPECT: (Blowing himself out like a summer squall, and more than a little intrigued by the superstar's imperturbability) *All right. Explain, please.*

SUPERSTAR: *Glad to. You see, program trading is just a way certain traders rush to catch up with whichever way the market is zigging or zagging at the moment. So, of course, you see exaggerated short-term moves in either direction, because these guys fall all over each other getting in or out.*

Funny, the newspapers only talk about program trading on the downside, like in October of '87. But program trading helped push the market to its biggest one-week gain ever, when the Allies attacked Iraq in January of '91, and nobody said boo about that. Well, never mind …

The bottom line, like any other aspect of the market's short-term zigs and zags, is that program trading is a total non-event to the long-term investor. Twelve years from now, when your boy is taking a double major at Harvard (when you're fishing in the Keys), neither program trading nor any other "headline" will matter. You see that, don't you?

Please note that program trading, like "volatility," can only affect you if you let it change *your* program — if you let it take you off the track. You can stand on a railroad platform all day long, watching trains go by. Trains have tremendous destructive force if you step onto the tracks in front of them. But if you use trains for the intended purpose, you'll be fine. If you just stand on the platform until the train stops, then get on and sit down ... you have harnessed all that power to take you where you want to go.

*   *   *

By the time you read this book, the program trading objection may be a laughable antique, like the Edsel. But, make no mistake about it: Another journalistically induced *objection du jour* will have arisen to take its place. Although this chapter has been devoted to handling today's main objections, don't take your eye off the big picture. The most important principles — the timeless ones — remain constant:

(1) **The stated objection isn't the real objection.**

(2) **Know the "General Principle of Response" to each major objection.**

(3) **Craft your individual responses using "The Patriot Missiles" to regain control of the agenda.**

SUMMARY

• Today's major stated objections are the sales charge, risk and volatility. But, the real issue is your relationship with the prospect.

• The sales charge objection is really a way of asking if your services — at the point of sale and in future times of stress— are worth it. Only you can answer that.

• The General Principle of Response to "risk" is that the ultimate risk is purchasing power. To "volatility," it's that volatility blows both ways, but only in the short run. Value is forever; value drives price, not the other way around.

• The Q&A/objections phase of the interview is a potential generator of anger in the planner/salesperson. Anger is the ultimate downward spiral because all anger is ultimately directed inward.

• The Three Patriot Missiles of Q&A rob an objection of all force by showing the prospect that the superstar is not perturbed by the issue.

• If the ultimate risk is purchasing power, then inflation is the dragon. Growth is St. George. And only equities grow.

• It's OK to tell the prospect volatility scares you, too. But, if growth is the only answer, what's the alternative? "VOLATILITY" IS THE GREEN CAR.

• Another common objection is the market-timing/current-events issue. Short term, the market is unknowable, and long term the event won't matter. The key issues are: (1) successful investing is always about time, never about timing; and (2) it's never the wrong time to hire the right guys.

• The overriding issue is, always, trust.

20

Q&A/Objections Handling 3: More Objections, The Most Powerful Response, And The Close

Where was the Dow Jones Industrial Average on the day your prospect was born? If you don't know the answer, find out and you'll have a powerful tool to help you conquer the amazing misconception that common stocks (and the mutual funds which own them) don't make money.

The average person's rather bizarre view of the stock market is primarily due to a loss of long-term perspective. What better way to restore perspective than to personalize the stock market's performance by showing where the market was on the day most people feel is extremely important — their date of birth.

The effect of this information is very startling, in an intensely personal way. For anyone born on or after July 8, 1932 (the day the Dow bottomed out for the century at 40.56), the message is clear:

THE STOCK MARKET HAS BEEN GOING UP ALL YOUR LIFE!

Of course the market went down at times, and long periods saw essentially sideways movement. So what? The basic trend of the American economy — and the equity market which mirrors the economy over time — has been pretty much straight up for 60 years. (And now, the economy is going global!)

This reality gives you the Basic Principle of Response to the next major class of objections:

GENERAL PRINCIPLE OF RESPONSE	
OBJECTION	PRINCIPLE
My neighbor/mother/ barber/lover/veterinarian lost money in an equity fund.	The poor result was caused by something the individual did to himself. Because, long term, how do you lose money in a market that's been going up for 60 years?

Let's try it in practice:

PROSPECT: *My brother-in-law lost money in an equity mutual fund.*

SUPERSTAR: *You always said your brother-in-law was stupid, and that proves it.*

(Only kidding. It's almost the end of the book, and I just wanted to see if you were still paying attention. Obviously, that response doesn't belong in a real conversation because it's too nasty ... even if it is true. Start over again.)

PROSPECT: *My brother-in-law lost money in an equity mutual fund.*

SUPERSTAR: (Obviously stunned) *Good heavens! ... HOW??*

The prospect (albeit unconsciously) postulated the following incredible hypothesis: I know someone who lost money in an equity mutual fund; therefore one can lose money in an equity fund; therefore I will lose money in the equity mutual fund you're recommending.

The superstar, as always, saw the objection coming a mile away and simply refused to be drawn. He not only declined to answer the stated objection, he didn't buy into the *implication*. Instead, he responds with a PDOOI (Public Display Of Obvious Incredulity), and turns the question around on the prospect.

In contrast, the washout accepts any question or objection, no matter how weird or outrageous, as serious and worthy of an answer. Instead of gaining credibility with the prospect, he loses it. Deep down the prospect knows his objection is shaky at best and can't imagine why the poor soul is taking it so seriously. The net effect of the washout's approach is to diminish whatever little communication was established previously and heighten the conversation's unmistakable sense of unreality.

The superstar hears the "I-know-somebody-who-lost-money-in-this" dodge, and says PDOOI:

- *"What?? Are you sure? How?"*
- *"How in the world did he do that?"*
- *"Amazing!"*
- *"How is that possible?"* (Optional: hold up the mountain chart while responding.)
- *"How, I wonder?"*

Follow the response with a particularly stunned version of the superstar's trademark magisterial silence. What's at issue here is trust. The prospect said he'd rather believe the fragmentary experience of a known jerk than what you are telling him. So the superstar knows the trust dipstick reads two quarts low. He turns the issue back to the client, with the clear implication that he has so much faith in his product he literally cannot see how anyone could *ever* lose money in it. Let's hear what happens next.

PROSPECT: *Well, uh, I don't know ... he just said ... uh ...*

SUPERSTAR: *Now that I think about it, there is a way you could, theoretically, have lost a little money — but I'd never let **my** clients fall into it. If you'd stampeded into a fund when everybody was bullish, in 1986 and early '87, and then stampeded out again after Black Monday ... I guess maybe you would have to say, "I lost money in a mutual fund."*

But clearly, the mutual fund isn't at fault; the investor did it to himself. Either he was badly advised, or simply made his own bad decisions.

You're not responsible for his result, and I'm certainly not responsible for it. Look again: Do you doubt the Gronsky Quality Growth has turned $25,000 into $150,000 since 1980? Do you think the numbers are flawed in some way, or some important truth is left out?

PROSPECT: *Well, no ... I, uh ...*

SUPERSTAR: (Clearly relieved) *I feel better. My practice involves finding the highest quality, most reliable ways to help investors like you reach their most important goals in life. Maybe I take myself too seriously, but my job, to me, is like a sacred trust. So I'd feel terrible if you thought I'd ever recommend something to you I wouldn't own myself or involve my own family in. You understand that, don't you?*

-OR-

SUPERSTAR: *Saying you don't want to own this portfolio because somebody, somewhere managed to lose money is like saying: "A guy threw himself in front of an oncoming train once, so I'm never going to ride a train again."*

> *Forget it. The guy was suicidal. I don't think you are. I'm certainly not, and neither are the Gronsky people. They've been making fortunes for serious long-term investors all my life. I'd be delighted to see them start doing the same for you today. I believe you deserve that! Do you believe it?*

Friends, you know how loath I am to burden you with facts and numbers, particularly when we're discussing the almost purely emotional issues of Q&A/objections. But I'm constrained to remind you that the Lipper Growth Fund Index — the S&P 500 of growth mutual funds — increased nearly three-fold, from 163.5 to 461.6, in the decade ending on December 31, 1990. You know somebody who lost money in funds? PDOOI! *The issue is trust.*

OBJECTING TO WHAT THE FUND ISN'T

The next great class of objections hangs the discussion up on what your proposed investment isn't. In a variation on this theme, the prospect suggests some other investment medium is "better."

Say you spend a lot of time building agreement with a prospect on the absolutely critical nature of holding long-term growth stocks in his portfolio. Then, you present Gronsky Quality Growth, in all its magnificence. Right at the end, the guy says, "3% yield? That's not enough." Since these objections come in an infinite variety, we must establish the central objection and the General Principle of Response.

GENERAL PRINCIPLE OF RESPONSE	
OBJECTION	**PRINCIPLE**
One particular aspect of the fund is objectionable or inadequate.	The fund is what it is. All benefits of the fund — and the underlying portfolio— are economic trade-offs. You give up something to get something else.

Let's apply the principle to the "low-yield-on-a-growth-stock-fund" objection:

PROSPECT: *3% yield? That's not enough.*

SUPERSTAR: *Enough for what?*

PROSPECT: *Why, I can get 7% from a money market fund!*

SUPERSTAR: *Yes, you could.* (Silence)

PROSPECT: *So why isn't 7% better than 3%?*

SUPERSTAR: *Because, after taxes and inflation, you're treading water— as we agreed when we talked about why you need equities in the first place.*

I think what you're doing — and it's perfectly understandable — is slipping back into a one-issue comparison; in this case, current yield.

But every investment involves an economic trade-off. You can have good growth from an investment, or you can have higher income. But you can't have both at the same time.

Here, you can give the prospect an example from the fund's portfolio to make the abstract more real.

SUPERSTAR: *Look at the fund's holding in Phillip Morris. The current dividend from the stock is $1.72. But it's earning $4.80 a share. So the vast majority of earnings go back into growing the business. And what happens when the business grows? The earnings go up, and so does the dividend. In fact, Phillip Morris' dividend has grown at nearly a 20% compound rate over the last 20 years ... more than three times the rate of inflation. Can you see why that's going to be so important for your retirement? Are you OK on this issue now?*

Here's another, more general example you can use.

SUPERSTAR: *Say you bought a business for a million dollars. And the business throws off $100,000 in earnings a year. You can pay all the earnings out in dividends. But, your business can't grow. Or you can pay $30,000 in dividends — the 3% yield you referred to a minute ago — and put the other $70,000 into growing the business. And in a few years, maybe the business will be worth $2 million. Do you see that's always the fundamental trade-off? Are you OK on this now?*

If the prospect is still objecting, he's telling you either his investment goals are not those he described, or psychologically, he needs a more conservative approach — a balanced fund, say, or an equity income fund, even if that choice means giving up some growth. (You must repeat that conclusion back to him, in so many words, and get agreement before proceeding.)

Or suppose you're showing someone a municipal bond fund, and you hear this:

PROSPECT: *This municipal bond fund only yields 7%. That's not enough.*

SUPERSTAR: *Enough for what?* (Silence)

-OR-

Strictly speaking, the fund doesn't yield anything at all. (Silence)

-OR-

The bond market doesn't seem to agree with you. (Silence)

-OR-

I'm not sure I understand. Are you saying you'd be prepared to come down in quality in order to pick up extra yield? (Silence)

All four responses say: That's all she wrote. Sufficient unto the day are the interest rates thereof. The *fund* doesn't yield anything; a portfolio of this quality gives you this much return right now — go argue with the bond market, not with me or the Gronskys. You aren't trying to predict the interest rate cycle here, are you?

The prospect's reaction to the first three responses above will be some combination of "What?" and "Huh?," perhaps spiced up with "What are you talking about?" His response to the fourth will probably be, "Heavens, no," or words to that effect. Then:

SUPERSTAR: *If you're going to stay with a portfolio of this quality, 7% is the market. Yields have been both higher and lower ... and will be again. But 7% is today's yield on paper of this quality.*

If your goals are the ones we've agreed on — the best income available from a beautifully diversified, superbly managed portfolio of high-quality municipal bonds — you should be happy with this fund. If your goals are different — if something

else is on your agenda — perhaps we have to look elsewhere.

But I don't think so. I think those really are your priorities. That's right, isn't it?

Here's another typical "what-the-fund-isn't" objection to a municipal bond fund:

PROSPECT: **If I buy your municipal bond fund, I'll have to pay state and local taxes on the income.**

SUPERSTAR: (Beaming) Yes. (Silence)

PROSPECT: *You don't seem to understand. That's a criticism.*

SUPERSTAR: (With a trace of horror) No, no, it can't be! You've just put your finger on one of the key reasons I love Gronsky Quality Tax-Free Income Fund: beautiful geographical diversification!

Of course you'll pay a little tax on the income from portfolio bonds outside your state. The alternative is to buy bonds all from the same state.

I could never, in good conscience, counsel you to put all your municipal bond investments in one state. Why, that's not an investment strategy, it's legislative Russian roulette!

You do see the wisdom of broad geographic diversification, don't you?

Ever hear this one?

PROSPECT: **I can't go long term. I have to keep my powder dry.**

SUPERSTAR: *Why?*

-OR-

Exactly! That's the real genius of open-end funds.

Clearly, the stated issue here is the prospect's liquidity *wants* as opposed to his liquidity *needs*. But, don't bother debating the point, because the real objection is, "I don't trust you." Just play along for a while.

PROSPECT: *Huh? ... What? ... I don't understand.*

SUPERSTAR: *The true genius of the open-end mutual fund is total liquidity. Any day you want to be gone, you're gone.*

I confess that, given the long-term nature of the goals we've agreed on, I don't quite see why you think you need much liquidity. But (beaming), heaven knows, in any Gronsky fund, you've got it!

PROSPECT: Yes, but ... you don't know what the fund will be worth.

SUPERSTAR: (With growing mystification) Sure you do; you'll get the value of the securities in the portfolio the day you sell.

PROSPECT: But you don't know how much that will be!

SUPERSTAR: Of course not. That's the price you pay for instant, total, guaranteed liquidity. It has nothing to do with mutual funds, or the Gronskys, or me. Heck, if you buy a one-year Treasury note, and need to sell in six months, you'll either get more or less than you paid. If you cash in a CD right away, you'll pay a penalty!

Listen, maybe it's my turn to let you talk, because I don't know where we're going with this. I don't think you're really worried about liquidity, because that's a non-issue. I think you're worried about something else, but I can't figure out what it is. Can you try to put your concern into words for me?

Let's try on a couple of "something else is better" objections:

PROSPECT: **Individual money managers do better than funds.**

SUPERSTAR: Actually, that depends on the investor himself. (Silence)

PROSPECT: What? ... Huh? ... What does that mean?

SUPERSTAR: Well, first of all, individual money management only starts to make economic sense at about $100,000. Since you initially indicated you had about $45,000 to work with, I ruled that out. But I'm happy to re-examine the issue, if you'll consider a substantially greater commitment. (Wait for response.)

Second, if you're going to be accumulating capital in the twelve years until you retire, a fund is the peerless vehicle. An individual money manager won't take $1,000 a month from you, because he couldn't efficiently invest or compound small sums.

For large sums of money, an individually managed account may make sense. But, in your case, a Gronsky fund still looks to me like the ideal solution.

In investments, you'll usually find no objective "better" and *"worse"* — only *"better for your situation,"* and *"worse for you."* That makes good sense to you, doesn't it?

Here's another beauty:

PROSPECT: **Mutual funds underperform Chinese ceramics ... real estate ... stamps ... Confederate autographs ...**

SUPERSTAR: *Everything outperforms everything sometimes. And then, the rest of the time, it doesn't.* (Silence)

PROSPECT: *What are you talking about?*

SUPERSTAR: *This goes to the heart of everything I've always said to you about asset allocation and proper diversification. During the 1970s, hard assets like real estate did great, stocks just lay there, and bonds got creamed. The '80s saw real estate, oil and precious metals get massacred; stocks and bonds soared. Art was the darling of the greed cycle of '82 to '89, and the next year they couldn't get a bid for Greta Garbo's Renoir.*

No asset class permanently outperforms any other asset class (after you adjust for risk and liquidity). So what do all the really wealthy investors own? You guessed it: a little bit of everything. You see the wisdom of that, don't you?

THE ULTIMATE WEAPON

We come now to the greatest, most wonderful, most liberating, most useful response imaginable — a response perfectly applicable to an almost infinite number of investor questions. During your superstar apprenticeship you may use this response at least once in every fund sales interview for the next two years. It is, of course ...

"I DON'T KNOW."

You really want to spend a lot of time practicing this answer, because its psychological and practical uses are so powerful. "I don't know" is the ultimate non-answer answer, which, when used properly, completely changes the direction of your conversation. With it, you will immediately regain control of the sales interview.

The superstar knows that "I don't know" is his best friend. The washout fears it pathologically. The superstar *can't wait* to be asked a question to which he doesn't know the answer. In fact, to hasten the interview to a successful conclusion, the superstar may say, "I don't know," even when he knows the answer. The washout not only doesn't use this tactic, he can't even believe it exists.

The superstar realizes that saying "I don't know" regains all the initiative. When the washout is finally forced to say, "I don't know," he feels he should have known and has failed. And yet both superstar and washout are reacting to the very same question.

How is this possible? Asked the same question they can't answer, how can one salesperson close the transaction in the next five minutes, while another lets his inability to answer zero out his ego and allow the sales interview to wind down into failure?

The difference certainly can't be product knowledge, since neither salesperson knows the answer. So the distinction must have something to do with *attitude.*

Even as he struggles up the learning curve, the emerging superstar is convinced he knows the most important conceptual truths about a fund and its managers. But he also knows he may be asked a question he can't answer. So, he prepares a fall-back position which works *every time.*

The emerging washout has never been able to shake the psychology which says: "I'm supposed to know this stuff." He has not accepted the probability of a question he can't answer. So, he has no fall-back. He has only fear — and fear kills confidence. So, the poor fellow is already on a downward spiral to failure.

(The other thing the washout never accepted was that prospecting is a numbers game. He has his ego invested in the outcome of every single presentation, so each failure is a real blow to his self-confidence. The washout takes rejection personally, and then wonders why he can't complete his prospecting program.)

Having a sure-fire, all purpose fall-back changes the emerging superstar's attitude ...

THE SUPERSTAR IS NEVER AFRAID.

Confidence is the critical commodity in selling managed money. During Q&A, the prospect is probing — not just for how much you know, but for a sense of your genuine *confidence* in the fund. The lighter, easier, and more succinct you are, the more the prospect receives the subliminal message: "I have perfect confidence in this fund's superiority and in the fact that it's a marvelous fit for you."

When you arrive at the moment of truth … **when you are asked a question you can't answer … the fact that you are not disconcerted has a tremendous impact on the prospect.** The ability to sit there, smile, shrug, and say, "I don't know" — and then not say anything else for a few moments — tells the prospect in the most forceful way that your unshakable conviction isn't based on an endless accumulation of small details but on the higher realities of the fund and its management.

This attitude says (nonverbally), "Stop! You're looking for the truth in all the wrong places. I don't know the answer to that question, and clearly the fact that I don't know doesn't concern me — or even particularly interest me."

In those few moments of silence, the prospect looks at you, sitting there in perfect calm … and suddenly hears what you have *really* said:

VERBAL: *I don't know.*

NONVERBAL: *And, therefore, the question is probably not important.*

That's the initial reason the superstar welcomes the question he can't answer. He is selling himself as opposed to selling the number of technical details he knows. The superstar wants to focus the conversation back on himself and on the paramount issue of the fund.

In this situation, owning a little bit of the fund you love to sell can pay extra dividends to you. When you've made your prospect aware you own the fund yourself during your conceptual presentation, then the nonverbal "other shoe" drops with an even louder thud:

VERBAL: *I don't know.*

NONVERBAL: *And I'm an investment professional who bought this fund for his own account. So if I didn't care enough to investigate this particular point, it must not matter.*

The "I don't know" response helps draw Q&A to an end. Your silence suggests you've been through all the major points, and the questions are now getting irrelevant.

Other than by instinct, how can you be sure the question isn't material to the investment decision? That's easy:

YOU ALREADY KNOW WHAT
ALL THE IMPORTANT QUESTIONS ARE.

Wouldn't you? After all, if you're committed to present this fund at least once (and perhaps more) every day, you wouldn't start without first sitting down with the wholesaler, or your firm's professionals, and asking:

"What are the ten most common, most important questions or objections about this fund?"

Don't accept fast answers to this question, either. Make everybody take time and really work out the big questions/objections and the answers. (If you ask more than one person, ask them separately. Then compare and contrast the lists, looking very hard at the differences and probing for reasons.)

Now, you know the answers to the major questions you will face. So, when Q&A wanders beyond your list, you'll have a pretty strong feeling the conversation is drifting, and you should regain control with your serene and imperturbable "I don't know."

Suppose you say, "I don't know" and sit calmly, saying nothing… but the prospect doesn't say anything either. His non-response creates a somewhat different kettle of fish. In this situation, go ahead and gently ask:

"Is that important to you?"

The answer may very well be, "I don't suppose it matters much," which is, in every case, a signal to begin your close. The prospect has acknowledged he's run out of important questions!

But suppose the prospect says, "Yes, I think I'd really need to know the answer." He thinks the interview is over, right? If he is talking to an emerging washout, he is correct. But with you … Wrong. Now comes the ultimate fall-back position:

GO TO YOUR BACKUP MAN.

THE BACKUP MAN:
DON'T LEAVE HOME WITHOUT ONE

This tactic is so elegant, so simple and so genuinely inevitable that only an intensely creative emerging washout would *not* think of it. Observe closely, please.

You've formulated and mastered your list of the ten most important questions/objections, so you are totally conversant with the genuine make-or-break issues in your fund. There's just one little problem: *The prospect's list may be different from yours.*

You realize the moment will inevitably come when you don't know an answer to a question the prospect thinks (or claims) is important. As Karl Malden says on the American Express commercials, "What will you do? ... What will you do?"

You look your prospect right in the eye, and say:

"I'm sure we can get the answer to that question by making a simple phone call. May I do that?"

The prospect can't say "No" without signaling that he doesn't really care about the answer. He has to let you make the call, or disqualify himself.

Who do you call? Your backup person, of course. Because under no circumstances should you, at any time during your superstar apprenticeship, go out on an appointment or have someone come into your office for a presentation, unless you ...

HAVE SOMEONE FROM THE FUND OR YOUR FIRM WAITING TO TAKE YOUR CALL.

Never make an appointment for a managed money sales interview without having a specific support person agree to be near his phone when you're out there trying to do business for him. Simple as that. The willingness and ability of a fund to provide you with nice, knowledgeable backup people is an acid test of whether you should work to raise money for them. If they can't be bothered with backing you up, you can't be bothered selling their fund. Over and out.

After all, **nothing is as effective as the third-party, call-on-the-expert close.** And when you know you have someone backing you up, you no longer have to be concerned about a question you can't answer. You have instant access to a friendly, knowledgeable voice who, as your prospect can clearly hear, knows who you are and welcomes your call. Given the backup person, why would you ever again worry about questions you can't answer?

When you invite your prospect to restate his question to your backup person, you'll find that half the force of the question has already dissipated. That's simply because the prospect now recognizes that you really are a super professional, and that this fund and its people really are quite well known to you. Remember, the question probably wasn't what was really bothering the prospect — he may have doubted the relationship among you, your firm, and the fund sponsor. Your ability to go effortlessly to the backup person alleviates all such concerns.

If enhanced credibility is all this technique accomplishes, it would be worth using. But there's more. **Going to the backup person moves the sales interview from Q&A to a close.** A little gentle prodding from you is all that's needed to make the transition.

When your client has restated the question you couldn't (or wouldn't) answer, your backup person will, of course, have a very logical and compelling answer. (Remember: There is no smoking gun.) Then, come back into the conversation by asking this question:

> *"Before we let (Mr. Backup) off the phone, are there any other questions or problems on your mind that would prevent you from making this investment today?"*

The idea is to keep everyone on the phone until all questions are smoked out and answered. Now the prospect is in a position to make an intelligent decision, *right then and there.*

This tactic is also an effective way of short-circuiting some stalls to which a prospect may resort. Picture someone sitting in your office on a conference call with an executive of a major fund company. After all that, will the prospect say he has to talk it over with his wife? Not likely.

The backup person is probably the single most effective tool you can use to overcome the constant anxiety of the infinite number of technical questions to which you don't know the answer. And you can't grow into a truly effective communicator/salesperson if you live under a cloud of concern. The day will surely come when the anxiety is gone — when you have learned the elusive answers and your need for the backup person withers away. But until that day comes: *No backup person, no appointment.*

THE ULTIMATE DISQUALIFIER

Let's talk about stalls a little longer. None are quite as ludicrous as the prospect saying he has to show a fund prospectus to his accountant or attorney. This stall is about as close as you come to the ultimate prospect disqualifier. In fact, let's postulate a rule on the subject:

THE PROSPECT WHO SAYS HE MUST CONSULT HIS CPA FOR AN INVESTMENT UNDER $25,000 IS NO PROSPECT.

(One possibly valid exception: pension plan sales.)

You can probe for a while, if you have the energy, but I doubt much will come of it. Respond as though you were hearing any off-the-wall comment. Ask, "Why?" in amazement. Usually, the prospect will say something like he wants the CPA to tell him whether or not the fund is a good investment.

Isn't that depressing? You've spent all this time establishing a need, talking about how well your firm knows the Gronskys and what makes them superior managers, telling the prospect (if it's true) that you own the fund yourself ... and he says he wants his CPA to tell him if it's good. What is he really telling you? Right. "You've told me it's good, but I don't believe you." Let him go. He's not going to show the fund to his CPA, and who cares? You're never going to do any significant business with this person because he's not prepared to trust you. The prospect has "Bond/CD Buyer" written all over him. He only believes, heaven help us, in "guarantees." In the time you sit there wondering what you could have possibly said to this bird, you can make two more hash marks on your "baseline" call chart.

MOVING PAST A COMMON STALL

Of course, there are some very effective stalls. The most common is:

PROSPECT: *I'd like to think it over.*

When you hear this one, all you say is:

SUPERSTAR: *Very good! And I'm here to help you with the process. This investment is going to be at the core of your education (retirement) planning, and you must be comfortable with it.*

On the other hand, we've both been in the position, I'll bet, of letting a great investment opportunity slip by, and then biting our tongue when we see what it's worth a year later. When you think this over, will you be focusing primarily on the integrity of the people?"

Now, go through a whole laundry list of the fund's greatest attributes, which, in every case, the prospect has heard and at least tacitly acknowledged earlier.

SUPERSTAR: *Do you need to think about the wisdom of owning great, dividend-growing companies?*

PROSPECT: *No, I see that.*

SUPERSTAR: *Do you need to think about the total flexibility and liquidity of the fund?*

PROSPECT: *No, that's clear.*

SUPERSTAR: *Is the ability to switch into different funds within the Gronsky family, at no charge, something you need to think about?*

PROSPECT: *No ...*

The prospect's inclination will be to keep saying no, since each of these aspects of the fund is actually quite good. And you will get to deliver a very quick summation of the best features of your fund. Then:

SUPERSTAR: *It's really just the difficulty of making an important decision like this, isn't it? I understand; I struggle with it all the time myself. What the decision comes down to — and there's no way around this — is a matter of trust. You have to find in yourself a belief that I'm as committed to your goals and as careful about choosing investments as I've told you I am. In the meantime, just think: You're retiring in twelve years. Look at what the fund has done for people in the last twelve years. And ask yourself:* **How would you feel today if you'd passed up the chance to buy the fund twelve years ago?**

The ultimate cruncher — one of the most powerful ideas the planner/salesperson has — is the fact that when people procrastinate and let great investment opportunities slip by, they regret it. So, be ready for the delaying objection, play it back through a list of benefits reinforcing your fund's attractiveness, and end by asking how the prospect would feel if he missed the opportunity to buy in some years ago. That will speed up his decision-making.

ISOLATE THE BLOCK AND CLOSE

My theory of closing is consistent with my Q&A theory: The reason that a prospect gives you for not investing is not the real reason. The challenge is to get him comfortable enough to tell you what's really bothering him, so you can then break up his real source of resistance.

The tactic is called "isolating the blocking objection" and consists of three parts:

(1) **Cushion the objection by reacting with sympathy and respect.**

(2) **Ask if the objection is the single one remaining that's preventing your prospect from making the investment.** In other words, if you could cause this objection not to be a problem, would the prospect buy the fund?

(3) **Only after hearing an affirmative answer to the previous question, proceed to do away with the objection ... then close again.**

Here's an example:

SUPERSTAR: *If you have no more questions, can I suggest a $25,000 investment to start with now?*

PROSPECT: *I don't think so. I'm still afraid that the deficit is going to drive up interest rates and kick the slats out from under the stock market.*

SUPERSTAR: *I very much respect your concern. We all respond emotionally to the idea of an unbalanced budget. And, even though our national debt is a little less as a percentage of GNP than it was five or ten years ago, the huge increase in dollar terms tends to disturb us, in a very visceral way.*

But tell me: If there were some way to relieve your concern — if I could make you reasonably comfortable even with the deficit uncertainty — **would you have any other concerns that would cause you not to want to own this fund?**

PROSPECT: *No. That's my big problem. I'm just not sure how the economy can handle the deficit!*

SUPERSTAR: *That's fine. I think the problem here — as it so often is when we're trying to make long-term investments — is simply one of perspective.*

My perspective is that at any given time, we're always faced with a problem which, if you listen to newspapers and other media, is insurmountable. The next time you turn around, the problem has been dealt with, and the economy is making new highs — and the market right along with it.

For instance, if the stock market ever went down 85% and there was 20% unemployment, could the economy survive?

PROSPECT: *No, of course not.*

SUPERSTAR: *And yet it did. I've just described the 1929-32 experience. What if, a few years later, we had the smallest standing army of any industrialized nation in the world and suddenly found that we had to fight a world war in both Asia and Europe? That might be curtains, right?*

PROSPECT: *Yes, I see what you're doing, but ...*

SUPERSTAR: *One American President shot to death, and another driven from office under threat of impeachment, within 11 years? Pretty grim. And, in between, one party's probable presidential candidate and the nation's greatest civil rights leader assassinated within a couple of months? Oil prices tripling one day, then doubling again six years later? Inflation in the low teens, and a prime rate in the high teens? That'd just about put us under, wouldn't it? How about a one-day 22% decline in the stock market? Armageddon?*

PROSPECT: *No, no; of course not.*

SUPERSTAR: *That's right. Of course not. Mr. Prospect, I can't tell you how, but in another ten years today's deficit will be woven into the tapestry of apparent disasters — ones that are troublesome in the short term and completely forgettable in the long run.*

I may have said this before, but if we'd been sitting here talking in 1980, I could never have predicted that a $25,000 investment in Gronsky Quality Growth Fund would have grown to $150,000. And I can't predict what the next ten years will be like (although, with the 40-year nightmare of the Cold War now over, I have my suspicions).

I just know this: For 60 years, whenever someone didn't commit to long-term growth in America's greatest companies, he lost the opportunity to make a fortune.

Nothing's changed. Will you tell me to go ahead and get started now?

PROSPECT: *You bet I will. And thanks.*

The foregoing is a nice, simplified example of a case where the stated objection actually turned out to be the real objection. But look how long and painstaking the superstar's answer was. Suppose the stated objection was not the real one; look how long you'd have labored for no productive purpose. Isolating the blocking objection helps insulate you from this risk.

Suppose the conversation had gone this way:

SUPERSTAR: *If you have no more questions, can I suggest a $25,000 investment to start with now?*

PROSPECT: *I don't think so. I'm still afraid that the deficit is going to drive up interest rates and kick the slats out from under the stock market.*

SUPERSTAR: *I very much respect your concern. We all respond emotionally to the idea of an unbalanced budget. And, even though our national debt is a little less as a percentage of GNP than it was five or ten years ago, the huge increase in dollar terms tends to disturb us, in a very visceral way.*

But tell me: If there were some way to relieve that concern — if I could make you reasonably comfortable with the deficit uncertainty — would you have any other concerns that would cause you not to want to own this fund?

PROSPECT: *Well, it's just that… you see, chucking the whole $25,000 in at once scares me to death. I just don't want to do that. Isn't there some other way?*

SUPERSTAR: *Sure there is. Why don't you put $15,000 in now, and park the other $10,000 in a money fund for six months. Does that make you more comfortable?*

PROSPECT: *Yes, it does. And thank you.*

Can you see what would have happened if you'd launched into that closely reasoned socioeconomic history of the U.S. since 1929, when all the poor fellow cared about was being able to invest gradually so he could sleep nights? The only way to reach nirvana is to isolate the blocking objection — **get the prospect's agreement first that you are dealing with his last remaining problem.**

SUMMARY

- Show the equity mutual fund prospect (using newspapers from the day he was born) that the equity market has been going up all his life. This ultimate defense powders the objection that a prospect "knows someone who lost money in funds." PDOOI: The investor who lost money in funds did it to himself.

- Learn to spot objections based on "what the fund isn't." The fund is what it is. All aspects of the fund and its portfolio are economic trade-offs. You give up one benefit to gain another.

- No matter what the stated issue may be, the real issue is always trust.

- The "I don't know" response is powerful. Say it unafraid and then pause.

- "I don't know" smokes out the prospect and promotes the start of the close.

- "I don't know" moves you into the best closing technique for your sale — using the backup person. Never leave home without one.

- Unless the proposed investment is over $25,000, or is aimed at a pension plan, the CPA stall is a disqualifier.

- Overcome the "I want to think about it" stall with an allusion to how the prospect would feel if he'd missed buying the fund in 1980.

- Isolate the blocking objection. Speak to an objection only after the prospect says he has no more.

APPENDIX I

Presenting Dollar-Cost-Averaging In Volatile Markets

Dollar-cost-averaging ("DCA") is one of those classic investment concepts that everybody professes to believe in, but almost nobody practices consistently. What's worse, people are eager to dollar-cost-average during (i.e. throw more money at) rising markets. But let the market take one of its increasingly frequent kamikaze dives, and suddenly all your long-term investors leave town.

And yet, dollar-cost-averaging works even better in volatile markets than in gently undulating markets — as long as the basic, long-term trend is up, which it always is. In other words, the greater the volatility of price movement, the greater the advantage of dollar-cost-averaging.

But you must be very careful explaining the concept to prospects and clients. Remember, we're living in an age that is obsessed with volatility. People aren't paying any attention to fundamentals, or values, or the long-term uptrend, or anything rational. In this psychology, risk attends upon the possibility that share prices can go down a lot in a hurry. The fact that prices can't *stay* down isn't part of this equation, nor is the recent phenomenon of extreme "upside" volatility.

You know from painful experience that you can't stand before a client and say, "Yes, now they're down a lot, let's load up — because *prices* can be as volatile as they like, but *value* always re-asserts itself in the long run." You are trying to talk someone out of a phobia, but you can't reason people out of irrational fears.

Nor can you ease "volatility phobia" by showing gradations, (i.e. X is half as volatile as Y). "Reduced volatility" is, as we've discussed in earlier chapters, a meaningless abstraction — a smaller caliber, but still deadly, bullet. All volatility is perceived to be fatal. The panic of claustrophobia is no less in a 30-square-foot elevator than in an elevator half the size. Panic is panic.

But you can use the incontrovertible mathematics of DCA to show people that, **when you're dollar-cost-averaging diligently, volatility is actually working for you.**

Here's how the presentation works. We all know that dollar-cost-averaging lets you buy more shares when prices are low and fewer when prices are high. If the portfolio experiences increased volatility — higher highs and lower lows — around a trend line, you'll buy even more at the lows and even less at the highs.

Say you put $1,000 a month into shares of a mutual fund. The fund starts at $10 a share at the beginning of the year, then trades as high as $12, as low as $6, and ends the year back at $10. (See table on next page.)

Now imagine you still invest $1,000 a month, but prices are more volatile. Let's say the starting and ending value is still $10 as in the earlier case, but the share prices are $1 higher in months of uptrend and $1 lower in down months.

Look at what happens in this "high volatility" case. You acquire 7% more shares in the high volatility case, at an average cost that's 6.6% lower. No lifestyle changer, by any means. But enough to suggest strongly that dollar-cost-averaging makes volatility your friend, instead of a screaming nightmare from which you can't wake up.

Never use all this data as the response to a stated objection. Remember, that's against the rules. Suppose you are showing an equity mutual fund to parents whose first child is ten years from college, and they say something like:

PARENTS: *We can't risk Junior's college education on the stock market. It's become much too volatile.*

SUPERSTAR: *Yes. And if you're going to be saving systematically for the next 120 months, you'd hope it would stay that volatile.* (Silence)

The effect of this non-answer answer is, of course, that the clients are immediately conscious of your calm professionalism and self-confidence. They don't understand why you hope the market stays

ADVANTAGE OF DCA INCREASES WITH MARKET VOLATILITY

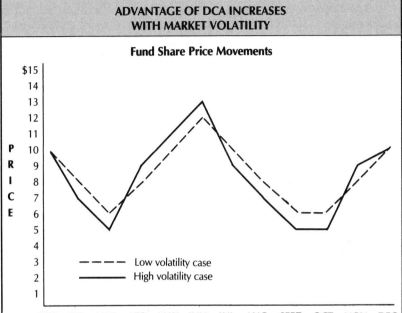

Fund Share Price Movements

- - - - Low volatility case
───── High volatility case

JAN. FEB. MAR. APR. MAY JUN. JUL. AUG. SEPT. OCT. NOV. DEC.

MONTH

$1000 Systematic Investment Per Month

Month	Lower Volatility Case Price	Number Of Shares	Higher Volatility Case Price	Number Of Shares
Jan	$ 10	100	$ 10	100
Feb	8	125	7	143
Mar	6	167	5	200
Apr	8	125	9	111
May	10	100	11	91
Jun	12	83	13	77
Jul	10	100	9	111
Aug	8	125	7	143
Sep	6	167	5	200
Oct	6	167	5	200
Nov	8	125	9	111
Dec	10	100	10	100
Total Shares Purchased		1,484		1,587
Average Cost Per Share		$8.09		$7.56

327

volatile. But they're not going to find out until they ask. Remember, after your non-answer answer, the client must speak next ... no matter how long it takes.

PARENTS: *Huh? Why would you hope for this kind of volatility?*

Then, and only then, would you take them through the example above. The point to stress, of course, is that as long as the basic trend is up, you can use all the "volatility" you can get. And the basic trend is always up.

Client still not convinced? Then maybe volatility isn't the issue that's really troubling him. Maybe, in his heart, he's afraid that the fund share price will go down one day and never come back. Again, just because the elevator has never fallen before doesn't mean a guy can't be afraid that it will as soon as he gets in. (In mutual funds, this is the phenomenon of "somebody else's mountain chart," also known as "it wouldn't have done that if I'd owned it.") So now you know you have a deeper fear to work on.

But maybe it's just that all illustrations are, to some extent, abstractions. Try giving the prospect a concrete example.

Say that your favorite clothing store carries a line of suits (or dresses) that you really like. You go in and buy a couple for $300 each. Two months later, they're marked down to $150 each. Same brand, same quality, same value, same everything. Well, not only will you not go in and buy any, you'll drive six blocks out of your way to avoid even passing the store! Luckily, three months later, these garments are priced at $400 each. Now, you'll go in and buy.

Crazy? Maybe, but this irrational parable exactly describes most people's behavior toward high-quality common stock funds. And that's why dollar-cost-averaging is so terrific: DCA turns all our worst instincts on their head. DCA tricks us into being aggressive (in terms of the number of shares we buy) near market bottoms and extremely cautious near tops.

And now you know: If markets are volatile ... DCA works even better.

Suggested Readings

Ours is, if we let it be, a phenomenally instructive business, because the forces we deal with are essentially cyclical. So, in the largest sense, President Truman's dictum should be our guide:

**THE ONLY THING NEW
UNDER THE SUN IS
THE HISTORY YOU DON'T KNOW.**

Experience is the best teacher. But, while you're accumulating experience, you can also learn a lot — and have a great deal of fun — by reading a few of the better books about the history of business, markets and investing.

One indispensable book is *Extraordinary Popular Delusions and the Madness of Crowds*, by Charles Mackay. The book was written in the 19th Century and chronicles the more dramatic mass manias in history. Particularly useful are the accounts of financial crazes like the South Sea Bubble and, best of all, the tulip mania. An excellent paperback edition is in print. And that's good, because rather than borrowing it once from the public library, you should own this one and read it again and again.

A favorite of mine is *Once in Golconda*, by John Brooks — a wonderfully written history of Wall Street in the 1920s. Brooks is, for my money, consistently the best writer working in the field of business and finance. I also recommend two of his other books, *Business Adventures* — featuring a great essay on "The Fate of the Edsel" — and *The Go-Go Years*, about the bull market of the 1960s and its terrible aftermath. John Kenneth Galbraith's *The Great Crash* is probably the definitive history of the events leading up to the 1929 debacle.

I've always loved Mathew Josephson's *The Robber Barons,* about the founders of the great industrial fortunes of the last century. If you're feeling ambitious, Ron Chernow's 1990 National Book Award-winning *The House of Morgan* is an excellent history of the last hundred years of American finance.

Before he was an establishment figure on PBS, "Adam Smith" (George J. W. Goodman) was an acute — and howlingly funny — observer of Wall Street in the 1960s. His *The Money Game* might have saved a lot of people a lot of grief in 1987. (And then again, maybe not.) "Smith" was also responsible for the re-publication (after it had been out of print for nearly half a century) of Gustave LeBon's classic *The Crowd.* LeBon was kind of "the Stone Age Freud" — in the late 19th and early 20th centuries, he was among the deans of world psychologists. LeBon was particularly fascinated — as you and I need to be — by crowd psychology.

I suggested earlier that extrapolation is the arch-enemy of the economic truth that everything cycles. The perils of extrapolation are superbly documented in David Halberstam's *The Reckoning.* The book chronicles how the Japanese auto industry got ready for the oil price explosion of the 1970s, and how the US auto industry didn't. For people in our profession, who have to guard against consensus thinking all the time, this is must reading.

Since this is a book about hiring other people to manage your clients' money, I've stayed away from recommending "how-to" books about investing. I do, however, commend two books to your attention. The first is Gerald M. Loeb's classic *The Battle for Investment Survival,* still as fresh and acute in many respects as it was thirty years ago. The other is Peter Lynch's immensely charming *One Up On Wall Street,* the most likable book about investing you'll ever read.

Much as we might wish to, we can't ignore Wall Street in the 1980s. I have two favorite non-fiction books: *Barbarians At The Gate,* the saga of the RJR Nabisco LBO, by Bryan Burrough and John Helyar; and James Sterngold's *Burning Down the House,* about the fall of E.F. Hutton & Company (the firm I joined as a stockbroker trainee on May 1, 1967). I still think, though, that the definitive book on the 1980s is a novel: Tom Wolfe's *Bonfire of the Vanities.*